The Story of the

Nottingham Suburban Railway

Volume 2
The Operational Years 1889 - 1951

David G. Birch

BOOK LAW PUBLICATIONS

ISBN 978-1-907094-36-1

Dedicated to Karen and Jennie
My two much loved daughters

ACKNOWLEDGEMENTS

I would like to express my sincere thanks to two of my dearest friends who many years ago generously gave both their time and archive resources to help me produce this series of books. Sadly, Tony Hill and Alf Henshaw have since passed away but these books will help to keep their photographs and knowledge preserved and available for all to enjoy forever. I also thank the late Sid Checkley for the interview he supplied for this book many years ago and the late John Wilson for some of his excellent photographs.

At the same time that Volume 1 of this series of books was launched, a group known as the 'Friends of the Nottingham Suburban Railway' was created. To date, over forty persons have joined, mostly from the Nottingham area but some from as far a field as John O'Groats, Australia and Canada. What is more important than the size of the membership is that the majority of the 'Friends' have contributed some of their knowledge about the NSR. This new information has generated many revisions to this and subsequent volumes of the NSR series. What is not included in these books will be included in the frequent 'Friends' Newsletters that are produced. Membership is free and if you are not already a member and wish to join just email david@nottinghamsuburbanrailway.co.uk with your request. I thank the 'Friends' who have contributed to produce this improved edition of Volume 2, especially Charles Weightman for the excellent chapter on NSR signalling, Graham Jelly for all the valuable information and photographs, Jeff Holt for the illustrated diagrams of the stations and the line, Alan Westby and Aubrey Gibson for their superb interviews and photographs, Hayden Reed for his knowledge and diagrams, Tony Etches for the photographs and loan of the single line tickets or tablets and Ian Askew for the images from his collection of tickets. My thanks also go to the staff of both the Nottingham Archive and also those at the National Archive at Kew. I also appreciate the valuable assistance of the librarians at the various libraries within the City of Nottingham and the County of Nottinghamshire, especially Carol Barnes.

Thanks to John Hooper for his marvellous publishing skills and David Allen for giving his approval for this series of books to be published by Book Law Publications.

I would also like to thank my dear wife Jane, who has spent many a lonely hour whilst these chapters were written and has given me her endless support both in proof reading and when I have given talks on the NSR.

Every effort has been made to trace the copyright holders whilst writing this book. However, if a copyright holder has been inadvertently missed, please let the publisher know and details will be amended in future editions.

Pete Waterman with the author, David Birch, at the launch of Volume One of *The Story of the Nottingham Suburban Railway*, at the Harvey Hadden Sports complex on Saturday 20th March 2010. *Jane Birch*

First published in the United Kingdom by
BOOK LAW PUBLICATIONS
382 Carlton Hill, Nottingham, NG4 1JA
Printed and bound by The Amadeus Press, Cleckheaton, West Yorkshire.

CONTENTS

Preface iv

Introduction 1

Chapter 7   **The Nottingham Suburban Railway Company**...3
         The Golden Decade 1889 to 1899

Chapter 8   **The Signalling on the Nottingham Suburban Railway Line**.......................25
         By Charles Weightman

Chapter 9   **The Nottingham Suburban Railway Company**...37
         The Threat from the Nottingham Victoria station
         and the Introduction of Electric Trams

Chapter 10   **The Nottingham Suburban Railway Company in Decline 1900 to 1909**.....................49

Chapter 11   **The End of the Nottingham Suburban Railway Company 1910 to 1922**....................65

Chapter 12   **The Early Years under the Ownership of
the London & North Eastern Railway 1923 to 1932** 81

Chapter 13   **The Later Years under the Ownership of
The London & North Eastern Railway 1933 to 1947** 95

Chapter 14   **Memories of the Nottingham Suburban Railway Line** 109

David Birch was born in the City of Nottingham, England in 1949 and educated at schools in Nottinghamshire. Like many young boys, his interest in railways began when he started trainspotting. He graduated with a B.Sc. Honours Degree in Civil Engineering in 1976 and subsequently became a Chartered Civil Engineer. Initially he specialised in the design of bridges and roads but later moved into managing their construction. To further his career, he progressed into management, where he gained a degree of Master of Business Administration. Since taking early retirement, he has devoted much of his time to writing about the Nottingham Suburban Railway, which he has been researching since 1983. He also provides illustrated talks and guided walks on the topic. He is currently putting the final details to the writing of the third volume of this series of books on his favourite railway.

PREFACE.

The Nottingham Suburban Railway (NSR) is my main interest; some call it my obsession.

It was back in 1983, whilst I was employed as the Site Agent on the A612 Carlton Road/ Porchester Road junction Improvement Scheme in Nottingham, that my interest in the line was conceived. The scheme included the demolition of the north parapet of the NSR Carlton Road Railway bridge No.7 and the filling in of about half of the cutting between the Carlton Road bridge and the Sneinton tunnel using materials that had been excavated from the road works. I had been interested in railways from an early age and I therefore decided that I should find something out about this closed railway line, which at that time I was assisting to destroy. Little did I realise then that this line would become such an important part of my life. My research still continues today, twenty eight-years later.

I was just two years old when the NSR closed on 1st August 1951 and although I lived only about a mile away from the line, I do not have any personal experiences or recollections of it during my young life. This included passing over the Carlton Road bridge twice a day, for seven years, on my journey to and from my senior school. I have tried to develop and maintain a photographic record of the slowly disappearing remnants of the line since 1983. However, most of the information I have collected has been sourced from analysing other peoples' writings and photographs and researching materials contained in various archives and libraries.

Volume 2 of my story of the NSR continues where Volume 1 left-off. The original Volume 2 text was written at the same time as the first volume. However, such has been the response from some readers of that first volume, and the interest generated from members of the 'Friends of the Nottingham Suburban Railway' that the original Volume 2 has subsequently been significantly edited and additional plans, photographs and content has been added.

I wish to thank all of you who purchased or read Volume 1. of my NSR story and also everyone who has contributed to Volume 2, not only improving the original version's content and quality but also creating a much more valuable book of reference for the future.

This is the continuing story of the Nottingham Suburban Railway line.

I hope you enjoy it.

David G. Birch M.B.A., B.Sc. (Hons.), M.I.C.E., C. Eng. (Retired).
Ruddington, 8th August 2011.

Abbreviations.

AN&B&EJR	Ambergate, Nottingham & Boston & Eastern Junction Railway Co.
BR	British Railways
GCR	Great Central Railway
GNR	Great Northern Railway
LD&ECR	Lancashire, Derbyshire & East Coast Railway
LNER	London & North Eastern Railway
LNWR	London & North Western Railway
MS&L	Manchester, Sheffield & Lincolnshire Railway
MR	Midland Railway
NPBC	Nottingham Patent Brick Company Ltd
NSR	Nottingham Suburban Railway
RCTS	Railway Correspondence & Travel Society
SRL	Sneinton Railway Lands
pass or Thr'u	Train does not stop at this station (as shown on timetables).

INTRODUCTION

The 2nd December 2009 marked the 120 year anniversary of the opening of the Nottingham Suburban Railway. Just over a year and a half later, on 1st August 2011, 60 years will have passed since its closure.

Prior to the publication of Volume 1 of this series of books, there had only been several magazine articles and individual chapters in books written about this line. In my view, one of the best articles about the line and the one which was incidentally my earliest source of information is the one by the late John Marshall in the June 1961 edition of the *Railway Magazine* entitled 'The Nottingham Suburban Railway'. A comprehensive bibliography will be provided at the end of the last volume of this series of books for readers who wish to look at all of the sources of information on the Nottingham Suburban Railway (NSR) that I have discovered. I can assure you it is a very long list.

Those of you who have read Volume 1 will now be aware of the line's conception, construction and the events which occurred on its official opening day. However, those of you who are more interested in the operational years of the line and haven't read the first volume may need a brief introduction to the railway.

The NSR, as you might expect, was located in the County of Nottinghamshire, which is in the East Midlands of England. It served the suburban areas of Sneinton, Thorneywood, St. Ann's, Sherwood and Daybrook, which are located approximately three miles to the east and north-east from the centre of Nottingham.

It ran, at its southern end, from the Trent Lane junction on the Great Northern Railway's (GNR) Nottingham to Grantham line, for a distance of three miles, six furlongs, five chains and fifty links, (about 3¾ miles) to a junction just east of Daybrook station on the GNR's Derbyshire & Staffordshire Extension Railway, or the 'Back line' as it is affectionately known by local railway enthusiasts today. The NSR was an independently owned railway company until 1923 but was operated by the GNR through an Agreement between the two companies. It provided a short cut for GNR passengers from Nottingham to Daybrook and all stations to the west and the Leen Valley, instead of having to traverse the longer route over the 'Back line' via Colwick and Gedling. In addition it provided freight services primarily to its three stations and three adjacent brick yards.

The Nottingham Suburban Railway Act was passed on 25th June 1886 and was officially opened on Monday 2nd December 1889, with the inaugural train departing from the GNR's Nottingham London Road station to Daybrook.

As you will read in some detail in this volume, it sadly took only just over ten years for serious competition for the line's passenger traffic to materialise. On 24th May 1900 the Nottingham Joint station (later to be called the Nottingham Victoria station) was opened, which reduced the distance travelled to Basford, Pinxton and Derby by four miles when compared with that over the NSR rails. Then from 1901 to 1915 Nottingham's electric tram routes were constructed and opened, which not only provided the public with a more convenient and cheaper transport alternative but eventually covered most of the NSR's stations and passenger catchments. As a consequence, on 13th July 1916, the three NSR stations located at Thorneywood, St. Ann's Well and Sherwood were closed to passenger traffic.

On the 1st January 1923 the NSR was absorbed by the London & North Eastern Railway Company (LNER) and the line was reduced to a single track from February 1930 for the majority of its length.

In May 1941 a German bomb exploded on the NSR's railway embankment, just north of its bridge No.3 over the Midland Railway line. As the embankment was never repaired, the NSR line was permanently severed and thus became two single track railways with no through traffic. Pick-up goods traffic continued to be supplied to the line from the north until July 1951.

On 16th June 1951, the *Railway Correspondence and Travel Society* (RCTS) organised a Special train, part of whose route included a return trip over the northern rails of the NSR.

The line officially closed on 1st August 1951 and dismantling and demolition began in 1954. The line's bridges continued to be demolished throughout the 1960's and tunnel mouths disappeared as cuttings were filled in. Housing developments have been built on several sections of the line but some areas have been preserved to some extent as linear walkways.

This second volume of the NSR series covers its operational years and takes the reader from the opening day of the line on 2nd December 1889 to its eventual closure on 1st August 1951. At the end of this volume there is a comprehensive list of the amendments that are required to correct Volume 1 of *The Story of the Nottingham Suburban Railway*.

As in Volume 1, I have tried to balance the information provided in this volume, so that there is something for everyone. I have included lots of timetable information for those who like to thumb their way through them, comparing timings and frequencies of trains. The photographs have taken many years to collect. You will most probably have seen a few of them before but I can guarantee that many will be new to you. Regrettably it is not possible to go back to those GNR, LNER and BR operational days with our digital cameras in order to take hundreds of photographs so that we can go through them later and delete both the poor ones or the ones that we have accidentally taken of the inside of our pockets. The operational photographs of the line between 1889 and 1951 are few and the quality of some of these may be considered as not very good. However, we have to be grateful for what we find and what people are willing to agree to let us publish. The search however goes on for there are most certainly more photographs and information out there to be discovered.

I have endeavoured in every case to get permission, where I could, to include every photograph in this book and I have tried to credit photographs with the correct name of the person who took them. Where this has not been achieved I have named the person's collection who has kindly lent me the photograph to use.

The third volume will continue the story of the NSR. It will commence where this volume finishes – 1st August 1951 – and take readers right up to the present day. In addition there will be an abundance of photographs of the line in its various stages of decay and dismantling. Also there will be financial accounts of the line when it was still an independent company as well as details of freight and passenger usage. The volume will end with a detailed walk along the line, giving clear instructions of the route and where all the remaining artefacts of the line can now be found and observed.

THE NOTTINGHAM SUBURBAN RAILWAY

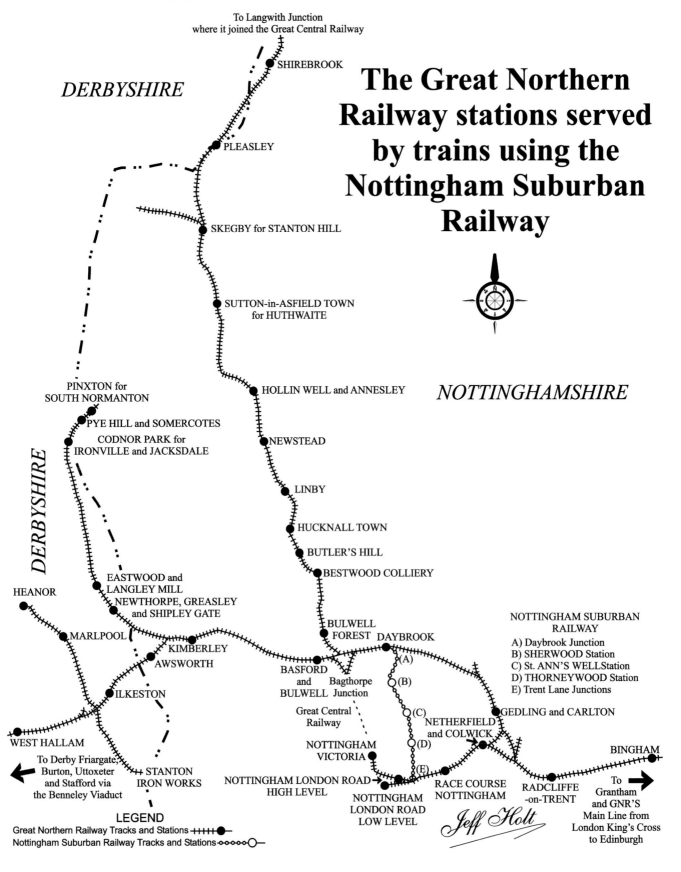

To Langwith Junction
where it joined the Great Central Railway

SHIREBROOK

DERBYSHIRE

The Great Northern Railway stations served by trains using the Nottingham Suburban Railway

PLEASLEY

SKEGBY for STANTON HILL

SUTTON-in-ASFIELD TOWN
for HUTHWAITE

NOTTINGHAMSHIRE

HOLLIN WELL and ANNESLEY

PINXTON for
SOUTH NORMANTON

PYE HILL and SOMERCOTES
CODNOR PARK for
IRONVILLE and JACKSDALE

NEWSTEAD

LINBY

HUCKNALL TOWN

BUTLER'S HILL

BESTWOOD COLLIERY

DERBYSHIRE

HEANOR

EASTWOOD and
LANGLEY MILL
NEWTHORPE, GREASLEY
and SHIPLEY GATE

BULWELL
FOREST   DAYBROOK

NOTTINGHAM SUBURBAN
RAILWAY

A) Daybrook Junction
B) SHERWOOD Station
C) St. ANN'S WELL Station
D) THORNEYWOOD Station
E) Trent Lane Junctions

MARLPOOL

KIMBERLEY

AWSWORTH

BASFORD
and
BULWELL   Bagthorpe
Junction

(A)

(B)

ILKESTON

Great Central
Railway

(C)   GEDLING and CARLTON

NETHERFIELD
and COLWICK

WEST HALLAM

NOTTINGHAM
VICTORIA

(D)

BINGHAM

To Derby Friargate,
Burton, Uttoxeter
and Stafford via
the Benneley Viaduct

STANTON
IRON WORKS

NOTTINGHAM LONDON ROAD →
HIGH LEVEL

(E)

RACE COURSE
NOTTINGHAM

RADCLIFFE
-on-TRENT

To
Grantham
and GNR'S
Main Line from
London King's Cross
to Edinburgh

NOTTINGHAM
LONDON ROAD
LOW LEVEL

Jeff Holt

LEGEND
Great Northern Railway Tracks and Stations ┼┼┼┼┼●
Nottingham Suburban Railway Tracks and Stations ○○○○○○○○○○○○○○○○○○○○○○○○○○

Chapter 7: THE NOTTINGHAM SUBURBAN RAILWAY COMPANY - THE GOLDEN DECADE 1889 to 1899

For its length, the construction of the NSR had been expensive and labour intensive. To complete the line, deep cuttings had to be excavated and high embankments constructed. Five tunnels, including the wagon-way to Thorneywood brickyard, had been built and impressive retaining walls created. On 2nd December 1889 the line opened and the fruits of the NSR Companies dreams and hard work started to be harvested.

In order to enable Volume 1. of this series to be a little bit more complete and add some new information, which has recently come to light, I am including here a couple of items which I am sure will be of interest.

The first is a free hand sketch drawn by Edward Parry, the NSR's Engineer. On it he was pondering how to solve the problems raised by the Board of Trade about the NSR's Up line traffic junctioning with the GNR Nottingham to Grantham line, on a down gradient of 1 in 48½. Parry's sketch shows the Grantham line horizontally across the drawing, with the LNWR Manvers Street on the left. He has drawn both tracks of the NSR coming off the GNR Grantham line with a note of the 1 in 48½ at its side. He has marked another set of lines in fainter and dashed lines for the additional set of GNR lines. These were never built but interestingly he labels them as 'Authorised Widening 1887', so he must have been aware that the GNR were intending to widen their Nottingham to Grantham line before he originally designed the NSR bridge No.2 as a single span. In very faint lines the revised Up line can be seen crossing the Grantham line where he has written 'Up Line' and 'Down Line'.

A delightful picture of the west face of bridge No.15 over Thackeray's Lane in 1905. *Clumber Postcard*

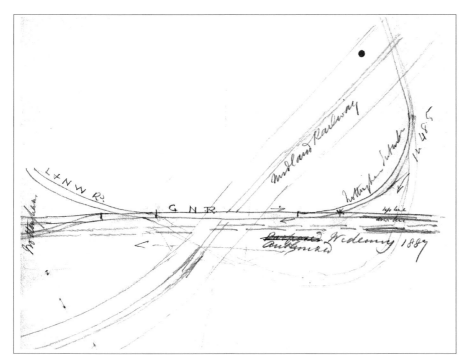

The second and third items have been kindly donated by Mike Chapman, the Manager of the Dorket Head Brickworks, owned by Ibstock Bricks Ltd. The first is the contract drawing for the construction of the 'Nottingham Patent Brick Company's Tramway to Carlton Brickworks'. It is signed by Edward Parry in the bottom right corner and dated as 28th July 1888. Considering the plan on the drawing first, the zero chainage is taken from the centre of the NSR siding behind the Up platform and proceeds under Thorneywood Lane and Private Road (note not Burgass Road) and then along the side of the Private Road, and over a pond before being laid over the Private Road to access

(left) **Edward Parry's free hand sketch showing the authorised widening of the GNR Nottingham to Grantham line and the Nottingham Suburban Railway Deviation No.3.**

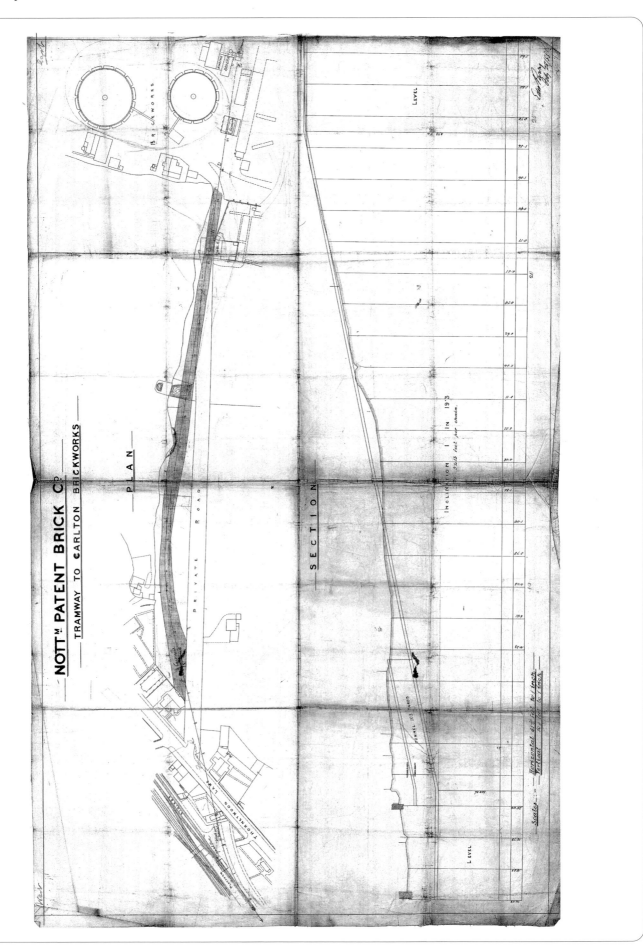

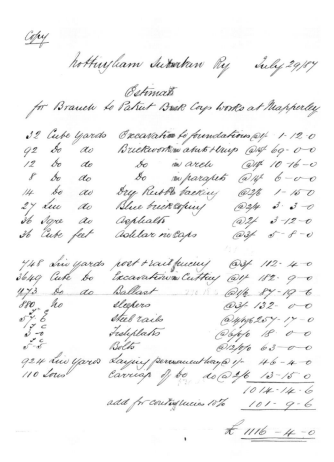

Reduced facsimile of Parry's Estimate for the Branch to the Patent Brick Co. works at Mapperley. *Mike Chapman coll.*

the brickworks; the details of which are quite interesting in themselves. The section reveals that the wagon-way tunnel was proposed to be 103 yards long and that a sewer had to be altered on Thorneywood Lane. The inclination of the track, which was 1 in 19.3 or 3.143 feet per chain, was the same from the west end of the tunnel through to the brickworks, point 25 on the plan, after which it was level.

The second item from Mike Chapman is Edward Parry's estimate (*above*) for the Branch to the Patent Brick Company's Works at Mapperley. The estimate dated 29th July 1887 is broken down for the quantities of materials required and their cost for the bridge (No.12) £101 6s 0d and then for the earthworks, fencing and construction of the inclined railway £913 8s 6d. The total cost for the incline and bridge, including an extra 10% for contingencies was £1,116 4s 0d.

The offices of the NSR Company were located on St. John's Chambers, a narrow passageway between Bridlesmith Gate and Fletcher Gate in Nottingham. This property was also the offices of Mellors, Basden, Mellors, an accountancy firm, which played a significant role in the life of the NSR Company.
NSR Board members at the time of the opening of the railway were:
Alderman Edward Gripper JP - Director and Chairman.
L. C. Probyn – Director.
Samuel Herrick Sands JP – Director.
Robert Mellors - Director.

In addition, the Engineer was Edward Parry and the Secretary was Duncan Frederick Basden.

It is important to recall that Gripper, Sands and Mellors were also all Directors of the NPBC, the main promoters of the NSR. The principal reason for the building of the NSR was to ensure transport to and from the NPBC's brickyards 365 days a year. If the brickyards had not existed, then the NSR would never have been built.

As far as the promoters were concerned, the main facility that the Suburban railway provided was the delivery of both sand and coal and the transportation for the bricks that were produced by both the Nottingham Builders' Brick Company (NBBC) and Nottingham Patent Brick Company (NPBC) brickyards.

The existence of the NBBC along the NSR was a bonus for the NSR. Significant in-depth research has been carried out to determine the history of the NBBC but unfortunately with little success. This is regrettable, especially as this company was responsible for contributing a fair amount of freight traffic on the NSR. The NBBC was formed in 1868 as manufacturers of bricks and tiles, along with chimney and flower pots. Up to 1876 their offices were at the Poultry Arcade on St. Peter's Gate, followed shortly afterwards with a move to Carlton Chambers at 6 Victoria Street, both being in Nottingham. In 1881 their offices moved to their Carlton Road brickworks where the Works Manager was James Whitehouse. In 1888 Frederick William Hollis, who lived on Meridith Street off St. Ann's Well Road, was the Secretary of the company. From December 1889 they were provided with rail transport by the new Suburban line and were also provided with goods sidings in the Thorneywood station. In 1894 Mr T.A. Whitehouse became Manager and he was replaced in 1902 by John Philips MRSA, who remained in the post until 1928. Mr William E. Phillips MRSA, then took over the management of the NBBC and continued until 1936. It is at this point that the story currently dries up. However, based on several eye witness reports, the brickyard apparently ceased operating either just before or during the Second World War.

The three stations along the line were named Thorneywood, St. Ann's Well and Sherwood. All were provided with small, but reasonable revenue earning goods sidings and facilities. They were all classed as passenger and goods stations, which could also handle the inward and outward conveyance of parcels, furniture vans, portable engines and machines on wheels, livestock, horse boxes and prize cattle vans!

Each station was initially provided with its own Station Master, who was accommodated in their own NSR owned house, adjacent to their station. The men who occupied the Station Master posts during NSR and the LNER periods, as far as I have been able to determine, were as follows:-

Thorneywood station
Address - Station Masters House - 1a, Thorneywood Lane.
Thomas Winfield (1891-1900)
Samuel Coningsby (1902-1904)
Frederick Allen (1905)
William Smith (1908-1910)
Leo O. Faunthorpe (1911-1922)
Harry Sparsholt (1926-1932)
J.E. Potts (1933-1948)

St. Ann's Well station
Address - Station Masters House – Station House, 459, The Wells Road.
Charles A. Smith (1894)
Cuthbert Felstead (1902)
William Henry Harrison (1904-1910)

(left to right) **The front elevation of King John's Chambers on Bridlesmith Gate, Nottingham. Home of the Mellors, Basden, Mellors and the NSR offices. The original entrance to the King John's Chambers. The rear entrance to King John's Chambers from Fletcher Gate with Bridlesmith Gate at the far end of the passageway.**

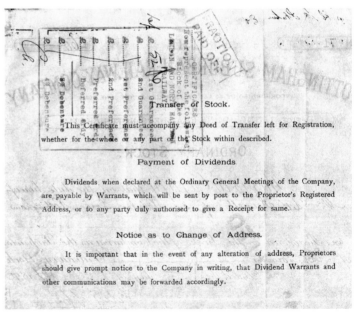

(left) **NSR Stock Certificate No.71 for £60.00 of NSR stock, dated 5th October 1891, with Edward Gripper, Samuel Herrick Sands (both Directors) and Thomas Galland Mellors (Secretary) signatures. *Bodleian Library and Ian Dinmore*. *(right)* Rear of Stock Certificate with LNER stock transfer details. The figures agreed for the transfer of stock from the NSR to the LNER was that £100 of NSR stock equated to £87.10s of LNER stock. Therefore for the £60.00 worth of NSR stock on the certificate No.71, it equated to £60.00 x 87.5/100 = £52.50 worth of LNER stock. *Bodleian Library and Ian Dinmore***

Three NSR signs, which were placed on structures and posts, have recently come to light. The first is the bridge number plate which used to be on the end of the parapet wall at the north east corner of the blue brick segmental arch section of bridge No.1 over Trent Lane. It was legitimately acquired by Graham Jelly, who has restored it to its original colours. The 'bill poster' sign came from the same bridge but was located beneath the bridge adjacent to the footpath. The other cast iron sign is a GNR 'Public Warning Not to Trespass' notice which was originally located at the top of the bank on the Down side adjacent to the north portal of Ashwell's tunnel. My thanks go to Barry Walker for giving me permission to photograph the plate. Barry also has loaned the Daybrook station Station Master's 'Thunderer' whistle.

A GNR warning notice from the Down side track of the NSR near the north portal of Ashwell's tunnel. Barry Walker collection. *D Birch*

The original bridge No.1 number plate rescued, and restored, by Graham Jelly. *Graham Jelly*

Graham Jelly proudly displays his bridge No.1 plate at the place from where it was rescued. *D Birch*

(above) **The 'bill poster' cast iron plate rescued from bridge No.1 and restored by Graham Jelly.** *Graham Jelly. (right)* **The GNR Daybrook station, Station Masters 'Thunderer' whistle. Barry Walker collection.** *D Birch*

Thomas Edward Alder (1912-1922)
J.E. Potts (1922-1948)
Sherwood station
Address – Station Masters House – Station House, Winchester Street.
Richard Addis (1893-1895)
Charles Edward Baker (1901-1920)
Frederick Martin, Relief Station Master (1922)
J.E. Potts (1922-1948)
Emsley Walt (resident) (1932)

All the above names and dates have been sourced from *Wright's, White's, Morris, Blair, Drake* and *Kelly's Directories*. As a consequence, it is not possible to determine the exact dates of changeover between the Station Masters or indeed if there were any short term appointments between the names listed. It is possible that some station masters could have been missed as the directories were only published at two to five year intervals. However, by utilising the many different publishers, this time interval has been reduced. Several years are still unknown and rather than filling in the gaps with the known names, which may be an inaccuracy, I have left them blank.

David Holmes in his book '*The Life and Times of the Station Master*' published by Silver Link Publishing, with contributions by Will Adams, gives some valuable information as to the life of a Station Master during this period. In 1910 there were apparently 8,688 Station Masters on the Railways of Britain with additional Relief Station Masters available to cover for illness, leave, or vacant Station Master posts.

The duties of a Station Master were many and varied and can be listed as follows:-

a). Station Facilities
  Seeing to all the station's train arrivals and departures;
  Booking tickets;
  Dealing with parcels including the delivery of urgent items;
  Covering porters' and clerks' jobs when they were absent from work;
  Assisting guards on trains;
  Assisting porters in attending to passengers and parcels;
  Cleaning windows, lamps and platforms;
  Painting edges of platforms white;
  Collecting tickets and excess fares;
  Putting up posters;
  Gardening;
  Checking, correcting and winding clocks daily;
  Using and securing barrows;
  Lighting and fuelling fires in the waiting rooms;
  Clearing ice and snow from the platforms and sanding as necessary;
  Replacing gas mantles;
  Filling fire buckets with sand in the winter or water at other times;
  Exchanging the single line token or staff with driver of each train (after the line had been singled);
  Dealing with and managing lost property;
  Dealing with public complaints;
  Opening and closing coach doors;
  Checking passenger facilities, waiting rooms, toilets, floors, seats and windows;
  Ensuring their staff deal with customers courteously;
  Dealing with excursion trains and
  Emptying litter bins.
b). Office Administration
  Dealing with the pay of station staff including collecting cash from the bank;

Accounting for booking and goods office receipts paid in;
  Maybe dealing with pay for other railway staff including permanent way operatives and signalmen;
  Ordering stationary, stores and fuel for the porter's room, signal boxes and waiting rooms;
  Ordering paraffin for lamps;
  Ordering cleaning materials and snow clearing equipment;
  Ordering tickets.
c). Goods Yard Facilities
  Shunting duties;
  Providing cover for the Shunter;
  Looking after the goods yard wagon sheets and tarpaulins;
  Fastening wagons' ropes securely;
  Dealing with coal merchants and ensuring the goods yard area is kept clean and safe;
  Managing the cattle dock area where appropriate;
  Managing the goods shed and its use;
  Managing the weighbridge, dealing with customers and receipting monies taken;
  Returning empty crates and boxes;
  Carrying out shunting, loading and unloading wagon duties;
  Taking rents from coal merchants and other users of the Goods Yard and Sheds.
d). Signal Boxes and Ground Frames
  Checking all clocks for the correct time every day both at the station and in the signal boxes;
  Checking signal box and ground frame operation, where appropriate.
e). Other Duties
  Dealing with fires on embankments;
  Dealing with animals on the line;
  Sanding of rail crossing points, steps and ramps;
  Dealing with vandalism;
  Checking signal lamps.

The three NSR stations' sidings were utilised by several businesses, which received incoming goods from wagons using the NSR. The companies and firms using the goods sidings and sheds, most of which I have been able to determine, were as follows:-

Thorneywood station:
Babbington Colliery Company, coal merchants (1893-1920).
Samuel Holden, milk dealer (1893-1908).
Edward Robert Reeve and Co., coal & corn merchants (1893-1932).
Elston and Co., coal merchant (1928-1932).
Bert Pickbourne, coal dealer (1936).

St. Ann's Well station:
Babbington Colliery Company, coal merchants (1894-1936).
Edward Robert Reeve and Co., coal & corn merchants (1894-1932).
E Burton & Son, coal merchants (1928).
Mr. Sanders, coal merchant.
Mr. Jones, coal merchant.
Mr. Heyhoe, coal merchant.
William Gell, coal merchant.
Somnus Bedding, bed mattress manufacturers.

Sherwood station:
Simms, Sons & Cook, timber stock yard.

[The dates given above have been taken from trade directories and therefore they may be incomplete and with either earlier or later dates than those quoted.]

E. Reeve & Co. 4-plank wagon No.132 with dumb buffers and the legend 'Empty to Watnall Colliery' written on the side.
(below) E. Reeve & Co. horse and cart No.5, Registered Office 31 Market Street, Nottingham. Taken on Canal Street, Nottingham in 1906.

(left) **Babbington Colliery 6-plank open wagon No.80 painted black. Located on the GCR preserved railway at Loughborough.**

The freight trains, which served the three goods stations and the three brickyards along the line, would have hauled wagons from a variety of railway companies, along with those which were privately owned by the various suppliers of minerals and goods. In addition to Edward Reeve, Babbington Colliery also had its own wagons and both businesses used the Thorneywood and St. Ann's Well goods stations. Coal and sand would have been brought in to the three brickyards along the line from collieries in the appropriate colliery company wagon or perhaps one hired from the GNR. The GNR wagons were generally painted a dark brick red colour with G N in large white letters on both sides, although liveries did change from time to time. The private owner wagons which contained coal or sand were emptied by hand in the brickyards, these wagons being returned empty to their respective owner. The brickyards had to hire empty GNR wagons from the Colwick marshalling yards and after these had been delivered to the appropriate brickyard, they were filled by hand with bricks and then transported back to Colwick, where they were sorted into trains for delivery all over the country. This separate use of wagons for the import of minerals and the export of bricks, meant that the sidings, adjacent to the two stations at Sherwood and Thorneywood, were always well used and had to be properly managed in order to ensure that incoming and outgoing wagons were efficiently and effectively marshalled and organised.

Following the eventful journey of the inaugural train, which left Nottingham (London Road) station, according to the timetable, at 7.45 a.m. on the 2nd December 1889, the remaining trains departing and arriving at the London Road station that day, which were either to stop at the NSR's stations or had passed over the Nottingham Suburban rails, completed their journeys without any further incident. The NSR main contractor Mr Edwards had made his point during the first journey, which as we will see later, had some justification.

The initial passenger timetable for the NSR commenced on that Monday morning, 2nd December 1889. It was designed by the GNR, the operating company, through Agreement with the NSR The timetable was clearly designed to be short-lived as it stated on the printed passenger timetable poster that this timetable 'will be revised and altered from Wednesday, January 1st, 1890.' It would appear that the GNR intended to carry out surveys of the passenger use of the line over the first few weeks following its opening.

For the first month of operation after the opening day, the GNR operated a shuttle passenger service of six Down trains (traversing northwards towards Daybrook) and six Up trains (travelling southwards towards the Nottingham London Road station) between the Nottingham (London Road) station and Daybrook station, plus five Down trains and four Up trains to Newstead. All of these trains had been previously routed via the 'Back Line' or 'Outer Circle' as it was also known and its Gedling and Carlton station and the Mapperley tunnel but were now transferred to run over the NSR's rails. In addition, contrary to many previously published writings on the NSR, four Sunday trains operated each way, but this service only lasted until the 31st December 1889. The timetable, as issued by the Great Northern on 26th November 1889, and published on the NSR Opening poster, is illustrated opposite.

E. Reeve and Co. was registered as a coal and corn merchant. Edward Robert Reeve was born in 1843, in Awsworth, Nottinghamshire. He married Hannah in 1869 and the couple had nine children, six girls and three boys, born between 1870 and 1886. One of his original business addresses was adjacent to the Nottingham Builders' Brick Company, who also had sidings on the NSR, on the south side of Carlton Road. Following office moves to Market Street and Angel Row, in 1936 he was at the Lloyds Bank Chambers on Beastmarket Hill, Nottingham.

He not only operated from both the NSR's St. Ann's Well and the Thorneywood stations but also had ten other railway goods facilities including the GNR wharf, the Great Central goods station on Kirke White Street East and New Basford station.

Edward Reeve operated his own fleet of privately owned wagons and registered a number of these with the Midland Railway. Details of his wagons, which were supplied to me by Mr. S.T. Turner, are as follows:-

Date: October 1888
Wagon running numbers 25 to 30
Register numbers 790 – 795.
Capacity 8 tons.
Builder - The Langley Mill Engineering Company.
Internal dimensions 14ft 6ins. long, 7ft 0ins. wide, 3ft 2ins. deep.
Side doors only.

Date: August 1890.
Wagon running numbers 36 to 43, 44 to 53, and 54 and 55.
Register numbers 2869 to 2876, 2883 to 2892, 2675 and 2676 respectively.
Capacity 8 tons.
Builder - S.J. Clay & Co. Ltd.,
Internal dimensions 14ft 6ins. long, 7ft 0ins. wide, 3ft 3ins. deep
Side and end doors.

Date: September 1902.
Wagon running numbers 143 to 172
Registered numbers 38704 to 38718, and 38790 to 38804 respectively.
Capacity 10 tons.
Builder - S.J. Clay & Co. Ltd.,

DOWN LINE		Weekday Working – 2 December 1889 to 31 December 1889						
		am						
London (King's X)	Dep		5.15		7.40	8.45	9.45	
Grantham	Dep		7.31		9.534	11.17	11.57	
Nottingham	Arr		8.03		10.33	11.53	12.30	
Nottingham	**Dep**	**7.45**	**8.44**	**9.50**	**10.43**	**12.00**	**12.40**	
Thorneywood	**Dep**	**7.49**	**8.48**	**9.54**	**10.47**	**12.04**	**12.44**	
St. Ann's Well	**Dep**	**7.52**	**8.51**	**9.57**	**10.50**	**12.07**	**12.47**	
Sherwood	**Dep**	**7.55**	**8.54**	**10.00**	**10.53**	**12.10**	**12.50**	
Daybrook	**Arr**	**7.58**	**8.57**	**10.03**	**10.56**	**12.13**	**12.53**	
Daybrook	Dep	8.13	9.05	9.09	10.10	12.20	1.03	1.07
Hucknall	Arr			9.24				1.21
Newstead	Arr			9.32				1.28
Pinxton	Arr			9.39			1.37	
Ilkeston	Arr	8.31			10.28	12.38		
Derby	Arr	8.50			10.47	12.56		
Burton	Arr	9.20			11.16	1.34		
Uttoxeter	Arr	9.40			11.50	1.48		
Stafford	Arr	10.19			12.30	2.29		

DOWN LINE cont.		Weekday Working – 2 December 1889 to 31 December 1889						
		pm						
London (King's X)	dep		12.30			3.00		5.30
Grantham	dep		2.55			5.25		7.38
Nottingham	arr		3.30			5.58		8.10
Nottingham	**dep**	**2.47**	**3.45**		**5.35**	**6.42**		**8.17**
Thorneywood	**dep**	**2.51**	**3.49**		**5.39**	**6.46**		**8.21**
St. Ann's Well	**dep**	**2.54**	**3.52**		**5.42**	**6.49**		**8.24**
Sherwood	**dep**	**2.57**	**3.55**		**5.45**	**6.52**		**8.27**
Daybrook	**arr**	**3.00**	**3.58**		**5.48**	**6.55**		**8.30**
Daybrook	dep	3.07	4.33	4.37	5.57	7.03	7.07	8.37
Hucknall	arr			4.52			7.22	8.51
Newstead	arr			5.00			7.30	9.00
Pinxton	arr			5.07		7.36		
Ilkeston	arr	3.25			6.15			
Derby	arr	3.44			6.34			
Burton	arr	4.45			7.17			
Uttoxeter	arr	4.57			7.25			
Stafford	arr	5.46			8.16			

UP LINE		Weekday Working – 2 December 1889 to 31 December 1889							
		am					pm	am	
Stafford	Dep								11.28
Uttoxeter	Dep								12.07
Burton	Dep			8.05					12.25
Derby	Dep			8.32					1.03
Ilkeston	Dep			8.50					1.23
Pinxton	Dep		7.35			9.54		12.55	
Newstead	Dep	7.30			10.01				
Hucknall	Dep	7.37			10.09				
Daybrook	Arr	7.51	8.07	9.06	10.23	10.26		1.27	1.41
Daybrook	**Dep**	**8.15**	**9.10**	**10.46**			**12.15**		**1.55**
Sherwood	**Dep**	**8.18**	**9.13**	**10.49**			**12.18**		**1.58**
St. Ann's Well	**Dep**	**8.21**	**9.16**	**10.52**			**12.21**		**2.01**
Thorneywood	**Arr**	**8.23**	**9.18**	**10.54**			**12.23**		**2.03**
Thorneywood	**Dep**	**8.25**	**9.20**	**10.56**			**12.25**		**2.05**
Nottingham	**Arr**	**8.29**	**9.24**	**11.00**			**12.29**		**2.09**
Nottingham	Dep	8.40	10.12	**11.08**					2.15
Grantham	Arr	9.15	10.44	**11.41**					2.47
London (King's X)	Arr	11.45	1.00	**1.55**					5.20

It was clear, even before the NSR had been opened, that trains which had destinations beyond Daybrook would benefit from shorter journeys, both in distance and time duration. However, after a couple of weeks of use, not quite long enough some may argue, the GNR determined that the use of the three NSR stations both for departures and arrivals wasn't as high as expected. This was particularly the case with regard to passengers using the line on a Sunday. As a consequence the GNR kept to its word and revised the timetable, the greatest alteration being the deletion of the Sunday passenger service. This would, in the future, only be reinstated on a passenger timetable on a couple of occasions during the rest of the NSR's operational years, one being a single train which ran from 1st November 1897 for a short period of time.

From January 1890, passenger services along the NSR consisted of ten trains daily from the Nottingham (London Road) station to Daybrook and to the stations west and along the Leen Valley line. Four of these trains continued on their journey from Daybrook and terminated at Newstead. The ten trains only stopped on the NSR on Mondays to Saturday. There was no Sunday service provided.

UP LINE cont.		Weekday Working – 2 December 1889 to 31 December 1889							
		pm							
Stafford	dep			2.27			4.50		7.20
Uttoxeter	dep			3.06			5.31		8.05
Burton	dep			3.15			5.41		8.08
Derby	dep			3.50			6.28		8.50
Ilkeston	dep			4.09			6.47		9.09
Pinxton	dep		2.08		5.20				
Newstead	dep	2.15				5.27			
Hucknall	dep	2.23				5.35			
Daybrook	arr	2.37	2.40	4.26	5.50	5,52	7.04		9.25
Daybrook	**dep**	**2.45**		**4.38**		**5.58**	**7.15**		**9.30**
Sherwood	**dep**	**2.48**		**4.41**		**6.01**	**7.18**		**9.33**
St. Ann's Well	**dep**	**2.51**		**4.44**		**6.04**	**7.21**		**9.36**
Thorneywood	**arr**	**2.53**		**4.46**		**6.06**	**7.23**		**9.38**
Thorneywood	**dep**	**2.54**		**4.48**		**6.07**	**7.25**		**9.40**
Nottingham	**arr**	**2.58**		**4.52**		**6.11**	**7.29**		**9.44**
Nottingham	dep	3.00		5.00		6.15			9.55
Grantham	arr	3.52		5.32		7.04			10.40
London (King's X)	arr	6.15		7.55		9.20			2.10

Later in 1890, the number of trains continuing to Newstead was increased to six a day with four extra trains on Saturdays. The 1890 passenger timetable for the trains from Nottingham (London Road) to Newstead via the NSR was as set out at the bottom of the opposite page. The two trains each way to Newstead that travelled on a Sunday, both went via Gedling.

Because of the NSR's steep gradients, only trains of a limited weight and hence length could use the line and many trains therefore continued to use the original, longer route via Gedling. The trains from Stafford, Burton-on-Trent, Derby and Pinxton continued to use the original longer route via Gedling so that passengers wishing to go to Grantham and London (King's Cross) could make their single change at Netherfield station. Passengers from Nottingham could travel by the Suburban and change at Daybrook for their connection. The cost of a single adult journey from Nottingham (London Road) to Bulwell and Basford in the first year was 1½d or 3d return.

Most passenger trains along the NSR consisted of varnished teak non-corridor carriages hauled by an engine from the GNR's Colwick shed. These were initially Patrick Stirling 2-4-0 tender and 0-4-4 tank locomotives, which although valiant, experienced considerable problems in negotiating the NSR's steep 1 in 48½ and 1 in 50 gradients, owing to the slipping of the coupled wheels when the rails were greasy in bad weather. It was often the case that the drivers of Daybrook bound trains would rush at the curve leading from the Trent Lane junction onto the NSR's Down line embankment. However, if the rails were greasy, the engine would start slipping as it passed over the Colwick Road bridge No.4, and occasionally the train would come to a stand by the time it had journeyed to Sneinton Dale bridge No.6. In order to get the train going again, the fireman would have to get down from the engine and use his shovel to sand the rails for some distance ahead of the locomotive. Towards the end of the existence of the NSR Company in the 1920's, these locomotives were replaced by Ivatt's 4-4-0 and 4-4-2 tank engines. Apparently Sherwood station was another trouble spot for engine drivers. It was particularly difficult to start from the station on the Up line. Likewise the St. Ann's Well station departures were difficult but this time in the Down direction. On many occasions, the heavier trains would give these two stations' local residents quite a spectacular firework display as they departed on their journeys. The Stirling 0-4-4 tanks were the best performers on the NSR, and they often pulled up to ten of the six-wheel teak coaches along the line.

Although the line had been open for nearly three months, it wasn't until 21st February that the NSR paid Henry Ashwell the sum of £3,570.00 for his 5 acres and 37 perches of land. The final agreement between Mr Ashwell and the NSR was signed by Samuel Hope Morley and Howard Morley for Mr Ashwell and Bernard Wells for the NSR Company. Although this appears to be a significant sum of

SUNDAY Working 2 December 1889 to 31 December 1889

DOWN LINE		am	pm			
Nottingham	dep	9.30	12.40	5.00	8.15	
Thorneywood	dep	9.34	12.44	5.04	8.19	
St. Ann's Well	dep	9.37	12.47	5.07	8.22	
Sherwood	dep	9.40	12.50	5.10	8.25	
Daybrook	arr	9.43	12.53	5.13	8.28	
Daybrook	dep	9.52	1.02	6.17	8.37	9.12
Hucknall	arr	10.06			8.51	
Newstead	arr	10.14			8.59	
Pinxton	arr		1.36			
Derby	arr			6.54		9.48

UP LINE		am		pm		
Burton	dep	10.00			4.45	
Derby	dep	10.26			5.12	
Ilkeston	dep	10.46			5.33	
Pinxton	dep			1.55		
Newstead	dep	10.30				
Hucknall	dep	10.38				
Daybrook	arr	10.51	11.02	2.27	5.48	
Daybrook	dep		11.08	2.35	5.52	8.40
Sherwood	dep		11.11	2.38	5.55	8.43
St. Ann's Well	dep		11.14	2.41	5.58	8.46
Thorneywood	arr		11.16	2.43	6.00	8.48
Thorneywood	dep		11.18	2.45	6.02	8.50
Nottingham	arr		11.22	2.49	6.06	8.54
Nottingham	dep		11.50	3.00	6.28	10.05
Grantham	arr		12.40	3.49	7.17	10.43
London (King's X)	arr			7.50	10.10	2.50

money for that time, it probably wasn't considered enough for Mr Ashwell, despite getting a seventy yard long tunnel constructed under his land to preserve both his coach road to his house and his farm yard area.

Born in Epperstone, Nottinghamshire, on 15th May 1828, Henry Ashwell was educated at Leicester Proprietary School. His parents had intended for him to be trained to enter the ministry but instead he studied at Bradford College before taking charge of his Uncle Heard's business. In 1853 he married Sarah Elizabeth Rogers who was the daughter of John Rogers of Nottingham. Henry and Sarah had four children, two girls and two boys born between 1854 and 1863.

Henry Ashwell was a hosiery dyer, bleacher and finisher by trade. In 1853 he acquired the works, which were founded by Mr. John Milnes that were afterwards carried on by Messrs Heard & Hurst. During the latter's ownership the works became the leading hosiery manufacturer in Nottingham, when compared with the other existing seven companies. Their successor, Mr Henry Ashwell, renamed the company Henry Ashwell & Co. Ltd. subsequent to his acquisition. He also continued using the Radford Road works in New Basford, Nottingham.

It is recorded that the Ashwell family lived in Mount Street, New Basford, between 1866 and 1874. They then took up residency at the Woodthorpe Grange house in 1874 and lived there until after 1891. Between 1891 and 1900 the family moved to 91 Waterloo Crescent followed by 117 Waterloo Crescent just before Henry passed away.

The Woodthorpe Grange property is of particular significance to the NSR story. The area occupied by the Grange house and the extensive grounds were originally forested grazing land, which was mainly used for pig farming during the nineteenth century. In 1871 an area of land, including that which the Woodthorpe Park would later occupy, came up for sale at auction. Mr. John L. Thackeray of Arnold, (who later had the road Thackeray's Lane and hence the NSR bridge No.15 named after him) purchased the land. Shortly afterwards, he sold the land to Henry Ashwell. Ashwell had major plans for the property with the purpose of creating for himself and his family a large estate, which would include a private house known as Woodthorpe Grange. The Woodthorpe house was completed in 1874 and became the Ashwell family home where, as the 1881 Census reveals, he was living there with his wife Sarah and his two daughters Mary and Frances, two of his nieces and four servants. In later years Henry Ashwell bought a small brickworks, which was situated on a neighbouring plot of land to the east, off Scout Lane. He paid Mr John Harrison the sum of £655 for it. He later transformed this land into rockery gardens utilising the topography of the quarry to great effect. This area became included within the boundaries of his private grounds. In the 1870's, Ashwell built a 20ft Victorian fountain within this new area of land, which had eight tiers of cascading water. This fountain is still functioning today.

From 1888 to 1893 Ashwell was a Borough Magistrate JP and from 1900 to 1908 he was a City Magistrate. He also served for some years on the Basford Local Board, and afterwards as a member and the Chairman of the Nottingham School Board. When

Down Line		am			pm						
Nottingham London Road	dep	5.30	9.03	11.15 SO	12.10 SO	12.55	2.30 SO	4.25	7.00	8.20	10.10 SO
Newstead	arr	6.19	9.40	11.55	12.50	1.32	3.10	5.02	7.37	9.00	10.49

Up Line		am		pm						
Newstead	dep	7.30	10.01	12.15 SO	1.30 SO	2.15	3.50 SO	5.27	7.57	9.20
Nottingham London Road	arr	8.11	10.38	12.37	2.12	2.32	4.32	6.04	8.34	10.01

(left) **Henry Ashwell (1828 to 1909) who built and lived at the Woodthorpe Grange.**

he died in 1909 at the age of 81, he left his shares to his eldest daughter Mary Helen Ashwell.

Under running powers, which were granted in an Act of 25th July 1890, the London & North Western Railway (LNWR) commenced working freight trains from 5th December 1892 out of their Manvers Street goods yard along GNR lines. It is possible that these running powers were used by the LNWR to transport goods from Manvers Street to Sheffield over the NSR rails, although evidence for this has not as yet been forthcoming.

The NSR Company underwent several changes as regards the membership of its Board in the initial years of operation, as will become evident further on in this chapter. The first change to the Company came about in 1890 when Duncan Frederick Basden, who was one of the partners in the company of Mellors, Basden, Mellors, moved to London to establish new London offices for the firm at 33 St Swithin's Lane.

Duncan Frederick Basden was born in 1855 in Deptford, Kent. Following a spell living in Suffolk, he moved to Nottingham and studied to be an accountant like his father. After qualifying as a Chartered Accountant, Estate Agent and Licensed Valuer he joined Robert Mellors firm, shortly afterwards entering into partnership with him as Mellors and Basden, Accountants. From 1885 to 1890 he was the Secretary to the Sutton-on-Sea and Willoughby Railway, which opened on 28th July 1884. As well as being the Secretary to the NSR from 1886 to 1890 he was also the Assistant Secretary to the Nottinghamshire and Midland Merchants' and Traders' Association.

His place as Secretary of the NSR was taken by Thomas Galland Mellors. He was the son of Robert Mellors born in 1866, one of

nine children. He became an Associate Member of the Institute of Chartered Accountants of England and Wales in 1887 and in the same year became the third partner in the now named firm of Mellors Basden Mellors. In 1892 he became a Fellow of the Institute of Chartered Accountants, becoming the President of the Institute in 1924 and 1925. He continued working for the firm until after 1932, at the same time being a JP and Secretary to many companies, including the Nottingham and District Tramways Co. Ltd. in 1893. He was to continue in this role as Secretary to the NSR until 1920.

It wasn't until December 1890 that Mr J.P. Edwards, the NSR's main contractor, had his outstanding financial contractual claims finally brought to a conclusion. The previous lack of agreement between him and the NSR Company resulted in a visit to the High Court of Justice, Chancery Division, where there were double proceedings, namely the cases of 'Nottingham Suburban Railway Company v Edwards and Edwards v Nottingham Suburban Railway Company – Terms of settlement of actions.' The proceedings settled the long standing claim arguments arising out of Mr Edwards's final account of 17th December 1889. Mr. Johnson, the Engineer of the GNR, was present and matters were referred to him for his opinions. He was directed by the Court to act as final arbitrator under the provisions of The Arbitration Act 1889 and arrange for all payments to be settled by 1st November 1890. On 24th October 1890, the date for making the award was extended to 1st December 1890, to give Mr Johnson more time to sort out the final issues. Each party was ordered to pay their own legal costs and other expenses. Edward Parry, the NSR's Engineer, was responsible for agreeing the final settlement with Edwards.

By coincidence both Edwards and Parry were born in Hendy, Mold, Flintshire and following the completion of the construction of the NSR, they were to both work on the Dore and Chinley Railway as Engineer and Contractor respectively.

As well as the NSR Company providing many new roads along its new line, the NPBC also financed and carried out several new road projects. In 1891 they built the new road, named by Mr. Robert Mellors as Mapperley Rise, which provided access from Woodborough Road on Mapperley top, down to the NSR's Sherwood station and to Sherwood Vale. [The section of Mapperley Rise between Sherwood Vale and Winchester Street, which bypasses the station site, was not constructed until much later.]

On the 2nd January 1893 the NSR received a boost to its traffic usage when the Manchester, Sheffield & Lincolnshire Railway (MS&L) opened the extension of its line from Staveley, through Annesley tunnel, to join the GNR's Leen Valley Line at Newstead, for which it received powers on 26th July 1889. The eleven year old Leen Valley Line was now no longer a branch line. The MS&L introduced a Sheffield to Nottingham passenger service, in accordance with their Agreement with the GNR, which ran via Chesterfield, with running powers over the GNR and the NSR lines, into the GNR's Nottingham (London Road) station. There were six trains in each direction Monday to Saturday, with two each way on a Sunday and the London Road station was taxed at times to deal with all the traffic.

(opposite, top) **One of Henry Ashwell's delivery trucks.** *(opposite, bottom)* **The house at Woodthorpe Grange built by Henry Ashwell in 1874 and later sold to Edward Parry in the mid-1890's.** *D.Birch*

14

From 28th January 1893, the GNR ran a few trains over the MS&L from Nottingham to Staveley but this lasted only a few months.

It was in 1893 that the first sign of a threat to the NSR was to present itself, for which it could have no response. Some may see this as the beginning of its long, slow end. It was certainly the birth of the first of the two major threats, which the NSR was to endure. It was on 28th March of this year that the MS&L had its Act authorised to construct a new line, which would pass through the centre of Nottingham from the north and on to Leicester and London. The NSR was to get first-hand knowledge of the MS&L proposals, for Robert Mellors, who was a NPBC's Managing Director and ex-Chairman and a NSR Director, was appointed by the MS&L in 1895 to acquire all the property for them along the whole length of the line of the new railway through all of Nottingham. In addition to this Edward Parry, also a future Director and Chairman of the NPBC and the Engineer to the NSR, along with his business partner T. Greenhalgh Walker, had drawn up the plans for the location of the new Nottingham Central station, which had been presented to the meeting of the Nottingham Council's General Purposes Committee way back on 3rd October 1881. Parry later became the MS&L's Resident Engineer for the section of the line from Annesley in the north to Rugby in the south. As the final design work for the MS&L must have been completed well before the Act of 1893, Parry was most probably appointed to this post well before this date, for it is certain that he was fully aware of the design of the new GCR and GNR lines prior to the introduction of the NSR's Deviations. Armed with the MS&L design information, he probably used it to change the design of the NSR's junction with the GNR's Nottingham to Grantham line, so that it would be to the east of the High Level's proposed junction with the same line. This was to ensure that the NSR would have future routes to and from the new Nottingham Joint station after it had opened. If my hypothesis is correct, this is why Parry withdrew his NSR Deviation No.2, which would not have been able to junction with the High Level route to Victoria station. The delayed and revised Deviation No.3 was designed so that the NSR would link with the route into Nottingham (Victoria) station, which it eventually did. The alternative scenario was for the NSR not to achieve direct access into the Victoria station from their Up line Deviation. If this had happened, then the GNR may have considered that the necessary track alterations, for the NSR to achieve access, would have been either too expensive or not cost effective. This would have meant that the NSR would have had to have terminated its traffic at the London Road station and consequently the NSR may have either received even less traffic after 1900 or the NSR may have been closed much earlier than it was.

The NSR accounts for the year ending 31st December 1893 showed deficits of £5,344 on the guarantee of £9,050 but the shareholders were paid their 3.5% dividend and the NSR Company, after paying its administration costs, still showed a positive balance in the bank. This was thanks to their Agreement with the GNR, who were legally bound to contribute the difference. The GNR Revenue Accounts part No.10 for the half years ending in 1894 and 1895 shows that the GNR contributed £4,525 to the NSR for both half years.

During the fourth quarter of 1894 the sad news was announced that Edward Gripper, the NSR's Chairman from 1888 to 1894 and Director 1885 to 1894, and the NPBC's Chairman 1882 to 1894 and Managing Director 1869 to 1894, had died aged 79. Gripper was born in 1815 at Layer Breton Hall, Layer Breton, Essex. His father was also named Edward and his mother was named Mary. Edward had seven younger siblings, four sisters and three brothers born between 1816 and 1833. The family were staunch Quakers. Edward Gripper never married. He remained at home living with his parents at Layer Breton Hall until 1855, were he was employed as a farmer on his father's farm.

He then moved to Nottingham and formed a company to manufacture bricks at The Mapperley Top Brickyard, on Mapperley Plains Road, which he purchased shortly after his arrival in Nottingham. By 1861 Gripper, who was then 46 years old, lived at Welbeck Terrace in Nottingham and he was then registered as a brick manufacturer, employing 43 men and 38 boys.

In 1866 he negotiated and was successful in securing exclusive local use of the Hoffman's continuous burning kiln, which was designed so that the surplus heat after burning was passed on to the next kiln chamber. In 1867 he entered into partnership with Mr William Burgass who owned brickworks at Carlton and Mapperley. Together they jointly founded the Nottingham Patent Brick Company (NPBC).

(below) **The GNR Revenue Account showing the GNR's contribution to the NSR for half years in 1894 and 1895.**

Dr.			No. 10.—NET REVENUE ACCOUNT.			Cr.
	Half-year ended 31st Dec., 1895.	Half-year ended 31st Dec., 1894.		Half-year ended 31st Dec., 1895.	Half-year ended 31st Dec., 1894.
	£ s. d.	£		£ s. d.	£
To Interest on Debenture Stock	194,591 9 1	193,034	By Balance brought from last Half-year's Account	3,161 2 4	6,396
„ Interest on Banking Balances [See Contra]	....	3,182	„ Do. Revenue Account, No. 9	1,011,142 18 9	919,813
„ General Interest Account	14,551 9 2	10,999	„ Interest on Banking Balances	1,136 17 7	....
„ Guaranteed rent of East Lincolnshire Railway	18,000 0 0	18,000	„ Dividends on Shares in other Companies	4,592 13 4	4,590
„ Do. Royston and Hitchin Railway	8,000 5 0	8,000	„ Amount received from Cheshire Lines Committee in respect of the North Liverpool Lines Guarantee Fund	4,400 0 1	4,395
„ Do. Nottingham and Grantham Railway	20,913 15 0	20,914			
„ Do. Nottingham Suburban Railway	4,525 0 0	4,525			
„ Do. Halifax High Level Railway	....	1,603			
„ Do. Ramsey Railway	806 5 0	806			
„ Do. Stamford and Essendine Railway	1,500 0 0	1,500			
„ Midland and Great Northern Joint Lines :—					
Western Section—Interest on Capital	8,010 3 10	8,010			
Eastern Section— Do.	4,864 11 9	3,479			
„ Rent of Navigations	5,272 10 0	5,273			
„ Manchester Sheffield and Lincolnshire Railway Company for proportion of amount of Interest on Capital expended at Manchester, &c., for accommodation of joint through traffic	2,187 10 0	2,187			
	£ 283,222 18 10	281,512			
„ Balance available for Dividend [See No. 13.]	741,210 13 3	653,682			
	£ 1,024,433 12 1	935,194		£ 1,024,433 12 1	935,194

Under Gripper's management, the NPBC reached an output of twenty seven million bricks in one year. Many of its best bricks were sent to London for the building of the St. Pancras Station, and used to construct various buildings and sewers for the London County Council. As a consequence the NPBC's bricks established a reputation to be described in specifications as standard.

He became a much respected gentleman becoming a Member of the Basford Local Board and when Basford was annexed to Nottingham he was made an Alderman and JP. From 1881 to 1893 he was a Nottingham City Corporation Alderman, from 1880 to 1881 he was Mayor of Nottingham and from 1881 to 1893 he was a Borough Magistrate and a Justice of the Peace. His activities also included Chairman of the Water Committee and for sixteen years he was a member of the School Board, becoming its Vice-Chairman from 1870-1873 and subsequently Chairman for thirteen years. Over twenty schools were built whilst he was on the Board and half a dozen were transferred to it on the extension of the Borough. He devoted six hours a day to public service business. In 1874 Gripper was on the Committee of Notts and Midland Merchants and Traders' Association for the Protection of Trade.

Despite all of these interests, he continued working for the NPBC and living at 144 Mansfield Road, Nottingham, where he had lived with his faithful housekeeper Emma Walton. She had been with him from the mid 1860's right up to his death in 1894. Edward Gripper was buried in the Friends' burial ground, in the Nottingham General Cemetery, near the junction of Waverley Street and Clarendon Street.

The loss of the NSR's Chairman necessitated a vote for a replacement. This privilege was afforded to Samuel Herrick Sands, who had been a Director of the Company since 1887. Sands was born in Nottingham in 1833 to Sarah and Harold Hall Sands, a civil engineer in the partnership of Sands and Walker of Basford. He married Phoebe Anne Ashwell, who incidentally was Henry Ashwell's sister, on the 3rd March 1859. In 1866 he became the manager at Copestake, Moore, Crampton and Company who were lace manufacturers in Hounds Gate, Nottingham. From 1895 to 1901 he was Chairman of the NPBC, 1896 to 1903 Director of the NPBC, 1886 to 1893 Nottingham Corporation Councillor for the Castle Ward and 1890 to 1891 the Mayor of Nottingham. In addition to these accolades he was a Town, City and County Magistrate, as well as a City Alderman for Bridge Ward. As can be determined from the above, Sands was a very influential man to have on your Board as your Chairman. He was also the partner of Jesse Hind, forming the firm of Wells and Hind who were the Solicitors for the NSR Company from 1886 to 1923 and also the NPBC.

The death of Gripper also created a vacancy on the NSR Company's Board of Directors. In 1894 Jesse Hind filled this vacancy and became a Director of the NSR. He was born in Sneinton, Nottingham in 1842, the son of William and Ann. He had four younger brothers. He was married in 1865 to Eliza and they had three sons and two daughters. He attended High Pavement School from 1852 to 1856. He later passed his law articles and was engaged as a managing clerk for Mr Enfield and was subsequently offered a partnership by Arthur Wells, forming the company of Nottingham Incorporated Law Society. In 1889 he became the first Clerk to the newly formed County Council. From 1893 to1904 he was the Clerk of the Peace for the County of Nottinghamshire from which he resigned due to increasing deafness.

By 1895 the NSR still had ten trains going north from Nottingham passing over its rails. Five of these travelled as far as Newstead, except on a Wednesday and Saturday when this figure was increased to six. In addition, one train travelled to Ilkeston, being extended through to Derby (Friargate) on a Friday only. There were also ten passenger trains a day travelling south over the Suburban. Four of

these originated from Newstead, which became five on a Wednesday and Saturday, and similarly one from Ilkeston, which departed from Derby on a Friday. On Saturdays the train from Ilkeston did not stop at any of the NSR stations and travelled from Daybrook station to Nottingham (London Road) station non-stop in just eleven minutes.

On 18th June 1897, as part of Queen Victoria's Diamond Jubilee celebrations, Nottingham was awarded 'City status', being signified in a letter from the Prime Minister, the Marques of Salisbury, to the Mayor of Nottingham. As a consequence of this, and as part of the Queen's Diamond Jubilee celebrations, a huge bonfire was built in the yard of the Mapperley Brickworks, as it was the highest point in Nottingham. The beacon could be seen for miles around.

The beacon constructed at the NPBC's Mapperley brickyard, one of the highest points in Nottingham, to celebrate the 1897 Queen Victoria's Diamond Jubilee. *Mike Chapman collection.*

The Act of 3rd June 1897 changed the title of the MS&LR to the Great Central Railway (GCR), which became effective from 1st August 1897.

During the mid 1890's Edward Parry and his family moved into Woodthorpe Grange and replaced Henry Ashwell J.P. as its owner. Parry was the son of Edward and Mary, of Hendy, Mold, Flintshire in Wales. Born in 1844, he had two younger siblings. Following education in a private school in Chester, Edward began his civil engineering career with the Midland Railway in 1869. Between 1875 and 1879 he was the Resident Engineer on the Midland Railway's Nottingham to Melton Mowbray railway line after which he joined Nottinghamshire County Council as their County Surveyor, holding the post until 1889.

By 1881 Edward, who was now classified as a Civil Engineer and Architect, had moved to Nottingham, where he was to spend most of the rest of his life, and lived at 56 Clarendon Street, Sherwood, Nottingham. He was now married to Mary Elizabeth and had three children, two girls and a boy. In 1884 he designed the Castle Gate United Reform Church.

Whilst occupying the role of County Surveyor, Edward also had a private business and it was through this that between 1886 and 1889 he designed and supervised the construction of the Nottingham Suburban Railway line as the Company's Engineer. The pressure of private work resulted in him resigning his post as County Surveyor in 1889, having previously accepted the post in 1879. It was about this time apparently that Parry had the idea of a joint central station in Nottingham, which eventually materialised as Nottingham's Victoria station.

Parry was a very busy man for during the late 1880's he also worked on the design of the Dore and Chinley line, which was part of the Midland railway route from Sheffield to Manchester which included the Totley tunnel, Britain's second longest tunnel, and Cowburn tunnel, Britain's deepest! In 1891 at the age of 46, Edward and Mary Elizabeth were now the parents of six children, the three additions being one girl and two boys.

The Great Central's London Extension from north of Nottingham at Annesley to Marylebone, London was designed and built between 1893 and 1899. Parry was engaged as the lines' Resident Engineer for the Northern section, which stretched south as far as Rugby. This included his dream Nottingham GCR/GNR Joint station which opened on Thursday 24th May 1900.

The new century still saw Edward Parry and his family living at Woodthorpe Grange but Mary, his wife, had now bore him another child making seven in all. In 1905 Edward Parry sold the Grange to Mr. John Godfrey Small, who was the son of the net manufacturer Mr. J.G. Small and whose factory was located at St. Mary's Gate, Nottingham.

In 1896 Parry became a Director of the Nottingham Patent Brick Company, which, as documented in Volume 1, was the main promoter of the Nottingham Suburban Railway. He was also a Director of the Digby Collieries near Eastwood, who also manufactured bricks. This Company also owned the Gedling Colliery, which was located on the Derbyshire & Staffordshire Extension Railway just east of Daybrook station and the Mapperley tunnel. It is also possible that Parry had family connections with Edward Parry & Co, the firebrick manufacturers, but this has yet to be established. Also it is known that Butterley Building materials marketed "Parry Blue" firebacks, which were made at their Catheralls works. From 1905 to 1909 Parry was the Engineer to the South Yorkshire Joint Railway, which was a subsidiary of the Great Central Railway.

Parry was renowned for his structures, which were faced with blue brindle bricks. This obsession, if that is what it was, allegedly began during the commencement of the construction of the Nottingham Suburban Railway. It is believed that the NSR bridge No.12, over the Mapperley Brickworks wagon-way incline and the extended culvert No.25 at Daybrook junction, were the first

structures to be completed in the late summer of 1887. They were faced with red brindle engineering bricks supplied by the Hathern Brick Company's works at Cliff, Tamworth, Staffordshire, which opened in 1882. It is thought that Parry found the colour of these bricks unacceptable and ordered that all the remaining structures would be faced with blue brindle wire-cut bricks bonded with a black mortar of which Parry stated '...it makes an excellent finish and imparts a less sombre colour to the structure than the more expensive Staffordshire blue pressed bricks. Being of a rougher grain, the brindle bricks bond better than the highly finished and smoother blue bricks, and are more easily handled.'

Sadly many of Parry's railways have been closed and their structures demolished. Their designs were noted for their elegant lines and well proportioned simplicity, as well as their fine durable construction, which made their demolition all the more difficult.

Happily one of Parry's structures has recently been re-discovered by Paul Clark on the NSR. This is of one of the original nine culverts, which were constructed to pass water courses under various railway embankments. None of these had been found to date but the one that has been located by Paul is in the corner of the playing field off Thackeray's Lane below the long radius curve where the NSR used to meet the 'Back line'. An aerial photograph shows a line of trees along field boundaries on both sides of the NSR at the same spot as this culvert, which may hide a stream which would have required the culvert. This culvert, which is about 2ft 0ins. span, is made out of blue brindle bricks and its ring is 15 inches or three bricks deep. The head wall is in a poor condition but can still be made out and is 11ft 0ins. long.

In 1897 the NPBC had the foresight to acquire an additional brickyard, which would ensure the life of the company for many years after the two brickyards at Mapperley and Thorneywood would prove to be uneconomical to operate. The brickyard, which they purchased, was at Dorket Head and was on the same outcrop of Keuper marl as the Mapperley brickyard but at its east end of the Mapperley Plains. Clay extraction for the manufacture of bricks at Dorket Head had been taking place for over 175 years. During the 1860's the Robinson family of Arnold established a factory there. When the brickyards at Mapperley and Thorneywood closed in the 1960's, the company moved its offices to the Dorket Head site. The word 'Patent' in the NPBC's name referred to the Hoffman manufacturing process which the company used to manufacture its bricks. When the Hoffman kiln was dispensed with at Dorket Head and more modern equipment took its place, the company changed its name to the Nottingham Brick plc. In 1987 the renamed brick company was acquired by Marley Brick. In 1993 Marley Brick was purchased by Tarmac and in 1995 the Dorket Head works were purchased by Ibstock Brick Limited, who remain as its owner to date.

My sincere thanks are given to Mike Chapman, the Manager of Ibstock Brick Ltd at the Dorket Head works, for his invaluable knowledge and assistance in recording the history of the NPBC in this series.

The remains of a blue brick culvert and headwall in the park adjacent to Thackeray's Lane; discovered by Paul Clark. *D Birch*

A brick manufactured by the Robinson brothers at the Dorket Head brickyard prior to it being bought by the NPBC. *Mike Chapman collection*

A brick produced by R Bennett the great grandfather of Charles Bennett who became the Manager at the NPBC. *Mike Chapman collection*

A brick produced by the NPBC. *Mike Chapman collection.*

A brick produced by the Nottingham Builders' Brick Company, Carlton Road. *Mike Chapman collection*

A group photograph of the horses and handlers at the NPBC's Mapperley brick yard, which were used to haul carts, tubs and standard gauge wagons around the brickyard. *Mike Chapman collection.*

Extract from the Great Northern Railway Working Timetables 1st November 1897:

LEEN VALLEY, EREWASH VALLEY, DERBYSHIRE & STAFFORD LINES

Down Line		Eng & Brakes	Pass	Goods	Eng	Pass	Pass	Pass	Pass	Pass
		am						pm		
Nottingham	dep	3.30	7.45	8.50	8.43	9.05	10.35	12.05	12.55	1.10
Thorneywood	dep	Thr'u	7.49	9.30	Thr'u	9.09	Thr'u	12.09	12.59	1.14
St. Ann's Well	dep	Thr'u	7.52	9.50	Thr'u	9.12	Thr'u	12.12	1.02	1.17
Sherwood	dep	Thr'u	7.55	10.10	Thr'u	9.15	Thr'u	12.15	1.05	1.20
Daybrook	arr		7.58		8.53	9.18		12.18	1.08	1.23
Daybrook	dep			10.15		9.19		12.19	1.09	1.24
Leen Valley Junction	arr			10.30						
Bulwell Forest	dep					9.25		12.25	1.15	1.30
Bestwood	dep					9.28		12.28	1.18	1.33
Butler's Hill	dep					9.31		12.31	1.21	1.36
Hucknall	dep					9.34		12.34	1.24	1.39
Linby	dep					9.38		12.38	1.28	1.43
Newstead	arr					9.42		12.42	1.32	1.47
To Pinxton	arr						11.15			
To Eastwood	arr	4.05								
		Monday excepted					Saturdays Only	Will run between Daybrook and Newstead on Wednesday and Saturdays only.	Saturdays excepted	Saturdays Only

Down Line		Cttle & Goods	Pass	Pass	Pass	Pass	Pass	Pass	Pass	GC Exp. Goods
		Pm								
Nottingham	dep	2.55	3.15	3.15	3.15	4.43	5.40	7.05	8.40	9.20
Thorneywood	dep	Thr'u	3.19	3.19	3.19	4.47	5.44	7.09	8.44	Thr'u
St. Ann's Well	dep	Thr'u	3.22	3.22	3.22	4.50	5.47	7.12	8.47	Thr'u
Sherwood	dep	Thr'u	3.25	3.25	3.25	4.53	5.50	7.15	8.50	Thr'u
Daybrook	arr		3.28	3.28	3.28	4.56	5.53	7.18	8.53	
Daybrook	dep		3.29	3.29	3.29	4.57		7.19	8.54	
Leen Valley Junction	arr	3.15								10.20
Bulwell Forest	dep					5.03		7.25		
Bestwood	dep					5.06		7.28	9.01	
Butler's Hill	dep	3.25				5.09		7.31	9.04	
Hucknall	dep					5.12		7.34	9.07	
Linby	dep					5.16		7.38	9.11	
Newstead	arr					5.20		7.42	9.15	
To Pinxton	arr				4.03					
To Ilkeston	arr		3.46							
To Derby	arr			4.01						
		Wednesdays Only	Friday and Saturday excepted	Friday Only	Saturday Only					To Manchester and Liverpool

Up Line		Goods	G C Goods	Goods & Coal	Pass & Cttle	Pass	Pass	Goods	Pass	Pass
		Am							pm	
From Annesley			2.35							
From Eastwood		12.15								
From Basford & Bulwell	dep							11.35		
Newstead	dep						9.55		1.35	2.15
Linby	dep						9.59		1.39	2.19
Hucknall	dep						10.03		1.43	2.23
Butler's Hill	dep						10.06		1.46	2.26
Bestwood	dep						10.09		1.49	2.29
Bulwell Forest	dep						10.12		1.52	2.32
Leen Valley Junction	dep	1.50						12.00		
Daybrook	arr	2.15	Thr'u				10.17	12.03	1.57	2.37
Daybrook	dep	2.19	Thr'u	7.20	8.15	9.10	10.18	12.35	1.58	2.38
Sherwood	dep	Thr'u	Thr'u	7.30	8.18	9.13	10.21	12.50	2.01	2.41
St. Ann's Well	dep	Thr'u	Thr'u	7.45	8.21	9.16	10.24	1.05	2.04	2.44
Thorneywood	arr	Thr'u	Thr'u		8.23	9.18	10.26	1.10	2.06	2.46
Thorneywood	dep	Thr'u	Thr'u	8.00	8.25	9.20	10.28	1.45	2.08	2.48
Nottingham	arr	2.40	3.16	8.08	8.29	9.24	10.32	1.53	2.12	2.52
		Monday excepted		Monday excepted					Will run between Daybrook and Newstead on Wednesday and Saturday only.	

Up Line		Pass	Pass	Pass	Pass	Pass	Pass	Pass	Pass
		Pm							
From Ilkeston	dep				4.53				
From Derby	dep		4.35						
From Pinxton	dep			4.38			6.25		
From Heanor	dep	2.30							
Newstead	dep					5.35			7.57
Linby	dep					5.39			8.01
Hucknall	dep					5.43			8.05
Butler's Hill	dep					5.46			8.08
Bestwood	dep					5.49			8.11
Bulwell Forest	dep					5.52			8.14
Daybrook	arr	2.59	5.13	5.13	5.13	5.57	7.56		8.19
Daybrook	dep	3.00	5.14	5.14	5.14	5.58	6.57	7.15	8.20
Sherwood	dep	Thr'u	5.17	5.17	5.17	6.01	7.00	7.18	8.23
St. Ann's Well	dep	Thr'u	5.20	5.20	5.20	6.04	7.03	7.21	8.26
Thorneywood	arr	3.05	5.22	5.22	5.22	6.06	7.05	7.23	8.28
Thorneywood	dep	3.07	5.24	5.24	5.24	6.08	7.07	7.25	8.30
Nottingham	arr	3.11	5.28	5.28	5.28	6.12	7.11	7.29	8.34
		Saturdays Only	Fridays Only	Saturdays Only	Fridays and Saturdays excepted		Saturdays Only		

Apart from NSR's Sunday passenger service, which ran during December 1889, according to the GNR Working Time Table dated from 1st November 1897, there was a late evening Sunday service along the line which only stopped at the Thorneywood station and passed through Sherwood and St. Ann's Well stations.

The GNR had obtained powers, through the Act of 20th June 1892, to construct the Leen Valley Extension from Kirkby South Junction initially through to Skegby (six miles north of Newstead), which it opened to goods traffic on 1st March 1898. Passenger services commenced the following month on 4th April from Nottingham to Skegby with trains running over the Suburban. Fast trains completed the journey in 40 minutes and stopping trains took between 50 to 55 minutes. There were seven Down trains to Skegby and six Up, with an extra train on Saturdays. In addition there were two each way to Sutton-in-Ashfield. Although there were two trains each way on a Sunday, these ran via Gedling and not via the Suburban.

Up Line		Pass.
		Pm
Newstead	dep	9.13
Linby	dep	9.17
Hucknall	dep	9.21
Butler's Hill	dep	9.24
Bestwood	dep	9.27
Bulwell Forest	dep	Thr'u
Daybrook	arr	9.34
Daybrook	**dep**	**9.35**
Sherwood	**dep**	**Thr'u**
St. Ann's Well	**dep**	**Thr'u**
Thorneywood	**arr**	**9.40**
Thorneywood	**dep**	**9.42**
Nottingham	**arr**	**9.48**

There is a frequently used photograph of the GNR's London Road station taken in October 1898 showing passengers crowding at the station to go to the annual Goose Fair in the Market Place, which was held there till 1927 before its move to the Forest off Mansfield Road in 1928. It is possible that the Suburban helped to feed the London Road station, and later the Victoria station, with Goose Fair passenger traffic.

In 1899, of the thirteen northbound and fifteen southbound passenger trains over the Suburban, seven went to or originated from Skegby. The Saturday service at this time included the 10.35 a.m. train from Nottingham (London Road) station to Pinxton which ran by way of the Suburban but with a first stop at Kimberley. Goods traffic along the line was light with only two or three trains a day each-way, travelling to and from the Nottingham London Road goods yard. There was also one daily train that serviced the NBBC and the NPBC's two brickyards by delivering to them wagons loaded with coal and sand and empty wagons. They collected for their return journey both empty sand and coal wagons and brick loaded wagons from the NBBC and the NPBC's Thorneywood and Sherwood wagon storage yards.

The October 1899 timetable gives an insight into the weekday London Road station passenger train departures and their final destinations, which left to travel over the Suburban rails before services were transferred to Victoria station. There were seventeen trains on a weekday but there were no trains advertised over the Suburban on Sundays.

Dep. Time	Final Dest.
7.57 am	Burton-on-Trent
8.30 am	Skegby
8.57 am	Skegby
10.35 am	Pinxton (SO)
11.15 am	Skegby
12.05 pm	Skegby
1.03 pm	Skegby
2.45 pm	Skegby
3.15 pm	Pinxton (SO)
3.15 pm	Derby (FO)
3.15 pm	Ilkeston
4.43 pm	Sutton-in-Ashfield
5.40 pm	Daybrook
6.05 pm	Skegby
7.10 pm	Skegby
8.40 pm	Skegby
11.20 pm	Skegby

In 1899 the NPBC sold some of their land around the Morley Avenue area, in order to provide new residential development adjacent to the new station.

There were probably quite a few specials that ran along the NSR prior to the *RCTS* Special in 1951. One that can be proved is the one advertising a trip to London on Saturday 20th May 1899, which picked up and set down day-trippers at all three of the NSR stations. They would have had to have got up early as the first departure on the NSR at Sherwood was at 5.20 a.m. and it was timetabled to leave King's Cross for the return journey at midnight. The charge was 4/3d (21.5p) and half price for children under 14 years old.

Great Northern Railway.

Jardine's Trip Committee have made arrangements with the Great Northern Railway to run a Trip to

LONDON,

King's Cross, stopping at Wood Green for Alexandra Palace,
— ON —

WHIT-SATURDAY, MAY 20th, 1899.

FARE **4/3** RETURN.

Children under 14 half-fares. A small extra charge will be made for printing and organising expenses.

☞ Tickets should be purchased on or before May 16th.

		A.M.
Hucknall	dep.	5·0.
Butler's Hill	,,	5·5.
Bestwood	,,	5·8.
Bulwell Forest	,,	5·11.
Daybrook	,,	5·17.
Sherwood	,,	5·20.
St. Ann's Well	,,	5·23.
Thorneywood	,,	5·26.
Nottingham (G.N.R.)	,,	5·45.
Colwick	,,	5·51.
Radcliffe	,,	5·56.
Bingham	,,	6·4.

Returning from King's Cross at 12·0 (midnight);
Finsbury Park, 12.6; Wood Green, 12·11.

EXTENSION OF TICKETS.—Passengers may return by ANY train, 10·0 a.m., 2·0 and 2·30 p.m. excepted, up to and including **Saturday, May 27th**, on payment of **2/- extra**, on presenting the Return Halves of their Tickets at the Booking Office, King's Cross. A few Extension Tickets may be had from F. Rushton, Deering Street Works.

TICKETS MAY BE OBTAINED FROM—
Messrs. W. W. Goodman, Raleigh Street; W. Lander, Cope's, Basford; G. Bennett, Victor Cycle Co.; G. Wright, Deering Street; E. Fowler, 61, Bruce Grove; W. Else, Wilford Road; W. Adkin, Music Warehouse, Arkwright Street; W. Ellis, West Street, Arnold; H. J. Williams, 55, Raleigh Street; J. Osmond, 32, Beauvale Road; J. Matthews, 14, Peas Hill Road; W. Crooks, 93, Norton Street; T. Hodkinson, 86, Alfreton Road; — Loverseed, 8, Ekowe Street, Basford; J. Barnes, Market Place, Bulwell; Mrs. Holroyd, Hucknall; G. Ward, Middle Marsh; J. Robinson, 16, Burton St.; J. T. Radford.
Applications for saloons to be made to F. Rushton, Deering Street Works.

GNR flyer advertising a day trip to London on Saturday 20th May 1899 with stops to pick and set down passengers at all three NSR stations. *GNR*

Down Line		am			pm								
Nottingham	dep	7.45	9.05	11.15	12.05	12.55	2.45	3.15	4.43	5.45	6.05	7.05	8.40
Thorneywood	dep	7.49	9.09	11.19	12.09	1.02	2.49	3.19	4.47	5.49	6.09	7.09	8.44
St. Ann's Well	dep	7.50	9.12	11.22	12.12	1.05	2.52	3.22	4.50	5.52	6.12	7.12	8.47
Sherwood	dep	7.55	9.15	11.25	12.15	1.09	2.55	3.25	4.53	5.55	6.15	7.15	8.50
Daybrook	arr	7.58			12.19			3.29		6.02			
Daybrook	dep		9.19	11.29		1.15	2.59		4.57		6.19	7.19	8.54
Bulwell Forest	dep		9.25	11.35		1.18	3.05		5.03			7.25	
Bestwood	dep		9.28	11.38		1.21	3.08		5.06			7.28	9.01
Butler's Hill	dep		9.32	11.41		1.24	3.11		5.09			7.31	9.04
Hucknall	dep		9.34	11.44		1.28	3.14		5.12		6.28	7.34	9.07
Linby	dep		9.38	11.48		1.32	3.18		5.16			7.38	9.11
Newstead	arr		9.42	11.52		1.38	3.22		5.20		6.34	7.42	9.15
Newstead	dep			11.58		1.35	3.28		5.26		6.40	7.48	9.21
Sutton In Ashfield	dep			12.02		1.42	3.32		arr 5.29		6.44	7.52	9.26
Skegby	arr			12.05		1.45	3.35				6.48	7.56	9.29

Up Line		am					Pm									
Skegby	dep		8.05			10.15	12.20		2.02		4.10					8.30
Sutton In Ashfield	dep		8.09			10.19	12.24		2.06		4.14		5.45			8.34
Newstead	dep		8.18		9.55		12.33		2.15		4.23	4.45	5.54			8.43
Linby	arr				9.59		12.37		2.19			4.49	5.58			
Hucknall	dep		8.24		10.03	10.33	12.41		2.23		4.29	4.53	6.02			8.51
Butler's Hill	dep				10.06		12.44		2.26			4.56	6.05			8.54
Bestwood	dep				10.09		12.47		2.29			4.59	6.08			8.57
Bulwell Forest	dep				10.12		12.50		2.32			5.04	6.11			9.00
Daybrook	arr		8.35		10.17	10.41	12.55		2.37		4.37	5.09	6.16			9.05
Daybrook	dep	8.15	8.34	9.10	10.18	10.42	12.56	1.59	2.38	3.00	4.38	5.14	6.17	6.57	7.15	9.06
Sherwood	arr	8.18		9.13	10.21		12.59	2.01	2.41		4.46	5.17	6.20	7.00	7.18	9.09
St. Ann's Well	dep	8.21		9.16	10.24		1.02	2.04	2,44		4.50	5.20	6.23	7.03	7.21	9.12
Thorneywood	dep	8.25	8.41	9.20	10.29	10.51	1.06	2.08	2.48	3.07		5.24	6.27	7.07	7.25	9.16
Nottingham	arr	8.29	8.45	9.24	10.32	10.55	1.10	2.12	2.52	3.11		5.28	6.31	7.11	7.29	9.20

It is interesting to observe that on the outward journey from Nottingham there is an approximately one hour service along the Suburban line, all of which stop at all three NSR stations. However, on the return trip, whilst the regularity of the Suburban service is about hourly, there are three trains that run through Sherwood and St. Ann's Well and only make a stop at Thorneywood station. This may be an indication that Thorneywood station had the highest patronage of passengers wishing to travel to Nottingham.

A horse, with its attendant handler, pulling a standard gauge wagon onto a wagon turntable at the NPBC's Mapperley brickyard. *Mike Chapman collection.*

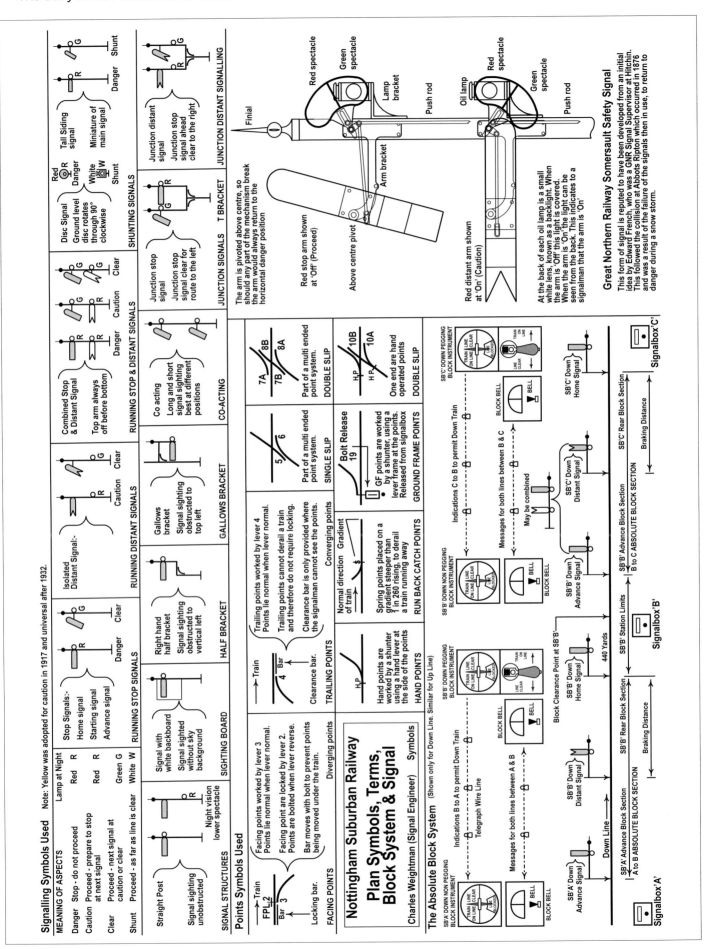

Chapter 8: THE SIGNALLING ON THE NOTTINGHAM SUBURBAN RAILWAY
By Charles Weightman

Introduction: Charles Weightman was, until 2001, the Signal Engineer of the London North Eastern Zone of Railtrack and at the time of writing in 2010 is still practising. He just remembers the Nottingham Suburban Railway line in existence. The route was converted to a single line on 9th February 1930, when all signalling (except at the extremities of the line) along with the intermediate signal boxes at Thorneywood, St. Ann's Well and Sherwood were closed. No formal signalling plans showing the signal and points' identities (lever numbers) have been found. This, 'The story of the signalling system' is therefore a composition, which is in the form of a plan of the line. Volume 1 of the *Story of the NSR*, contains 1/2500 Ordnance Survey maps of the whole line. These accurately show the positions of the bridges, tunnels, platforms, mile posts, signal posts and the track layout of the line including point end positions. The whole line has been drawn to a variable scale in the style of a signalling detailed sketch. The fixed infrastructure, which includes the signal and point positions, has been accurately placed on this plan. Many photographs have been studied to determine the 'form of the signals' so that they are correctly shown. Some of the photographs show the signal identities. Where no photographs exist, professional knowledge has been applied. This chapter's author, while working in the offices of the Signal Engineer at London Road (Low Level) station in 1966 (photograph in NSR Volume 1, page 6, the first floor office at the extreme right), has seen an 'invitation to tender' contract document for the signal box structures and lever frames and remembers them as each for 30 levers. Also seen was a GNR 'notice to traffic' document issued by the GNR on 26th April 1915, simplifying the junction distant signalling arrangements throughout the company. In order not to mislead future historians and to expose the degree of accuracy of this record, each description details those signal and point identities which are certain, those which are most likely and those which have been assumed.

Note: In the following reference (1.44.U or C or L) means that a photograph appears in *The Story of the NSR* Volume 1, page 44, Upper, Centre or Lower. Also (R1.172) refers to Alfred Henshaw's book *The Great Northern Railway in the East Midlands: Colwick Yards–Nottingham London Road–Gedling–Basford* published by RCTS, Figure 172. Also (HGN.29) refers to Michael Vanns book *An Illustrated History of Great Northern Signalling* Figure 29.

Requirement for Signalling: Steel wheels running on steel rails is a low friction form of transport, enabling heavy loads to be moved economically using a relatively low powered source of traction. However, because of this low friction, stopping requires a considerable distance. It is therefore not possible to safely drive on sight. A driver needs advanced information as to where he is expected to stop. Hence the need for a signalling system which integrates all the requirements for the safe movement of trains.

The Principles of Signalling used on UK railways had been well established by the 1880's. Those basic principles are still applied today although using relay and micro processor technologies

with colour light signals and now cab signalling. (However, 490 mechanical signal boxes, similar to those on the NSR, most with semaphore signals, were still open at the start of 2010). The basic elements of the system are:-

Signal boxes each contain a mechanical interlocking lever frame, at an elevated level on the operating floor. The lever frames on the NSR were at the front of the signal box to give the signalman a good view over the controlled area. A lever is considered to be 'normal' when it is back in the frame and 'reverse' when pulled over by the signalman. At the bottom of a lever is a spring catch arrangement, which holds the lever in each position, this is released by pulling a catch handle at the back of the lever. Signal levers are connected to the signals by flexible galvanised wires, wheels, pulleys and weights. When a signal lever is pulled, the wire is tightened and a weight bar at the signal is raised, this weight bar pushes the signal arm to the 'off' (proceed) position. When the lever is replaced back to the normal position, the wire is slackened and the weight bar pulls the wire back, also placing the signal arm to the 'on' (stop or caution) position. Point levers are connected to the points by iron rods on rollers and a series of cranks and adjusters. The levers are interlocked so that the signal levers can only be moved if the point levers are in the correct position and no conflicting or opposing signal levers have been pulled and vice-versa. Communication between the signal boxes was by the 'telegraph'. This electrical instrument enabled the signalman to cause a magnetic needle to move to the left or right, passing messages using a form of Morse code. Similar instruments were provided to regulate the safe passage of trains; these are known as block instruments. Electric indicators are provided to show the signalman the action of signals and the lamps of those signals, which cannot be viewed from the signal box. The instruments and indicators are arranged on a shelf above the lever frame, along with a diagram of the layout.

Signals (known as semaphore signals) which require to be read by a driver when on the move are known as 'running signals'. Such signals were mounted on a signal post (sometimes very high); the arms are large enough and positioned so as to enable the driver sufficient time to read the signal and to act upon its message in good time. Stop signals (home, starting or advance) have a red arm with a square end with a coloured glass spectacle moving in front of an oil lamp to give a red or green light at night. Stop signals show 'off' (proceed – green light) with the lever pulled and 'on' or 'danger' (stop – red light) with the lever normal. Caution (distant) signals had a red arm with a fish tail end. These also displayed a red or green lamp (From 1917 onward distant arms were yellow and the night display became a yellow or green lamp). A distant signal shows 'off' (clear ahead) with the lever pulled and 'on' (proceed at caution) with the lever normal. Running signals are sometimes mounted on brackets or bridges (gantries). Bracket mounted posts are known as 'dolls'. Mechanical signals may be up to 1,500 yards from the signal box. Shunt signals are usually at ground level (variously known as: - dwarfs, dods, dollys or discs), with a red face and red lamp to show 'stop'. To show 'shunt proceed' these signals rotate

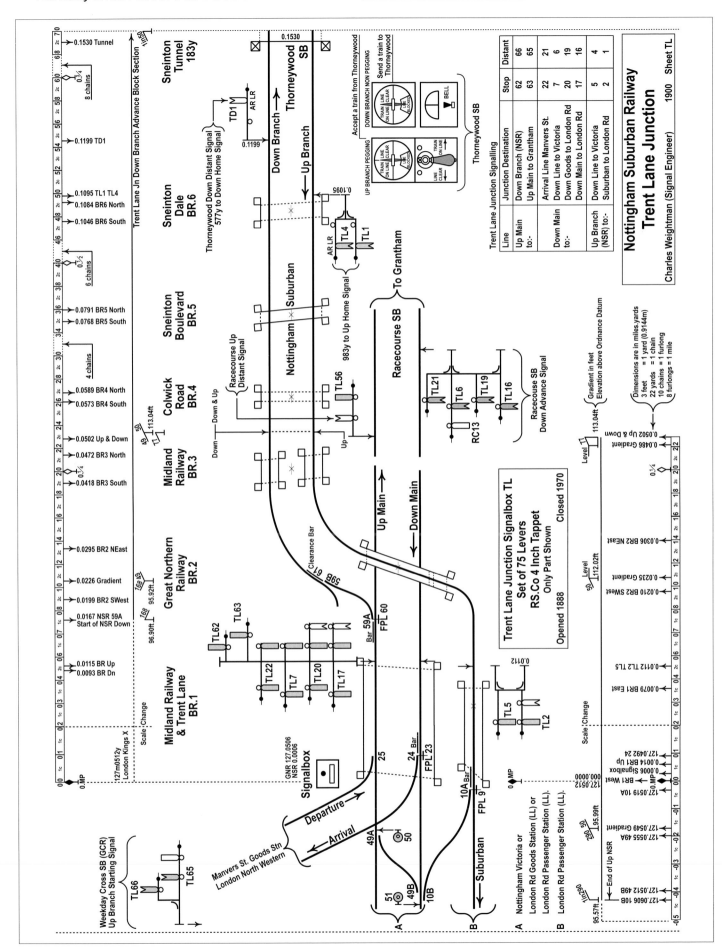

and show a white lamp at night. ('Shunt proceed' indicates to a driver that the move is only as far as the line is clear and must be prepared to stop short of any obstruction).

Points: Are located at the junction between lines. Where trains run in the diverging direction, these are known as 'facing' points, and if the line carries passenger trains these require to be separately locked. This locking is done by a bolt known as a 'facing point lock' (FPL). This is driven through a 'lifting bar', which prevents the signalman from unlocking the points with a train present. Points where trains only run in a converging direction are known as 'trailing' points and do not have a separate lock. However, where the signalman cannot see the whole junction, the points are provided with a 'clearance bar'. This prevents the junction points from being moved until the train has passed clear. Points are said to lie 'normal' (usually but not always, for the straight route) when the lever is normal, and 'reverse' (usually for the diverging route) when the lever is reverse. There are also levers for facing point locks, bolts and clearance bars. These are also connected by rods. Points could be operated by direct mechanical connection up to 200 yards from the signal box (later extended to 350 yards).

Ground or Shunting Frames: These are used where points in running lines are more than 200 yards from the signal box or there is an operational reason for the points to be operated by a shunter. The levers of points operated by the ground frames are locked 'normal' until they have been released from the signal box. The main signal box always retains control of the running signals. This release is through a 'midway bolt'. There is a solid rod from the ground frame point lever for a distance of approximately half way to the signal box (The position of the midway bolt). From the release lever in the signal box, there is also a solid rod to the midway bolt. Once the release in the main signal box is pulled, the point lever at the ground frame may also be pulled. This point lever must then be placed to normal before the release lever in the signal box can be replaced to normal.

Block System: The NSR line was originally double track and each line could only be used in one direction with left hand running. The lines were named 'Up' or 'Down', with Down being towards Daybrook. Each line between the signal boxes (say A, B & C) is divided into 'block sections', through which only one train is permitted to pass at a time (the system being known as 'Absolute Block'). The block section from the previous signal box A is known as the 'rear block section', this terminates at the first stop signal at B, known as the 'home signal'. The last stop signal at B is known as the 'advance signal' and marks the commencement of the 'advance block section' to the next signal box C. The area between these two signals may contain other running signals and is known as the 'station limits' of signal box B. Within the rear block section is the 'distant signal' at which trains are not required to stop. If the distant signal is off (at clear), this informs the train driver that all of the stop signals at the next signal box (B) are off (clear) and that the train will not be required to stop at B. If the signal is on (at caution) the driver must be prepared to stop at the next signal. (The term 'advance signal' for the signal reading to the advance block section, was a term only used by the GNR. The more usual term is 'starting signal'. The GNR used both, in this text for signals placed at the 'starting' ends of platforms).

Block Working: To permit a train to approach signal box B through the rear section (from the previous signal box A) the signalman at A uses the single stroke block bell to request permission to send the train to B using the code (is line clear). If at B the distant and home signals are at caution and danger respectively and the line is also clear for one quarter of a mile beyond the home signal (known as the overlap or block clearing point), then it is safe to permit a train to approach. Signalman B acknowledges (is line clear) and places the rear section (pegging) block instrument to 'line clear', thus granting permission for the train to approach. This causes the repeating (non-pegging) instrument at A to also show 'line clear', permitting signalman A to send the train. Once the train has entered the rear section, signalman A uses the block bell to send the code (train entering section). Signalman B acknowledges the code and places the (pegging) instrument to 'Train on Line'. The (non-pegging) instrument at A then also shows 'Train on Line', thus reminding signalman A not to offer a further train. If the train is to pass through to the next signal box at C, signalman B similarly offers the train to the signalman at C. If C accepts the train, signalman at B clears the home signal, any intermediate stop signals within the station limits, and then clears the advance signal. This enables the distant signal to be cleared, allowing the train a clear run through the station limits at B. If the train is not accepted by C, signalman at B maintains the home signal at danger, until the train has nearly stopped. The home signal may then be cleared and the train may move to the advance signal which is kept at danger until the signalman at C is able to accept the train. Once the train has passed one quarter of a mile beyond the home signal (known as the block clearing point), signalman B will inform signalman A that the train is clear of the section, by placing the rear section (pegging) block instrument to the normal 'Line Blocked' and sending the code 'Train Out of Section'. At A this causes the advance section (non-pegging) instrument to also show 'Line Blocked'. The section is now normal and A may offer a further train.

Telegraphic Communication: The communications between the signal boxes only required very small currents of electricity, which would be provided by 'Leclanche cells'. These cells consisted of a glass jar containing a carbon rod set in a sac containing manganese dioxide. Within the jar but clear of the sac is a zinc rod. All is immersed in a liquid suspension of sal ammoniac (ammonium chloride). The carbon rod is the positive and the zinc negative at 1.5 volts. Several cells would be connected in series to obtain the required voltage. The sal ammoniac required periodic replacement. The telegraph wires would have been soft iron or, in areas of air pollution, copper carried on ceramic or glass insulating pots. The telegraph route was of six wires (1.53.C) or eight wires (1.73.U). Unusually,

A poor enlargement but necessary to prove the existence of the small posted signal at the bottom of the Mapperley brickworks rope hauled incline, taken in June 1951. *F E Quenby*

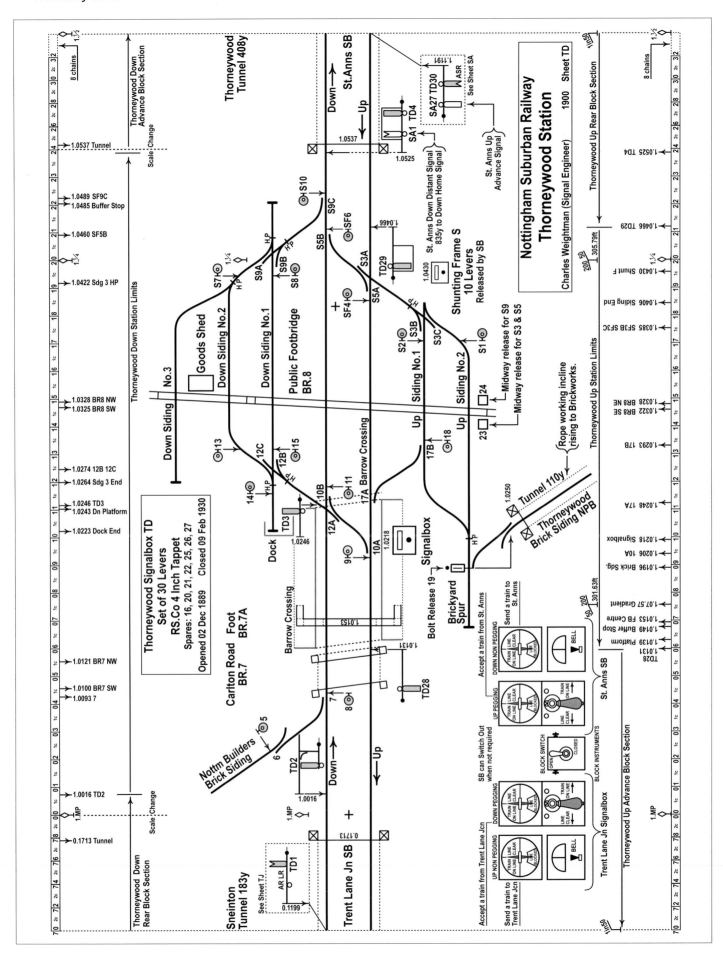

Nottingham Suburban Railway
Thorneywood Station
Charles Weightman (Signal Engineer)   1900   Sheet TD

on the NSR the wires were carried through the tunnels in a wooden trough, which would contain copper wires insulated by gutta-percha (a form of rubber) wrapped in a cloth braid. The more usual way at the time would have been to carry the telegraph route over the top of the tunnel on telegraph poles. In places, such as north of Sherwood tunnel, the wooden trough continued along the ground beyond the tunnel (1.73.L). Railway telegraph routes have now virtually disappeared and Leclanche cells are not used.

Signalling Contractor: The signalling on the NSR was provided by the GNR. Although they had their own signal works at Retford (the building still stands), this work was sub-contracted to the Railway Signal Company of Liverpool. This company manufactured interlocking lever frames (HGN.88), running signals (HGN.70 and 71), shunt signals (HGN.73) and point fittings. Site work commenced on 27th September 1889 and was completed on 11th October 1889. All systems and equipment would have been prefabricated and tested prior to arrival on site. The systems involved the three signal boxes on the line (Thorneywood, St. Ann's Well and Sherwood) and one at each of the junctions to access the line, Trent Lane Junction to the south, Daybrook Junction to the north.

Note: The number which is shown against each signal, point end, bar or bolt is the 'lever identity' (ID). Some signal IDs are correct as they can be seen in photographs. Some, from the rules of signalling are likely correct. The remainder are assumptions!

Trent Lane Junction signal box (1.44.U & C) was opened in 1888 (a 1918 record of this signal box still exists) and was built to control the complex of junctions between the Grantham to Nottingham (London Road) line (1857), the LNW Manvers goods station (1888), the Suburban Railway (1889) and the spur to Nottingham (Victoria) station (1899). The signal box was built by the Railway Signal Company and had 75 levers. The Down Main homes and Up Starting signals were carried on a large signal bridge (gantry), located at the east end of the bridge carrying the GNR over the MR and Trent Lane. Sighting of this signal was obstructed by NSR bridge No. 2, for the drivers of trains approaching from Grantham. The Down direction signals were therefore provided with (higher) co-acting arms. The Down home had arms applying for routes to London Road passenger station No.17, London Road goods station No.20, to Nottingham (Victoria) station No.7 and Manvers Street goods station No.22. The Up starting had routes applying to the Suburban (Down Advance to Daybrook) No.62 and to Grantham No.63. The Up Suburban home signal was carried on a small signal bridge to the east of the NSR bridge No.1. Although physically the track layout would have permitted routes to every destination except Manvers Street, arms were only provided applying to London Road passenger station via the Suburban Line No.2 and to Nottingham (Victoria) No.5. Each of these signals had a corresponding junction distant signal to give the driver of a train a pre indication of the route set at the junction ahead. These were taken out of use in 1915 as a wartime measure to reduce the cost of maintenance, leaving one distant signal which could be cleared only for the main route (the last remaining semaphore junction distant signal on the network was taken out of use in 2005). The junction facing points to the NSR Down line No.59A worked with a run-back catch point no.59B, this being provided to derail any train which may have run back from the extreme rising gradient (*See* later paragraph on gradients). Because this point could not be seen from the signal box, it was provided with a clearance bar No.61, which prevents the points from being moved while a train is still on them. Small alterations caused the lever numbering to change slightly over the years. The signal box closed in 1970, upon closure of the original 1857

extension of Grantham line from Netherfield. The railway at this point survived as a siding until 1972, to enable trains to serve the MOD Depot at Ruddington and the British Gypsum works at Hotchley Hill.

Thorneywood signal box was built of brick (1.58.U) accommodating (an assumed) 30 lever frame, located on the north end of the Up platform. Due to the extended area of control, the signal box was supplemented by an elevated shunting frame (small signal box) accommodating (an assumed) 10 levers. This was 212 yards north of the main signal box, was only manned when required for shunting and controlled all the points and shunting signals north of the public footbridge No.8. The main signal box controlled all the running signals and the points and shunting signals south of the public footbridge and released the points controlled from the shunting frame. The shunting frame appears in photograph (1.65.U), above the nearest wagon. In (1.66.U) it can be seen through Thorneywood tunnel. This signal box and shunting frame controlled a three-road goods yard with access to an end loading dock, on the Down side. On the Up side there was a two-road yard accessing the rope worked incline to the Nottingham Patent Brick Company's Thorneywood brick works. This incline passed through a tunnel, a photograph of the lower portal shows point-rodding to a trap point at the bottom of this incline, it is assumed that this was locally controlled by the shunter, released by a bolt from the signal box. The signal box also controlled access to the Nottingham Builders' Brick Company's brickyard siding from the Down line, south of the Carlton Road bridge No.7.

Historical Accuracy: For main running signals; No.1 Down Distant, No.2 Down Home, No.3 Down Starting (1.61.C) and No.4 Down Advance (1.65.L): the lever frame low numbers are at the south end of the frame and these identities are almost certainly correct. If the frame had 30 levers, then running signals; No.28 Up Advance, No.29 Up Home (1.65.U) and No.30 Up Distant will also be correct. The only running signals not photographed are No.28, which is located at the south end of the Up platform and believed to be a straight post and No.30 which is at St. Ann's Well. Although not clearly visible to the reader, the original of the photograph to the south, Sneinton tunnel (1.53.L) shows signal No.1. It was a tall straight post to the left of the line with a lowered spectacle. The Up Junction Distant signal for Trent Lane can also be seen, as an equal bracket with lowered spectacles. The photograph to the north through Sneinton tunnel (1.53.C) shows the post of No.2 Down Home. Because this signal is at the exit from the tunnel, it is a gallows type (similar to that at Sherwood). Photo (1.57.U) through Carlton Road bridge to the north, shows the shunt signal No.8 (marked on the back) leading to the Nottingham Builders' Brick Company's siding. Because there are two point rods through the bridge, the trailing points in the Down line and the trap points in the siding (not visible) are almost certainly lever Nos.7 and 6, with the exit shunt signal No.5 (also not visible). This photograph also shows the change of gradient in the platforms. Shunt signal No. 9 and the south main lines crossover No.10 (assumed IDs) are shown in photo (1.61.C). Photograph (1.65.U) shows many details: - Shunt signal No.18 from the Up sidings and points No.17B (assumed ID), also shunt signal No.15 from the Down sidings. On the extreme right can be seen two rods, each entering a small box below the public footbridge. These contain the midway releases to the shunting frame Nos.23 and 24 (assumed IDs). The back of signal No.29 can be seen. This is on a short post for sighting through the tunnel and has a white backboard, which is immediately adjacent to the shunting frame. Although at a distance, this illustration also shows the north main lines crossover Nos.S5A and B and shunt signals

The small signal placed on the Back Line at Daybrook Junction after the NSR became single track. The ground frame and LNER summersault signal with block instrument above the ground frame levers to communicate with the signal box approximately 300 yards away. Taken on 24th October 1954. *A.G. Cramp*

Nos.S1, S4, S6 and S8, all worked from the shunting frame (all assumed IDs). In the centre of the photo, near the tunnel, can be seen the 1¾ mile post. Photograph (1.65.L) shows signal No.4 with the lower arm being the Down Distant signal for St. Ann's Well. The weight bars at the bottom of the post show (because the weight on the right is raised) that at the time the photograph was taken, St. Ann's Well signal box Down distant lever is pulled (which most likely means that the signal box was switched out), thus when Thorneywood signal box pulled the other weight on the right (which also clears the top stop arm), the weight on the left would drop and the distant arm would clear as well. The crank attached to the distant arm is connected to the switch for the electrical signal indicator, which shows in the St. Ann's Well signal box that the arm has returned to caution. The battery for this circuit is contained in the box attached at the back of the bottom of the post. This signal is approached on a left-hand curve and in order to give sufficient time of sighting, the signal is located to the right of the railway. Had the signal been on the left, the sighting could have been obstructed by wagons in the Down yard, giving the driver insufficient time to read the signal and bring the train under control.

St. Ann's Well signal box was a low timber-built structure (1.70.C) accommodating a 30 lever frame, located just beyond the north end of the Up platform. All points and signals at St. Ann's Well were directly controlled from the signal box, all points being within the 200 yards permitted distance. The signal box controlled a three-road goods yard on the Up side and access to an end loading dock, on the Down side.

Historical Accuracy: For the main running signals; No.1 Down Distant ((1.65.L), No.2 Down Home, No.3 Down Starting (1.70.C) and No.4 Down Advance (1.70.L): are almost certainly the correct IDs. Photo (1.74.U) shows the lever number of St. Ann's Well Up Distant as being No.30 (number attached to post), so it is definite that the lever frame was of 30 levers. It then follows that No.27 Up Advance, No.28 Up Starting and No.29 Up Home are the correct lever numbers. The only running signals which are not photographed are No.2, which is located at the south end of the Down platform and No.27, which also carried Thorneywood Up Distant and was located at the south end of The Wells Road bridge No.9, also No.28, located at the south end of the Up platform. All are believed to have been straight posts. No photograph shows the south end arrangement of St. Ann's Well before 1930, which would contain the south exit from the yard points Nos.7 and 8 (from a photograph of the south yard points, post 1930 ground frame, it has been concluded that 'long points' were single ended – as at Thorneywood), the south mains crossover Nos.11A and B, shunt signals Nos.6, 10 and 12, also the tall siding signal No.9 (All these IDs are assumed). Signal No.3 (1.70.C) was a right hand half bracket for sighting through the footbridge and station awning. This photograph also shows points No.16A from the dock, the north mains crossover Nos.18A and B and the north entrance to the yard points Nos.23 and 24. Also shunt signals Nos.17, 19, 22 and 25 (not all clearly). Photograph (1.70.L) shows the base of signal No.29 which was almost certainly a tall straight post and signal No.4 which also carries Sherwood SB Down Distant. This illustration also shows the 2 mile post.

Sherwood signal box was also a timber structure (1.82.U) accommodating (an assumed) 30 levers frame, located beyond the north end of the Down platform. All points and signals at Sherwood were directly controlled from the signal box, all points being within the 200 yards permitted distance. The signal box controlled a two road goods yard, with access to an end loading dock, on the Down side and a two road yard on the Up side accessing the rope-worked incline to the brick works. To prevent runaways from the incline reaching the main line, unless transfers were actually taking place, the points from the incline were set for an arrestor. The points to the arrestor were locally operated but bolted from the signal box. Photo (1.82.L) shows the box containing the bolt, just inside the left of the arch of bridge No.12. A later photograph taken looking through this bridge shows a 'points indicator' associated with these points, believed to be so that the signalman at Sherwood, could see that the points were in the correct position, before using the bolt No.14.

Historical Accuracy: For main running signals; No.1 Up Distant, No.2 Up Home (1.86.U), No.3 Down Advance (1.74.U): the lever frame shows low numbers at the north end and these identities, because the lever number can be seen on the back of the post in photo (1.74.U) are certainly the correct lever numbers. If the frame had 30 levers, then running signals; No.27 Down Advance (1.86.U), No.28 Down Starting (1.82.U), No.29 Down Home and No.30 Down Distant (1.70.L) will also be correct. The only running signals which are not photographed are No.1, which is located just to the south end of the Marlborough Road bridge No.14 and believed to be a straight post with lower spectacle. Also not photographed is No.29, which is located just beyond the northern exit from Sherwood tunnel. It is expected that this was a low signal for sighting from the tunnel and because of the presence of Sherwood Vale bridge, which prevents a sky background, may well have had a white sighting board, similar to that on the Up home at Thorneywood. Photograph (1.83.L) showing the north end of Sherwood yard, shows the shunt signals Nos.12 and 13 (another copy of this photo shows the numbers clearly) and photo (1.86.U) shows shunt signal No.6 (marked on the back). It is therefore most likely that point identities Nos.7A and B, 9A and B, 12A and B and shunt signal identities Nos.8 and 10 are correct. For shunt signals Nos.15, 17, 18, 19, 21, 23 and 25, and for points Nos.16A and B, 21A and B, 22A, B and C and bolt No.14, the identities are assumed.

Daybrook Junction signal box is of timber construction, and taller than those on the branch (1.9.U) & (R1.172) accommodating (an assumed) 20 lever frame. (No good close-up photograph of the signal box has been found). The signal box was located on the east end of Daybrook station on the Up side. It controlled the right hand double junction between the GNR Derbyshire Line and the Nottingham Suburban Railway, as well as a trailing crossover.

Historical Accuracy: All lever IDs here are assumed. The form of Down main signals; No.1 Down Main Distant, No.2 Down Main Home (R1.172) are known to be correct, being shown on a signalling 'new works' plan dated 1st March 1935, which is in the possession of this chapter's author. This shows the resignalling between Daybrook and Colwick which was commissioned in 1937 (which removed both of these signals). No.18 Up Main Advance (R1.174) is also shown on this plan, although it was changed to a distant signal only as part of this re-signalling and remained until the line closed in 1960. No.3 Down Branch distant was the only signal

(right) **The NSR signal providing access into the London Road (Low Level) station goods yard.** *Graham Jelly.*

remaining on the line when the NSR closed in 1951, it became a 'fixed at caution' signal upon the closure of Daybrook Junction. Up Homes junction signal Nos.16 and 19 (R1.172) was the junction directing signal and was carried on a signal bridge. Because the sighting was obstructed by the station footbridge, this signal carried two high co-acting arms for the long distance sighting and two 'hanging' lower arms for sighting from the station platform. At some time the right hand top arm was removed and the corresponding bottom arm replaced by a shorter one (1.9.U). This was probably as part of the GNR's company wide signal rationalisation after 1915. This signal also had junction distant signals from both the Up Main and Up Goods lines between Daybrook station and Leen Valley junction, these being Nos.17 and 20 which worked with Nos.16 and 19 respectively. This was to give the train driver a pre-indication of route set ahead at Daybrook junction. The diverging arms, No.17 were also removed after 1915. These signal structures (which were very high) remained until this section of line closed in 1964. The only signal for which no photograph exists is No.15 Up Branch Advance; this is assumed to be a standard straight post signal. The complete layout of Daybrook junction, which consists of a standard right-handed double junction with a main lines' trailing crossover to the east, can be seen in photograph (R1.172). Due to the 1 in 100 gradient on the Suburban Line, a train standing at the Up Advance signal No.15, could run back foul of the main line. To protect against this, it is assumed that the junction also had a worked catch point No.11B (similar to that at Trent Lane).

Gradients: By any standards, the gradients on this line would be considered as extreme. A requirement of the Regulation of Railways Act of 1889 was that passenger trains be fitted with a 'fail safe' continuous brake (on all vehicles). As a result of this act most

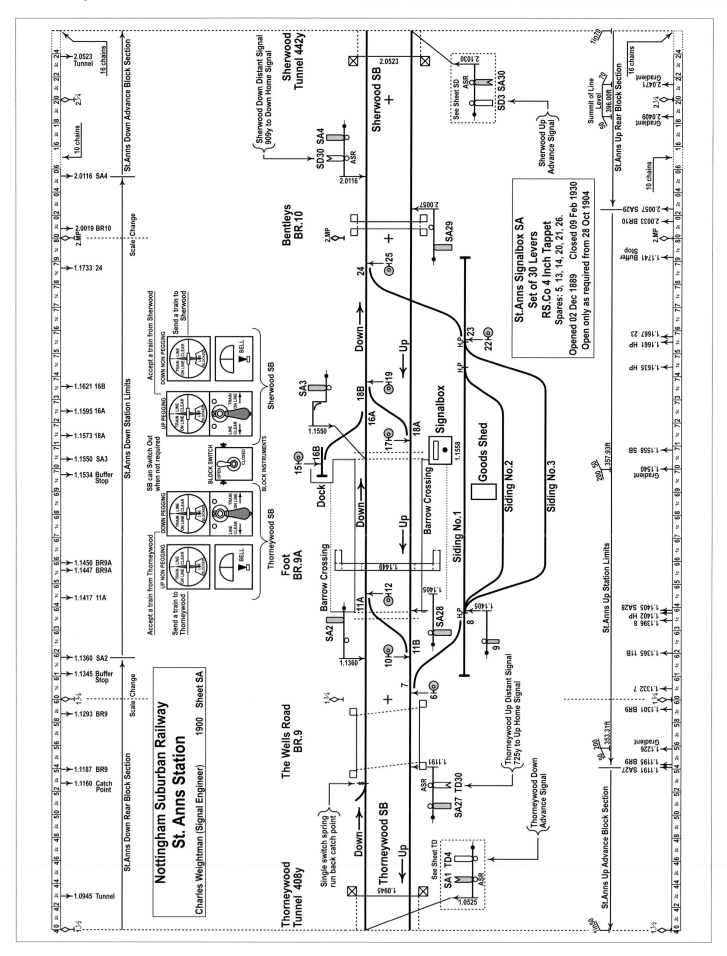

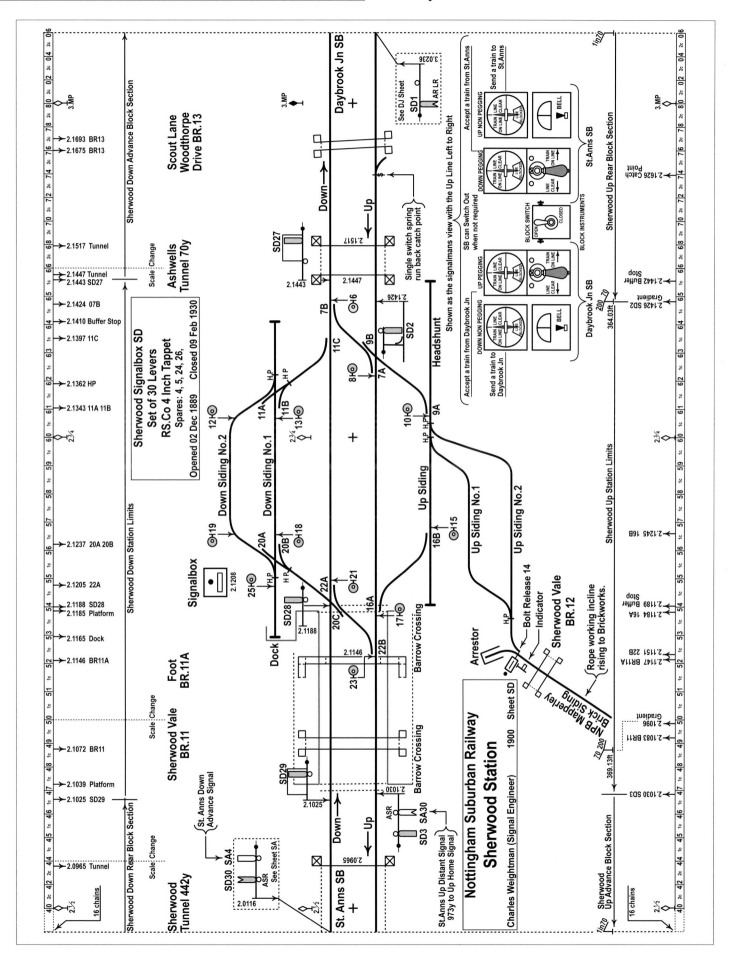

Sherwood Signalbox SD
Set of 30 Levers
RS.Co 4 Inch Tappet
Spares: 4, 5, 24, 26,
Opened 02 Dec 1889   Closed 09 Feb 1930

Nottingham Suburban Railway
Sherwood Station
Charles Weightman (Signal Engineer)   1900   Sheet SD

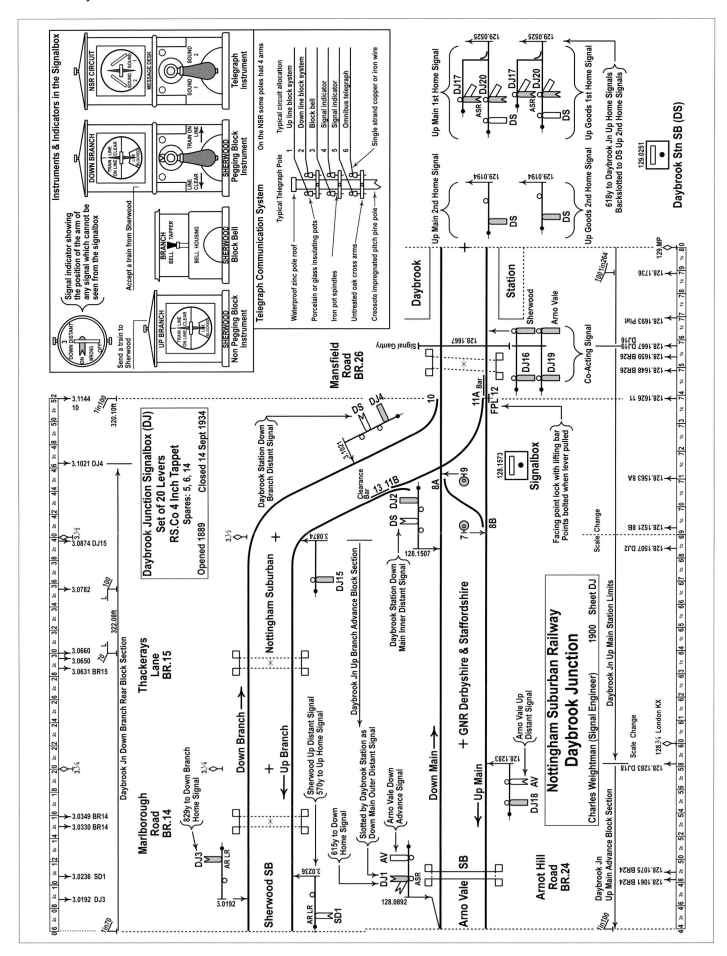

railways fitted continuous vacuum brakes. Should a passenger train become divided by a broken coupling, both parts of the train would stop automatically. However, it was not until the 1970s that freight trains were universally similarly fitted. Unfitted freight trains had a 'brake van' (fitted with a brake) attached at the rear of the train. On steep falling gradients, the guard would assist with the braking using the 'brake van' brake and may also have been required to pin down a number of wagon brakes before the train started down the gradient. If the train stopped on a rising gradient, the guard was required to manage the 'brake van' brake to prevent the train running back.

Catch Points: Photograph (1.87.L) looking through Scout Lane bridge, a catch point can be seen on the Up line consisting of a single switch (only on one rail) which is sprung to the open position. Should anything run back on the 1 in 70 rising gradient approaching Sherwood, it would be derailed at this point, which is approximately 200 yards in rear of the Up Home signal No.SD2 (which would limit the maximum train length permitted). This gives protection to an Up train standing at Daybrook Junction Up Advance No.DJ15. It is assumed that there was also a catch point on the 1 in 50 rising gradient on the Down Line approaching St. Ann's Well. This would be a similar distance to the rear of the Down Home signal No.SA2 and would protect Down trains standing in Thorneywood station. There appears to be no similar point on the approach to Thorneywood Down Home No.TD2 (also on a 1 in 50 rising gradient) where the 200 yard position is in Sneinton tunnel. Such a catch point would not be provided in a tunnel due to the difficulties of re-railing a derailed train. However, because there is no signal in advance of the junction at Trent Lane Junction, which is provided with a 'worked catch point' No.59B, no further protection would be necessary.

Permitted Speed: This is the speed at which it is safe for a train to move. This is governed by the distance available to safely stop and is related to the gradient and the curvature of the track. The distance between each distant signal and the home signal to which it applies, is theoretically at least the required braking distance. By 2010 standards, some of the distant signals on the line would be classed as 'underbraked' (Thorneywood Up Distant, grossly so). It can also be determined, by examining photographs which show the number of signal wires passing though each tunnel, that no use was made of additional 'outer' distant signals, which would extend braking distances. However, at the time, it was permitted for the 'sighting distance' to be considered as part of the required braking distance. No quoted permitted speed for the Nottingham Suburban Railway is known. The timetable suggests that a non-stop passenger train would not need to exceed 35 m.p.h. and a stopping passenger trains much less. The permitted speed over the junctions would be unlikely to have exceeded 20 m.p.h. and all crossovers and siding connections 15 m.p.h. This is all theoretical as locomotives at the time were not fitted with speedometers. Drivers of the day would adopt a style of driving according to their intimate knowledge of 'the road' and the weight of the trailing load.

Finally: After the withdrawal of most passenger services, when the line was converted to a single, 'single line block section' extending from Trent Lane Junction signal box to Daybrook Junction signal box, the line became worked by a system then known as Staff and Ticket Working. Authority to occupy this line was by the driver of the train being shown the 'Train Staff' (usually a circular staff or metal about 2 feet in length) engraved with the name of the section (for example: Nottingham Suburban Railway) and then handed a metal ticket. The last train through in one direction would also carry the staff. The staff always has to be at the end at which a train enters the single line, thus ensuring no head-on collisions. The NSR's Up line was retained and sidings remained at all three stations. These were controlled by a series of ground lever frames, which could only be unlocked and opened by the use of an 'Annett's Key', of which only one existed, attached to the train staff.

The details of the revised arrangement for the single line operation will be covered in Volume 3.

(top, left) **The Daybrook junction and Trent Lane junction ticket used after the NSR had been reduced to single line working.** *(top, right)* **Trent Lane Junction and Daybrook Junction ticket.** *(above, left)* **Daybrook junction and Thorneywood station ticket.** *(above, right)* **Thorneywood station and Daybrook junction ticket. All Tony Etches coll. *D. Birch.***

Final preparations take place in readiness for the 24th May 1900 opening of the Great Central Railway & Great Northern Railway Joint Nottingham passenger station. *Unknown.*

An interior view of the new Joint station on Opening day.

Chapter 9: THE NOTTINGHAM SUBURBAN RAILWAY COMPANY: The Threat from Victoria Station & the Introduction of Electric Trams.

The start of the twentieth century heralded the beginning of the decline in the use of the NSR, primarily in passenger train usage but also to a lesser extent in freight transport. The two main causes were the opening of the GCR/GNR joint railway station in Nottingham, later to be called Victoria station, and the introduction of electric trams across the city. Although the planning processes for both these alternative modes of travel had been publicly known for some time, there was little the NSR Company could have done about it to either reduce or minimise their negative affects on their line. There was no excuse for the NSR if they had not been fully briefed about the proposals. For a number of years both Robert Mellors and Edward Parry were involved in the design for the new Nottingham station, besides the securing of affected properties. Several of the NSR's and NPBC's Directors too were either Nottingham City or County Councillors and they would have been fully aware of the tram proposals.

The new Victoria station, and the introduction of electric trams, jointly played a very significant part in the decline of the NSR and the demise of its passenger service. Consequently the threat they presented to the NSR is presented here in some detail.

The Great Central and Great Northern Joint Station

The Nottingham Joint station was opened on 24th May 1900, Queen Victoria's 81st birthday, and was to have a major impact on the future use of the NSR lines and the existing GNR London Road station. The GNR Kimberley services were immediately transferred to the new Nottingham station via the Basford/Bagthorpe junction connections, consequently shortening the journey to Basford and Bulwell to three miles. Shirebrook trains now went by the Suburban and the Leen Valley junction or via Bulwell Common and Moorbridge junction; into the Victoria station one way, and out the other. As a consequence the Gedling route became a backwater and the nickname of the 'Back Line' probably originated as a result.

The new Nottingham station occupied about 13 acres of land in the heart of the City of Nottingham and the cost of the land and properties, negotiated by Robert Mellors (of Messrs. Mellors, Basden, and Mellors), and was over £473,000, which was just under the cost of building the station. The construction of the station, supervised by the GCR Engineer, Edward Parry, included the demolition of 1,300 houses, 20 public houses and a workhouse, displacing some 6,000 people in the process. Most of the area which was demolished could have been termed as a slum and as the GCR had to provide homes elsewhere for the displaced persons, it may initially be seen to have been a good outcome for the City and that area's population. However, the reality was that other persons were given these new dwellings and the displaced persons were actually relocated into less desirable properties. Subsequently, there was excavation of around 600,000 cubic yards of sandstone in order to produce the cutting in which the station was built. The station had twelve platforms and was constructed partly in Darley Dale stone and pressed brick, which was mostly supplied by the Nottingham Patent Brick Company, for which Edward Parry incidentally was now a Director.

Earlier in 1892, the MS&LR had invited other railway companies to partake in joint ownership of their proposed stations at Leicester and Nottingham. Only the GNR had accepted the offer in the case of Nottingham and an agreement was duly signed on 30th April 1892. By participating in the construction in the Nottingham Joint station/Victoria station, the GNR was rescued from its remote station on London Road. In 1895 further Acts were passed in favour of both the GNR and MS&LR for additional connecting lines between their respective systems. Subsequently, the GNR's connecting 'High Level' route, which was built entirely on bridges and viaducts, was constructed in 1899 from the Trent Lane West junction through a new station at Nottingham (London Road High Level) and on to the junction with the GCR at Weekday Cross. This new link between the GNR's Nottingham to Grantham line and the

(right) **Opening day for the new Nottingham Joint Railway station from the street side. The clock tower has yet to be completed but the train shed was ready for business.**

Shortly after opening day, after the clock tower and other finishing touches to the station had been completed.

A few weeks after the opening of the GCR/GNR Joint station. Note how the smoke from the locomotives has already left its mark on the glass panelling.

Nottingham Joint station was apparently opened to traffic on 15th March 1900. The existing GNR London Road station was renamed as the Nottingham (London Road Low Level) station. To enable the NSR to use this new 'High Level' viaduct, a facing crossover was constructed between the Up Suburban and the Down Main Line. This now provided the GNR with access to the new Joint station from Colwick, Grantham and London, and of course the NSR, something which Edward Parry had dreamed of for so long since pursuing the various deviation designs for the NSR. The engineers in charge of the connections works were Sir John Fowler and Richard Johnson, the Chief Civil Engineer of the GNR, and Edward Parry (still the Engineer for the NSR) on behalf of the GCR. All the track work from Trent Lane to Weekday Cross was completed during the first two months of 1900.

The opening of the Victoria station was a major blow for the London Road Low Level station for most of its train services were transferred to the new station. As a result it went from a peak traffic flow of over 135 movements a day in the 1890's to only ten a day by 1910, which were mainly the GNR/LNWR Joint line workings.

The new GCR main line gave the GNR direct access to Basford via New Basford and a spur from Bagthorpe junctions and to the Leen Valley line by a connecting line from Bulwell Common to Bestwood junction. From the opening day, the GNR transferred all its Nottingham (London Road Low Level) services to the new Joint station, via the London Road High Level station. The transfers included most of the trains with destinations both north and west of Nottingham. This meant that the Derby and Pinxton trains no longer ran over the Suburban. As a consequence the services over the NSR, stopping at all three stations, were reduced in the Down direction to four to Basford and Bulwell and three to Skegby, with another to Basford at noon on a weekday and an extra train to Skegby on a Saturday. In the Up direction there were five trains from Basford and Bulwell and three from Skegby, with an additional train from Basford and Bulwell on Saturdays. The new junction of the GCR with the Derbyshire Extension at Bagthorpe was now only a travelling distance of three miles from Nottingham, as opposed to seven miles by the Suburban and ten miles via Gedling. The opening of the Victoria station had done to the NSR what the NSR had originally done to the 'Back Line'. The NSR line was thus reduced to providing permanent way facilities for the Leen Valley trains whilst the 'Back Line' through Gedling was reduced to servicing the local trains between Basford and Nottingham. The consequence of all this, was that the main reason that the NSR Company had originally given to the GNR to persuade them to construct the NSR line by having a more direct route to the north and west instead of using the Gedling route had gone and whilst still classed as a double track main line, the NSR had very little use in serving the GNR local regional services. However, one service did remain and that was the service that in my view was the main reason for the vision and development of the line in the first place and that was the freight services to and from the NPBC's two brickworks.

The timetable for the NSR from the opening of the Nottingham Joint station from 24th May to 30th June 1900 can be found on the page over. Meanwhile, the GNR Working Timetable operating from 1st October 1900 was similar to that schedule but for a few changes which were:-

The 12.55 p.m. departure from Nottingham (Victoria) now left at 1.00 p.m. leaving the three NSR stations at 1.09 p.m., 1.12 p.m. and 1.15 p.m.

The 6.05 p.m. departure from Nottingham (Victoria) was re-routed via Gedling and in its place along the NSR were the 5.50 p.m. Victoria departure, which left the three NSR stations at 5.59 p.m., 6.02 p.m. and 6.05 p.m. and the 7.03 p.m. Victoria

departure which left the three NSR stations at 7.11 p.m., 7.14 p.m. and 7.17 p.m.

The 9.05 p.m. departure from the Victoria station was re-scheduled to stop at the three NSR stations at 9.14 p.m., 9.17 p.m. and 9.20 p.m., a minute later than previous.

There was a new departure from Daybrook leaving at 12.30 p.m. stopping at the NSR stations at 12.33 p.m., 12.36 p.m. and 12.39 p.m., arriving at Victoria at 12.48 p.m.

The 12.55 p.m. departure from Basford and Bulwell, which passed over the NSR was discontinued.

The 5.40 p.m. from Basford and Bulwell now left 15 minutes earlier at 5.25 p.m. with corresponding earlier times along the Suburban.

The 7.08 p.m. from Basford and Bulwell now left 10 minutes earlier at 6.58 p.m. with corresponding earlier times along the Suburban.

The 8.56 p.m. from Basford and Bulwell now left 24 minutes later at 9.20 p.m. with corresponding later times along the Suburban.

THE THREAT FROM PUBLIC ROAD TRANSPORT.

Whilst the 1900 opening of the Victoria station and its northerly route through Carrington and onwards to Bagthorpe junction was to take many trains away from the Suburban, 1901 was to bring the second of the two major threats to the NSR in the form of the electric tram, which ultimately was to take away many of its few remaining passengers.

The eastern fringes of Nottingham had not developed as quickly as the NSR Company had originally envisaged or perhaps hoped. However, despite this, competitive electric tram services were to be eventually introduced very close to every one of its stations, providing a more frequent and cheaper form of public transport. The trams' routes were of course on the roads around which the housing developments had been constructed or were taking place, and with more frequent and convenient stops to pick up and set down passengers than trains. Passengers had little walking to do in order to take a tram ride, which was not always the case with the railways.

The development of Nottingham's electric tram network is a very important element in the story of the Suburban and a précis of its history, particularly relating to those routes adjacent to the Suburban, is related here. It is true that the promoters of the NSR could have foreseen this threat, as an Act enabling the town of Nottingham to introduce trams had been passed back in 1870. The author believes that their main concern though was to improve the transport facilities for their goods traffic to and from their two brickyards, and the potential threat to their future passenger usage may not have been considered as too high a priority to them. Besides, by putting potential future competition for their passenger service into their portfolio, it may have put the GNR off from accepting the operating agreement they were to have with the NSR.

Public road transport had been in existence in Nottingham and its suburbs since the early 1800's. As early as 1839 the dashing Hansom carriages, designed by Lord Brougham, were gracing the streets of Nottingham. By 1848 hackney carriages were in competition from omnibus services with one of the first services running from the Maypole Hotel to the Midland Railway station meeting each train, as it arrived or departed, at the convenience of the passengers. Another service ran five times a day to Arnold from Milton Street. These services, operated by entrepreneurs, were to expand and by 1899 ten operators were providing seven minute services to Arnold, Carlton, Colwick and the St. Ann's Well Road area.

The timetable for the NSR from the opening of the Nottingham Joint Station from 24th May to 30th June 1900 was as follows:-

Down Line		Pass	Pass	Goods & Empts	Pass	Pass	Pass	Cttle & Goods	Pass	Pass	Pass
		am				pm					
Basford and Bulwell	dep	7.28			11.48						8.52
Nottingham Joint Station	arr	7.37			11.58				4.38	5.36	9.03
Nottingham Joint Station	**dep**	**7.40**	**8.55**		**12.00**	**12.55**	**2.48**		**4.40**	**6.05**	**9.05**
Nottingham High Level	**arr**	**7.43**	**8.58**		**12.03**	**12.58**	**2.51**		**4.43**	**6.07**	**9.07**
Nottingham High Level	**dep**	**7.45**	**9.01**		**12.05**	**1.00**	**2.53**	**2.55***	**4.45**	**6.09**	**9.09**
Thorneywood	**dep**	**7.49**	**9.05**	**9.30**	**12.09**	**1.04**	**2.57**	**Thr'u**	**4.49**	**6.13**	**9.13**
St. Ann's Well	**dep**	**7.52**	**9.08**	**10.05**	**12.12**	**1.07**	**3.00**	**Thr'u**	**4.52**	**6.16**	**9.16**
Sherwood	**dep**	**7.55**	**9.11**	**10.45**	**12.15**	**1.10**	**3.03**	**Thr'u**	**4.55**	**6.19**	**9.19**
Daybrook	**dep**	**8.00**	**9.15**	**Thr'u**	**12.19**	**1.14**	**3.07**	**Thr'u**	**4.59**	**6.23**	**9.23**
Leen Valley Junction	arr			10.53				3.15			
Basford and Bulwell	arr	8.04			12.23		3.12			6.29	9.28
Bulwell Forest	dep		9.21		12.25	1.21			5.05		
Bestwood Colliery	dep		9.24		12.27	1.24			5.08		
Butler's Hill	dep		9.27		12.30	1.27			5.11		
Hucknall	dep		9.30		12.33	1.30			5.14		
Linby	dep		9.34		12.37	1.34			5.18		
Newstead	dep		9.38		12.41	1.38			5.22		
Sutton-in-Ashfield	dep		9.47		12.50	1.47			5.31		
Skegby	arr		9.51		12.54	1.51			5.34		
								* From Nottm. Goods		From Derby	

Up Line		Coal	Goods & Coal	Pass	Pass	Pass	Pass	Pass	Goods	Pass	Pass	Pass	Pass
		am				pm							
Skegby	dep				9.40			2.05			5.42		
Sutton-in-Ashfield	dep				9.46			2.09			5.45		
Newstead	dep				9.55			2.18			5.54		
Linby	dep				9.59			2.22			5.58		
Hucknall	dep				10.03			2.26			6.02		
Butler's Hill	dep				10.06			2.29			6.05		
Bestwood Colliery	dep				10.09			2.32			6.08		
Bulwell Forest	dep				10.12			2.35			6.11		
Basford and Bulwell	dep			8.15		12.55	2.05			5.40		7.08	8.56
Leen Valley Junction	arr	1.50							1.25				
Daybrook	**dep**	**2.05**	**7.20**	**8.20**	**10.18**	**1.00**	**2.10**	**2.41**	**2.42**	**5.45**	**6.17**	**7.15**	**9.01**
Sherwood	**dep**	**Thr'u**	**7.30**	**8.23**	**10.21**	**1.03**	**2.13**	**2.44**	**3.00**	**5.48**	**6.20**	**7.18**	**9.04**
St. Ann's Well	**dep**	**Thr'u**	**7.45**	**8.26**	**10.24**	**1.06**	**2.16**	**2.47**	**3.20**	**5.51**	**6.23**	**7.21**	**9.07**
Thorneywood	**dep**	**Thr'u**	**8.00**	**8.29**	**10.28**	**1.09**	**2.19**	**2.50**	**4.00**	**5.54**	**6.26**	**7.25**	**9.11**
Nottingham High Level	**arr**		**8.08***	**8.33**	**10.32**	**1.13**	**2.23**	**2.54**		**5.58**	**6.30**	**7.29**	**9.15**
Nottingham High Level	**dep**			**8.35**	**10.34**	**1.15**	**2.25**	**2.56**	*****	**6.00**	**6.31**	**7.31**	**9.17**
Nottingham Joint Station	**arr**			**8.38**	**10.37**	**1.18**	**2.28**	**2.59**		**6.03**	**6.34**	**7.34**	**9.20**
Nottingham Joint Station	dep			8.40	10.40	1.20	2.30	3.01		6.05	6.36	7.36	9.22
Basford and Bulwell	arr				10.46	1.31	2.38				6.46		
		From Eastwood to Nottm. Goods. To go via Gedling if too heavy for NSR	*To Nottingham Goods Yard					Saturdays excepted	To Nottm. Goods Yard	To Skegby		To Skegby	To Skegby

40

In 1870, an Act of Parliament was passed, under Prime Minister William Gladstone, to permit the construction of tramways in Nottingham. This eventually facilitated the general introduction of both domestic and commercial electricity, introducing home and street lighting to replace candles and gas lamps. Street lighting was to be provided in the centre of many of Nottingham's main roads from wires suspended between tramline posts.

In 1875 another group of prominent local businessmen, under the chairmanship of Alderman J.Gilpin, carried out a feasibility study to consider the possibilities of constructing a tramway to convey passengers within the Borough of Nottingham. Following its application to the Board of Trade in 1877, authorisation was granted on 23rd July 1877. On Thursday 17th September 1878 the new Company, known as the Nottingham and District Tramway Company, ran the first horse-tram service from St. Peter's Church to Trent Bridge and London Road. Later a five minute service operating between 8 a.m. and 10 p.m. was introduced to both the GNR London Road and the Midland stations. Demand from the public for more services increased and this led to the introduction of further horse bus services to Carrington, St. Ann's Well Road, and Sneinton amongst others. In order to satisfy the high demand for the horse-tram services, they were sometimes supplemented with horse drawn buses. The next route to open was on 11th August 1879 to Carrington.

The Tramways Act of 1870, Section 43, stated that where the local authority were not the promoters of a tramway, they could within six months of the passing of twenty-one years after the tramway company were empowered to construct the tramway, require the present owners to sell the undertaking to them at its present day value. The Nottingham Corporation seized the opportunity to acquire this well maintained system and on 14th June 1896 they took over the undertaking and then, exactly a year later on 14th June 1897 they purchased it for £80,000; the official handover taking place on 16th October of that year.

In March 1898 a new horse drawn service from the Market Place to the Carlton Road Brickworks [probably the Nottingham Builders' Brick Company] was approved and then in May 1900 another new horse drawn service was opened to Colwick, having been previously rejected in 1898. However, due to the introduction of the electric trams, the last Corporation horse tram was to run on 30th April 1902. The horse tram system was purchased by John Commons, a private operator, who agreed to continue operating the service from 1st May at the existing fares and timetable. Despite the demise of the horse-tram, horse drawn vehicles continued to be used for public transport in those areas where electric trams did not or could not operate.

The Corporation continued to use horse power for its trams and it wasn't until under the Nottingham Improvement Act 1897, Sections 41 and 42, that the Corporation obtained powers to construct and operate an electric tram system. At a cost of £425,000, on 28th March 1898 eight routes in the city were sanctioned with three of these passing close to two of the Suburban stations. Powers for the tram lines' construction was granted in the Nottingham Corporation Act 1899, and the initial order for twenty-five trams was placed with the Dick Kerr Company in 1900. The first route to have its track laid was from the Market Place to Winchester Street, in Sherwood, which commenced on 1st June 1900. Work on the Sherwood depot had started a few weeks previously. During October 1900, the first nine trams were delivered to the Sherwood depot for assembly and trials began on 17th November. The Sherwood route was sanctioned by the Board of Trade on 16th December 1900.

On 1st January 1901 the electric tram made its debut in Nottingham when a service was introduced from the Market Place

(below) **The first electric tram having just left the Sherwood depot following the completion of its construction from the kit that was delivered. Note that as yet there are no adverts on the tram.**

to Mansfield Road, running as far as the west end of Winchester Street, which was already served by the NSR at its easterly end. The tram service had a frequency of 5 minutes, which was increased to three minutes at peak times. The fare for the two-mile journey was 2d and operated for seven days a week. It was impossible for any railway company, let alone the NSR, to compete with this level of service.

At the start of the electric tram services, the drivers initially received 5½d per hour for a six-day week, averaging 62 hours; conductors received 4d per hour.

After a route to Station Street had opened on 21st October 1901, work started on the St. Ann's Well Road tracks, which were to terminate at Coppice Road (latterly Ransom Road). This was the first all-new tram line as the previous one, to Sherwood, had been partly converted from the horse drawn route to Carrington.

In November 1901 an ambitious proposal was put forward for a 'Nottingham Suburban Light Railway' with routes to Carlton, Arnold, Hucknall and Ilkeston but owing to substantial opposition by the MR, the scheme was turned down by the Light Railway Commission in February 1902.

Towards the end of 1901 construction work commenced on the electric tram route to Mapperley, via Woodborough Road, which was to terminate at its junction with Porchester Road. On 12th February 1902 a successful trial run was made on the St. Ann's Well Road route, and following the Board of Trade's inspection and approval on 20th February 1902, a five minute service commenced the next day to and from the Market Place. Although this did not have such a great impact on the NSR as the Sherwood route, with regard to loss of passengers, the small affect it did have in competing for the St Ann's Well station passenger trade, all added to the NSR's eventual decline.

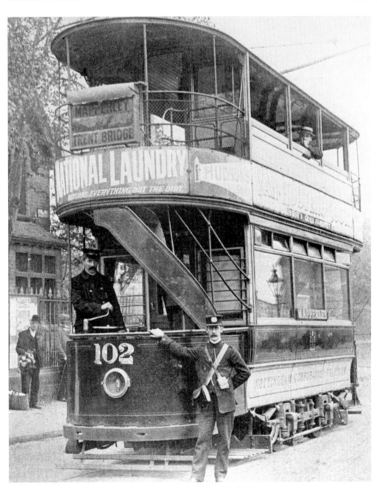

The introduction of new tramways and services was now gathering pace and, bit by bit, provided additional competition for the NSR. The next tram route to be commissioned was the one to Mapperley and, completing its trials on 1st May 1902, the service opened on 13th May following the Board of Trade's inspection on the previous 6th May. The route was from Mapperley to the Market Place and continued to Trent Bridge. The frequency of service was 12 minutes and the fare from the Market Place to Mapperley being 2d, with 1d intermediate stages. This route took some passengers away from the Suburban especially those who would have previously walked down Mapperley Rise to the station from Woodborough Road. The Sherwood station was now threatened by two tram routes.

On 30th July 1903, the St. Ann's Well Road route was joined to the Lenton and Radford 'Boulevard Circle' which improved its service to a tram every six minutes!

On 26th March 1906, the Corporation introduced a motorbus service, under powers that were granted in the Nottingham Corporation Act of 1905, which ran to the Crown Hotel on Carlton Road. This replaced the previous horse bus operation provided by a Mr Bamford, which the Corporation removed. However, after only a few months of operation, this service was giving considerable trouble as bus servicing costs were too high and the service became very haphazard. Consequently on 15th June the motorbus service was withdrawn and Mr Bamford agreed to reintroduce the horse bus service until such time as electric trams could be substituted.

On 22nd August 1906 track laying began on the Colwick Road route, which was completed on 6th March 1907 and on which date the first trials were carried out. In the Corporation's usual efficient way, the inspection of the line was carried out on 13th March 1907 and the tram service started the next day. Although this service was not in direct competition with the NSR, as the public in this area were unlikely to walk to Thorneywood to get transport to Nottingham, it would have been a threat if the proposed station at Sneinton had been built on Earl Manvers's land.

In April 1907 the Sherwood to Station Street service was extended to Colwick Road but after only one month of operation this service was discontinued.

A Bill was passed through Parliament in April 1908 which authorised the Corporation to not only take over some of the powers of the Nottinghamshire and Derbyshire Tramways Company but also to construct tramways to Arnold and Carlton.

Minor competition to the NSR was to rear its head on the 17th February 1908 when the first motor taxi ran in Nottingham. Costing a shilling a mile, it was only for the more affluent of the population. The first Beeston Humber cab, costing £350, parked up on the taxi rank in the Market Square amongst the hansom cabs and growlers. Mr. Harold Lees, the driver of the Humber, was forced out of his cab by the hansom cab drivers and then they drove him under his car using their whips. He was kept there until the daily crowds of workers and shoppers arrived after which they released him. They told him it would never pay and that *Trams go everywhere; there's no room for cabs in Nottingham'*. They could not have been more wrong.

Bill Knight the driver and conductor Alf Burton pose proudly with tram No.102 at the Mapperley terminus.

The Mapperley tram terminus at the junction with Porchester Road taken during the 1914 to 1918 war. *W. H. Smith post card.*
(below) **Tram No.100 at the Mapperley tram terminus in 1906 with the Wesleyan Chapel and the Mapperley brickyard chimneys to the left.**
Clumber Postcard No.149.

TRAM TERMINUS, MAPPERLEY, NOTTINGHAM.

The opening of the Sneinton Tramway on 14th March 1907 at the terminus on Colwick Road just to the east of NSR bridge No.4. *(below)* A tram bound for Nottingham leaves the Colwick Road terminus to pass under NSR bridge No.4.

The opening of the Nottingham to Carlton Road motor bus service on 26th March 1906. *E. Hamel postcard.*

It wasn't until 31st August 1910 that the laying of track on the Carlton Road route commenced with a revised terminus located at Thorneywood Lane, adjacent to the NSR's Thorneywood station. The line was inspected on 16th December and the service commenced the same day. Thorneywood was the final NSR station to be threatened by the electric trams and unlike the other two stations, this time the trams stopped right outside the door. As a consequence, passenger numbers using this station plummeted. This also resulted in the withdrawal of Mr. Bamford's horse-bus service. Now, most of the horse drawn trams in Nottingham had been superseded by electric trams.

In November 1912 tram route service numbers were allocated and those affecting the Suburban were as follows:-

Route No.	Route Termini
1	Winchester Street, Sherwood to Trent Bridge
2	Porchester Road, Mapperley to Trent Bridge
4	Basford to Colwick Roa
6	St. Ann's Well Road to Lenton and Radford
8	Carlton Rd at junction with Thorneywood Ln to Market Place

The Nottingham Corporation Bill of 1913 authorised several extensions to the Nottingham tram system, namely along Sneinton Road to Sneinton Dale; from Winchester Street, Sherwood via

Daybrook Square to Arnold; along Carlton Road to Newgate Street and from Porchester Road to Sprout Lane (now Coppice Road) on the Mapperley route. The subsequent Act gave powers to operate motor buses within the City boundary.

Expansion of the tram network now accelerated apace particularly on the east side of the city. In September 1913 construction commenced on the Carlton Road extension from Thorneywood Lane to Standhill Road at the top of Carlton Hill. Following inspection on 1st January 1914, it was opened on 5th January for public service. The Council then held a meeting in the same month and authorised the commencement of a further extension from Standhill Road down the east side of Carlton Hill. As well as immediately commencing work on this, the Corporation at the same time started work on the extension to Arnold. The Carlton extension was opened on 14th June 1914, which would have had little affect on the usage of the NSR.

Despite the commencement of the Great War, the Arnold extension was inspected on 29th December 1914, in time for the service to be available to the public on New Years Day 1915, the service being numbered 9. This was the final 'nail in the coffin' for the NSR, for now the electric trams went by Daybrook station, the NSR's northern terminus. The Nottingham Corporation electric tram network, which serviced the east side of the City of Nottingham, was virtually complete and was in direct competition with every station on the Nottingham Suburban Railway!

Tram usage was ever on the increase which was partly due to them expanding their network and taking clients away from the local railway systems. Their steady increase in passenger use is explained with the following usage figures:-

Year run	Electric Tram Passengers	Miles
	per annum	
1903	24,552,000	2,117,000
1904	27,876,879	
1905	27,518,200	
1906	28,833,311	
1907	31,218,691	
1908	34,411,860	
1909	33,813,997	
1910	34,647,238	
1911	35,259,067	3,389,000
1912	36,026,471	
1913	38,484,082	
1915	41,211,000	3,790,000

Many of these tram passengers would have used alternative public road transport conveyances such as horse drawn buses, trams, and cabs if the electric tram had not been introduced into Nottingham. Some would have continued to use the local suburban trains and many would probably walk as the cheapest alternative. However, these figures do show that the trams were catering for over half a million journeys a week, which goes some way to explain why the NSR was loosing so much revenue from all three of its stations where an alternative tram service had been provided nearby.

The Nottingham Corporation continued to improve its public transport services adjacent to the line through the introduction of motor buses to Sneinton Boulevard, Carlton Road and Mapperley in 1927 and trolleybuses, also in 1927. It was the initial introduction of a network of electric trams, however, which along with the construction of Victoria station and its associated rail links, that brought about the loss of the Suburban's passenger service. The last tram ran in Nottingham on 6th September 1936. A summary of the electric tram services competing with the Suburban is as follows:-

Electric Tram Route	Construction Start	B-of-T Inspection Date	Service open to Public
Winchester Street, Sherwood to Market Place	1st June 1900	16th December 1900	1st January 1901
St. Ann's Well Road to Market Place	21st October 1901	20th February 1902	21st February 1902
Woodborough Rd, Mapperley to Market Place	Towards end of 1901	6th May 1902	13th May 1902
Colwick Road to Market Place	22nd August 1906	13th March 1907	14th March 1907
Thorneywood Ln, Carlton Rd to Market Place	31st August 1910	16th December 1910	16th December 1910
Carlton Road 1st extension	September 1913	1st January 1914	5th January 1914
Carlton Road 2nd extension	January 1914	?	14th June 1914
Daybrook and Arnold extension	January 1914	29th December 1914	1st January 1915

By the time of the closure of the three NSR stations to passenger traffic, the trams were operating a service which could not be have even been contemplated by the railways. Their first trams in a weekday morning started at about 5.40 a.m. and the last ran at 10.45 p.m., whilst on a Sunday they ran from about 9.10 a.m. to 11.00 p.m. depending on the route.

Whilst on the subject of other forms of NSR competitive transport, one should consider the private motor car. In fact, the 'horseless carriage' as it was otherwise known, never posed a threat to the NSR. The first motor car did not appear in Nottingham until 1897 and very few were in the Nottingham area in the Edwardian era. Compulsory car registration came into force in 1903 and in Nottingham only 125 vehicles were listed which included motor cycles and tricycles. This may have been due to the fact that the early vehicles were very unreliable and noisy, which presumably frightened the numerous horses which were found using the city streets.

(below) **Tram No.200 having just travelled under NSR bridge No.4 on Colwick Road. Photograph reproduced by kind permission of Phil Atkins.** *G.H.F. Atkins.*

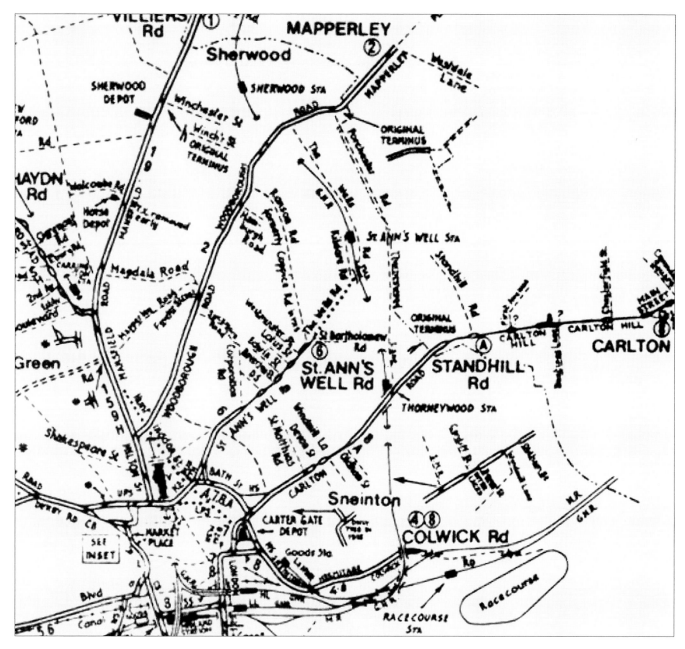

A map of eastern Nottingham showing the line of the NSR and the tram routes which provided an alternative mode of transport for the NSR customers.

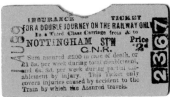

1

2

3

4

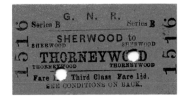

5

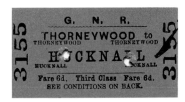

6

7

8

9

10

11

12

13

A selection of tickets issued by the Great Northern Railway relating to stations on the NSR or passage along its tracks.

1 - GNR insurance ticket dated 1st August 1889 issued by the GNR London Road station, coloured beige. *Ian Askew.*

2 - The rear of the previous ticket. *Ian Askew.*

3 - GNR ticket St. Ann's Well to Kimberley 3rd Class, dated 16th April 1904, 6d, coloured turquoise. *Ian Askew.*

4 - The rear of the previous ticket. *Ian Askew.*

5 - GNR ticket Sherwood to Thorneywood 3rd Class, dated 29th April 1904, 1½d, coloured turquoise. *Ian Askew.*

6 - GNR ticket Thorneywood to Hucknall 3rd Class, 6d, coloured turquoise. *Ian Askew.*

7 - GNR ticket Sutton-in-Ashfield to St. Ann's Well, 3rd Class, 1½d, coloured turquoise. *Ian Askew.*

8 - GNR ticket Nottingham (Joint St'n) to Sherwood, 3rd Class, 3d. *Alfred Henshaw.*

9 - GNR ticket Nottingham (Joint St'n) to Newstead via Trent Lane Junction, 3rd Class, 1s. 3d. *Alfred Henshaw*

10 - GNR return ticket St. Ann's Well to Skegby Via Annesley, 3rd Class, coloured grey. *Ian Askew.*

11 - GNR ticket Nottingham (Joint St'n) to Newstead via Trent Lane Junction, 3rd Class, 1s. 0½d. turquoise. *Simon Swain.*

12 - GNR ticket Thorneywood to Netherfield & Colwick, 3rd Class, 3d, coloured turquoise. *Simon Swain.*

13 - GNR ticket Sherwood to Netherfield & Colwick, 3rd Class, 3d, coloured turquoise. *Simon Swain.*

Chapter 10: THE NOTTINGHAM SUBURBAN RAILWAY COMPANY IN DECLINE 1900-1909

The 25th November 1900 saw the completion and opening of the Leen Valley Extension to Shirebrook and the Lancashire, Derbyshire & East Coast Railway at Langwith. As a consequence, from 1st November 1901 the GNR's passenger services to Skegby were extended to Pleasley and Shirebrook. Four trains ran each way daily using the Suburban, with two each way on Sundays travelling via Gedling and the 'Outer Circle'. The daily service was soon increased to ten each way with an additional train on Saturdays.

It is recorded in the NSR minutes that in 1901 Mr. G. B. Kid commenced the role as Auditor for The NSR Company.

As the NSR was operated by the GNR, the tickets that were issued to the traveller were the standard GNR tickets of the time. Several have been provided as examples, primarily from Ian Askew's collection, and are illustrated opposite.

As mentioned earlier, extensive track alterations were carried out at the Trent junctions (*see* pages 54-57) in order to accommodate the link between the GNR and the new London Road (High Level) and Victoria stations. In order for the NSR to also gain access to Victoria station a link was put in between the NSR's Up line and the GNR Nottingham to Grantham Down line. It was also around this time

that a new line was constructed from the end of the NSR's Up line just west of Trent Lane through to the London Road Low Level goods yard. It is believed that in order to accommodate this single line the GNR bridge over Meadow Lane was widened and given an extra two track wide span.

In 1902 Lesley Charles Probyn K.C.V.O., who represented the GNR on the NSR Company's Board, resigned. His place was taken by Harry L. Birkin. Also, in this same year, Mr. W.J. Grinling took up the role of Auditor for the Company's accounts.

Also in 1902, the Mapperley brickyard was again used for the site of another huge bonfire, this time to celebrate the Coronation

The view looking west to London Road (Low Level) station in 1957, with the NSR bridge No.1 to the rear, showing the new NSR Up line on the left of the picture which is believed to have been put in around 1899 following track revisions for the LNWR goods station on Manvers Street (note the guards van far right) and the GNR link via Weekday Cross to the Nottingham Victoria station - twin track to left of signal. *Tony Hill.*

A further view from 1957. Travelling further west along the new NSR Up line, on the left of the picture, and approaching closer to the London Road (Low Level) goods yard. Note the small semaphore signal on the left for NSR traffic. Taken in 1957. *Tony Hill.*

of King Edward V11. The bonfire was originally programmed to be set alight on 26th June along with other beacons located throughout the country. However, owing to the King taking seriously ill, the Coronation Festivities had to be postponed and alternative arrangements were made. The Mayor of Nottingham therefore declared that the 30th June would be a public holiday and that the bonfire would be lit at 10.00 p.m. at the original site at the Mapperley brickworks.

In 1903 the NPBC made a substantial donation towards the building of the Wesleyan Chapel, which is on the north side of the Woodborough Road, at its junction with Woodthorpe Road, which is just to the west of the Porchester Road junction. The ground on which it still stands was donated by Charles Bennett, one of the NPBC's Managers, who was mentioned in Volume 1. Prior to this, the NPBC's Mapperley offices were used in the evenings as reading rooms and on Sundays for religious services.

The NSR received a letter on 20th October 1904 from the solicitor representing Colonel Thackeray, who had recently acquired land from Mr. C.G. Hill with whom the NSR already had an agreement. The solicitor was drawing the NSR Company's attention to Clause 14 of the Agreement dated 24th June 1889, under which the NSR acquired certain lands from Mr C.G. Hill, a portion of which now belonged to Colonel Thackeray. The clause mentioned the erection of fifty houses, which they said had now been erected, and they were stating that the time had now come to erect the new station. This information was reported to the Company Directors' meeting

of 9th December 1904 who were also advised that a site visit had shown that only 34 houses had actually been built and that a copy of the letter and the NSR's Agreement had been sent to the General Manager of the GNR by the Company Secretary. It was agreed that the matter should be reconsidered when the reply was received from the GNR. This matter was still ongoing in March 1906 and a decision regarding the Breck Hill station, as it was now called, had not been reached. It was also reported at this meeting that the Nottingham Corporation had made an application for powers to construct tramways along Colwick Road which included passing under the Company's bridge No.4 on Colwick Road. This matter was also referred to the GNR.

On 28th October 1904, the signal box which was located at the north end of the Up platform at St. Ann's Well station was withdrawn from service, after which the Station Master at St. Ann's Well was required to work the siding's points for all traffic.

Although not directly pertaining to the NSR, one of its most prominent merchants was E. Reeves & Company. Just before 29th April 1905 one of this company's wagons was involved in a serious incident (*see* illustrations later). The accident occurred at Nuthall sidings and was recorded on camera. A copy of a post card and another photograph in the collection of Tony Hill shows one of Reeves's wagons upended and resting on the top of another wagon. A GNR crane is lifting a guards van and an unidentified GNR single-wheeled locomotive waits to give assistance in the background.

(above) **Trent Lane junction and a Nottingham to Grantham train crosses the Midland Railway's Nottingham to Lincoln line on 21st May 1902. Immediately to the right of the home and distant somersault signals – in the 'off' position for the train – is the home signal controlling trains onto the Suburban line.** *Rev. Thomas Parley (1876-1951), Michael Vanns collection.*

(right) **Official Programme front cover for the Local Celebrations for the Coronation of King Edward VII and Queen Alexandra, 26th to 29th June 1902.** *Nottingham City Town Clerk.*

(below) **A circular advertising the Coronation Bonfire to be held on 26th June1902 at the NPBC Mapperley brickworks, one of the highest points in Nottingham.** *Nottingham City Council.*

Coronation Bonfire,

THURSDAY EVENING, June 26th.

Arrangements have been made for a large Bonfire to be constructed on one of the highest points on Mapperley Plains (in the yard of the Nottingham Patent Brick Company's premises).

This fire will be lighted at 10 o'clock p.m., punctually, in accordance with a scheme prepared by a Central Committee, formed for the purpose of securing the simultaneous lighting of Coronation Bonfires all over the Kingdom.

City of **Nottingham.**

· **Official Programme** ·

OF THE

LOCAL CELEBRATIONS

ON THE OCCASION OF THE

Coronation of Their Majesties

King Edward VII. and Queen Alexandra.

26th, 27th, and 29th JUNE, 1902.

SIR SAMUEL G. JOHNSON,

TOWN CLERK.

Alteration of Celebrations
IN NOTTINGHAM.

Owing to the serious illness of His Majesty the King the whole of the Coronation Festivities in Nottingham were postponed.

His Majesty having now been pronounced out of danger, the Mayor has declared Thursday, July 3rd, a Public Holiday, and approved of the Celebrations to take place as follows.

Bonfire
Mapperley Plains, Monday, June 30, 10 p.m.

Display of Fireworks on the Forest,
Wednesday, at 9.30 p.m.

PEACE DEMONSTRATION

THURSDAY MORNING, JULY 3rd,
leaving Trent Bridge at 10.30.

ORDER OF PROCESSION, etc.,
the same as contained in the Programme.

Will all those who have so generously worked and promised their support endeavour to make this Demonstration a complete success.

Water Fete
THURSDAY AFTERNOON, July 3rd.

The Fete will commence at 2.30 instead of 1.30 as announced in the Programme, and all the events will be one hour later than the advertised time.

(left) Circular advising of alterations to the Coronation Celebrations, due to the illness of the King. *Nottingham City Council. (right)* Declaration of the Mapperley Plains bonfire at the NPBC on 30th June 1902. *Nottingham City Town Clerk.*

CITY OF NOTTINGHAM.

CORONATION BONFIRE

Monday Evening, JUNE 30th.

In accordance with the suggestion of the Chairman of the Central Committee that all the Bonfires throughout the United Kingdom should be lighted at 10 o'clock this (Monday) Evening, the Bonfire on Mapperley Plains will be lighted accordingly.

BY ORDER,

SAMUEL G. JOHNSON,
TOWN CLERK.

LEEN & SON LTD., PRINTERS, NOTTINGHAM.

(below) The 1902 beacon at the NPBC yard at Mapperley was constructed very high so that, in accordance with the procedures laid down, 'beacons shall be visible one to another'. *(right)* The 1902 NPBC beacon burning.

It was around 1908 that agreements were finally reached with Earl Manvers and Mr Hill that the provisionally proposed stations at Sneinton and Woodthorpe should not be constructed as the population in the immediate vicinities had not reached the certain numbers specified by that time or in the foreseeable future. In the case of Earl Manvers, he was paid by the NSR Company in order to redeem the Agreement. In the case of Mr Charles Gray Hill, he had sold off some of the land included in the Agreement and the NSR and GNR said the Agreement had been solely with him and could not be passed onto future owners. As a consequence the Agreement with him was redeemed but no payment was made.

The 1st October 1907 to 30th June 1908 GNR Passenger Timetable, a 232 page book costing 1d, highlighted the principal train alterations, including cancelled trains. There were, as you will probably guess or expect, not only changes to the NSR's services but also some trains which were discontinued. These can be summarised as follows:-

The 9.10 a.m. and the 12.08 p.m. Shirebrook to Nottingham (Victoria) via the Suburban would run on Wednesdays and Saturdays only, instead of daily.

The 4.55 p.m. Nottingham (Victoria) to Shirebrook via the Suburban would now leave at 4.47 p.m. and run correspondingly earlier throughout the journey.

The 12.00 noon and the 2.48 p.m. Nottingham (Victoria) to Basford via the Suburban were discontinued.

The 5.23 p.m. Basford to Nottingham (Victoria) via the Suburban was also discontinued.

As a consequence, the revised Suburban timetable was as reproduced on pages 60 and 61.

As stated above, the services from the Suburban's passenger stations were now all duplicated by more frequent electric tram services which all had quicker, more direct routes to the Nottingham City centre without having to pass through the additional miles travelling through the Sneinton area and the High Level route to the east and south of the City. Tram fares were also cheaper than those on the Suburban. It appears harsh that the NSR's passenger services were partially ruined by the Nottingham's Corporation's tram services, especially as it was the Nottingham peoples' money which helped to finance the line in the first place and the Corporation still held shares in the Company.

On 18th June 1907 the NSR and GNR made an agreement with the City of Nottingham Corporation to give them, without charge, 14 square yards of land adjacent to the Colwick Road bridge No.4, so that the Corporation could carry out a road widening scheme.

(right) **The Wesleyan chapel, now a Methodist church, which cost £2,850 to build and stands upon land donated by Charles Bennett, the Manager of the NPBC.** *D. Birch.*

Charles Bennett (1832-1909) Manager of the NPBC. *NPBC.*

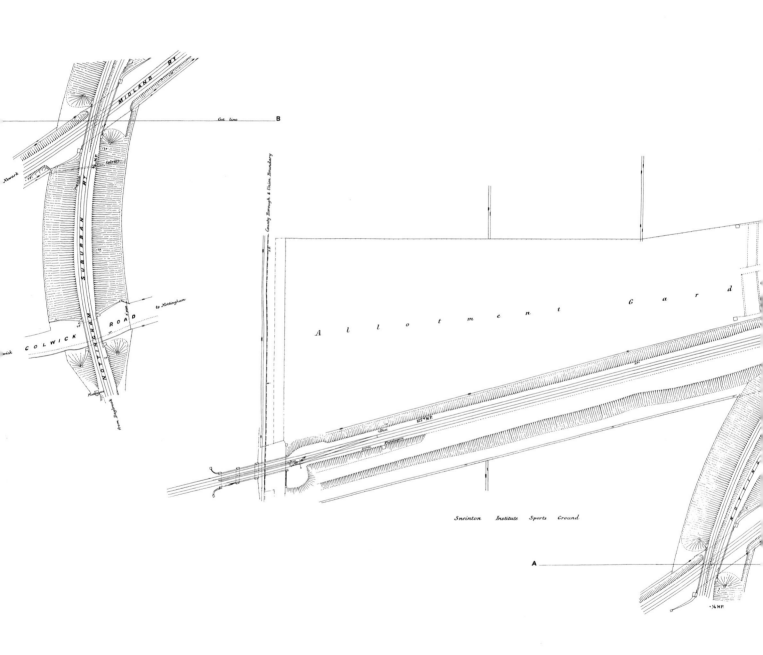

MIDLAND RY

SUBURBAN RY

NOTTINGHAM

Newark

Colwick

to Nottingham

COLWICK ROAD

Cut line   B

County Borough & Union Boundary

A l l o t m e n t   G a r d

MP

Sneinton   Institute   Sports   Ground

A

¼ MP

The GNR Passenger Timetable for 1st July to 30th September 1905 gave the following information for the Suburban services:

PINXTON, BASFORD AND BULWELL, NOTTINGHAM AND SHIREBROOK.
(Via THORNEYWOOD)
Monday to Saturday Only (No Service on Sunday)

Down Line		am			pm								
Basford and Bulwell	depart	7.33							5.43				
Nottingham Victoria	arrive	7.40	8.39					4.30	5.50				
Nottingham Victoria	**depart**	7.42	9.05	11.25	12.00	1.08	2.48	4.55	5.52	7.03	8.30	9.35	11.10
Nottingham London Rd High Level	**arrive**	7.44	9.07	11.27	12.02	1.10	2.50	4.57	5.54	7.05	8.32	9.37	11.12
Nottingham London Rd High Level	**depart**	7.46	9.08	11.28	12.04	1.12	2.52	4.59	5.55	7.06	8.33	9.38	11.13
Thorneywood	**depart**	7.51	9.13	pass	12.09	1.17	2.57	5.04	5.59	7.11	pass	pass	pass
St Ann's Well	**depart**	7.54	9.16	pass	12.12	1.20	3.00	5.07	6.02	7.14	pass	pass	pass
Sherwood	**depart**	7.57	9.19	pass	12.15	1.23	3.03	5.10	6.05	7.17	pass	pass	pass
Daybrook	**depart**	8.02	9.23	11.37	12.19	1.27	3.07	5.14	6.09	7.21	8.42	9.47	11.22
Basford and Bulwell	arrive	8.06			12.23		3.12		6.13				
			to Shirebrook	to Shirebrook		to Shirebrook		to Shirebrook	from Pinxton	to Shirebrook	to Shirebrook Weds & Sat only	to Shirebrook	to Shirebrook Sat only

SHIREBROOK, PINXTON, BASFORD AND BULWELL AND NOTTINGHAM
(Via THORNEYWOOD)
Monday to Saturday Only (No Service on Sunday)

Up Line		am			pm						
Basford and Bulwell	depart	8.13			2.08				5.23	7.05	
Daybrook	**depart**	8.18	9.54	10.36	12.56	2.13	2.45	5.20	5.28	7.10	9.07
Sherwood	**depart**	8.21	9.57	10.39	pass	2.16	2.48	5.23	5.31	7.13	pass
St Ann's Well	**depart**	8.24	10.00	10.42	pass	2.19	2.51	5.26	5.34	7.16	pass
Thorneywood	**depart**	8.27	10.04	10.46	pass	2.22	2.54	5.31	5.37	7.20	pass
Nottingham London Rd High Level	**arrive**	8.31	10.08	10.5	1.04	2.26	2.58	5.35*	5.41	7.24	9.15
Nottingham London Rd High Level	**depart**	8.33	10.10	10.52	1.06	2.27	3.00		5.43	7.26	9.17
Nottingham Victoria	**arrive**	8.35	10.12	10.54	1.08	2.29	3.02		5.45	7.28	9.19
Nottingham Victoria	depart								5.50	7.34	
Basford and Bulwell	arrive								5.56	7.40	
			from Shirebrook	from Shirebrook			from Shirebrook	From Newstead not Bank Holidays *Arrives at Nottm. Low Level Station		from Pinxton	from Shirebrook

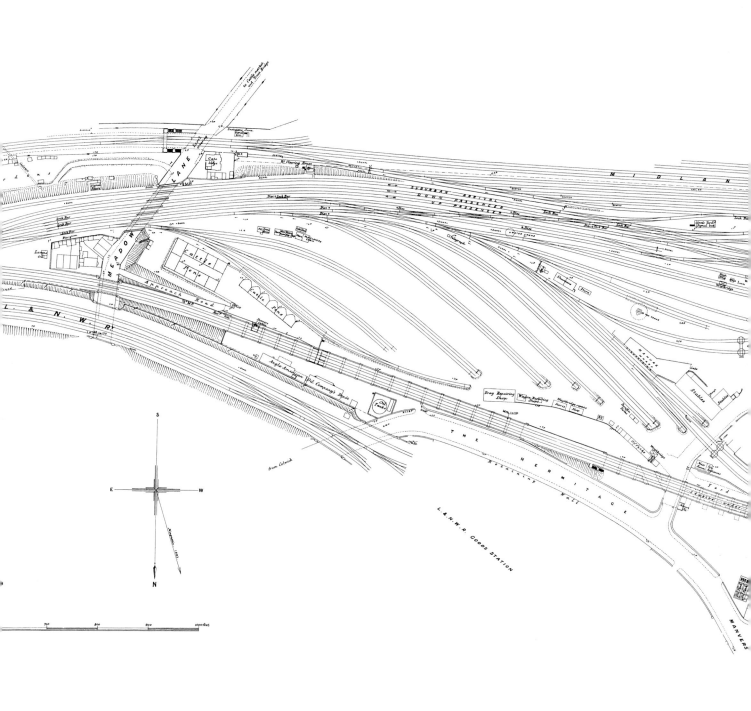

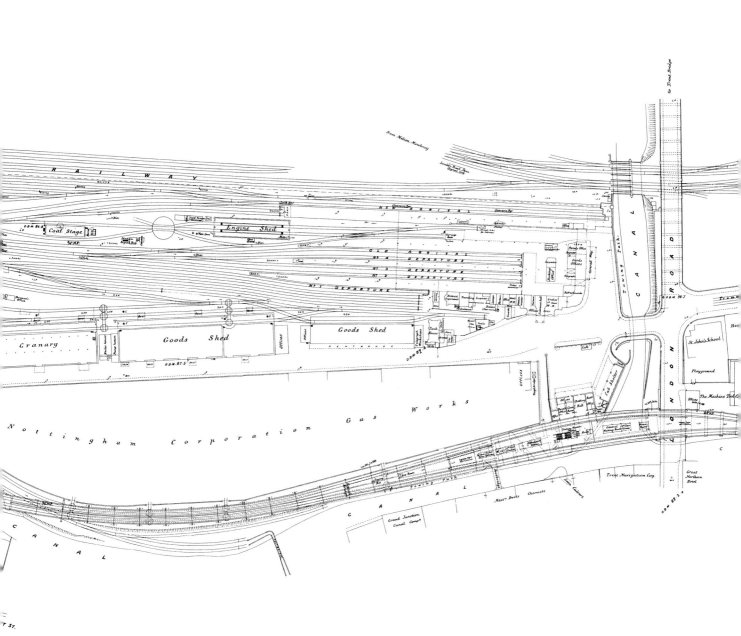

A latter day view of the row of houses on Eaton Terrace, which were built by the NPBC to accommodate the families of some of its workers employed at the Mapperley brickworks. *D. Birch.*

A railway accident at Nuthall sidings just before 29th April 1905 involving an E.Reeve & Co. wagon. The rear of this post card reads 'We do things in a form here'..

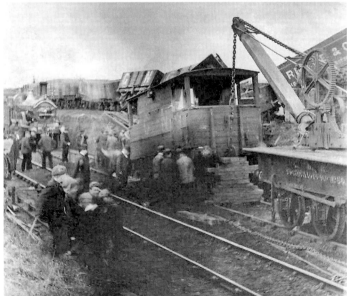

Another view of the railway accident at Nuthall sidings just before 29th April 1905.

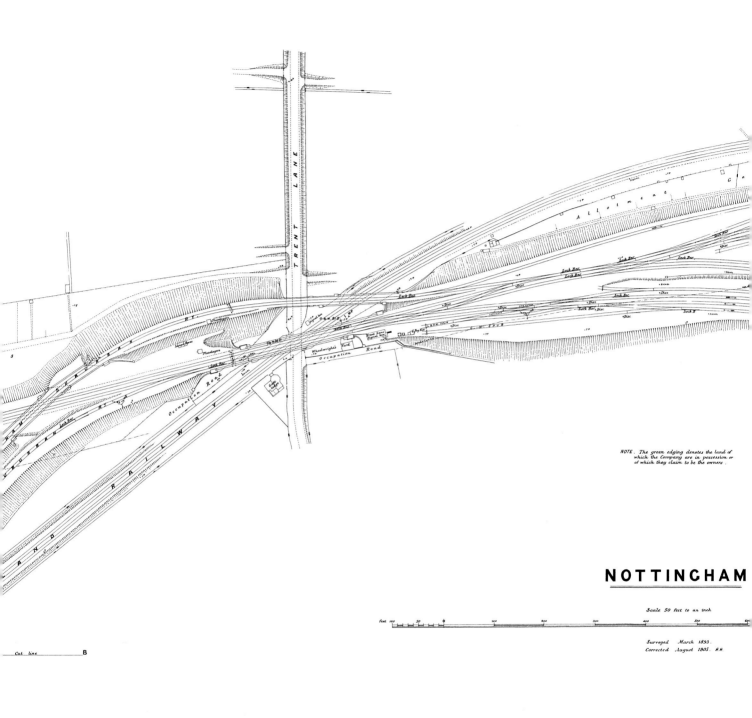

NOTE. The green edging denotes the land of
which the Company are in possession or
of which they claim to be the owners.

NOTTINGHAM

Scale 50 feet to an inch

Feet 100   50   0   100   200   300   400   500   600

Surveyed   March 1893.
Corrected August 1905.

Cut line   B

Nottingham Victoria to Shirebrook

Down Line		Pass	Pass	Pass	Pass	Pass	Pass	Pass	Pass	Pass
		am		pm						
Nottingham Victoria	dep	9.00	11.25	1.08	4.47	7.03	8.30	8.30	9.37	11.10
Nottingham High Level	dep	9.03	11.28	1.12	4.50	7.06	8.33	8.33	9.40	11.15
Thorneywood	dep	9.08	Thr'u	1.17	4.55	7.11	Thr'u	Thr'u	Thr'u	Thr'u
St. Ann's Well	dep	9.11	Thr'u	1.20	4.58	7.14	Thr'u	Thr'u	Thr'u	Thr'u
Sherwood	dep	9.14	Thr'u	1.23	5.01	7.17	Thr'u	Thr'u	Thr'u	Thr'u
Daybrook	dep	9.21	11.38	1.27	5.03	7.21	8.43	8.43	9.50	11.23
Bulwell Forest	dep	9.27	Halt	1.33	5.11	7.27	Halt	Halt	Thr'u	Thr'u
Bestwood Colliery	dep	9.30	Thr'u	1.36	5.14	7.30	8.50	8.50	9.57	11.30
Butler's Hill	dep	9.33	Thr'u	1.39	5.17	7.33	8.53	8.53	10.00	11.33
Hucknall	dep	9.36	11.47	1.42	5.20	7.37	8.56	8.56	10.03	11.36
Linby	dep	9.40	11.51	1.46	5.24	7.41	9.00	9.00	10.07	11.40
Newstead	dep	9.44	11.55	1.50	5.28	7.45	9.04	9.04	10.11	11.44
Sutton-in-Ashfield for Huthwaite	dep	9.53	12.06	2.01	5.40	7.56	9.15	9.15	10.22	11.55
Skegby	dep	9.58	12.09	2.04	5.43	7.59		9.18	10.25	11.58
Pleasley	dep	10.03	12.14	2.09	5.48	8.04		9.23	10.30	12.03
Shirebrook	arr	10.08	12.19	2.14	5.53	8.09		9.28	10.35	12.08
							Saturday excepted	Saturday Only	Leaves Victoria 5.30pm B/hols.	Saturdays Only

(above) **Nottingham (Victoria) to Shirebrook - Down.**   *(below)* **Shirebrook to Nottingham (Victoria) - Up.**

Shirebrook to Nottingham Victoria

Up Line		Pass	Pass	Pass	Pass	Pass	Pass	Pass
		am		pm				
Shirebrook	dep	9.10	9.48	12.08	1.57		8.20	9.55*
Pleasley	dep	9.16	9.54	12.14	2.03		8.26	10.01*
Skegby	dep	9.22	10.00	12.20	2.09		8.32	10.07*
Sutton-in-Ashfield for Huthwaite	dep	9.25	10.04	12.24	2.13		8.36	10.11
Newstead	dep	9.35	10.14	12.34	2.22	4.55	8.46	10.20
Linby	dep	9.39	10.18	12.38	2.26	4.59	8.50	10.24
Hucknall	dep	9.43	10.22	12.42	2.30	5.03	8.54	10.28
Butler's Hill	dep	Thr'u	10.25	12.45	2.33	5.06	8.57	10.31
Bestwood Colliery	dep	Thr'u	10.28	12.48	2.36	5.09	9.00	10.34
Bulwell Forest	dep	Thr'u	10.31	12.50 Sat only	2.39	5.14	Thr'u	Thr'u
Daybrook	dep	9.53	10.37	12.57	2.45	5.20	9.08	10.42
Sherwood	dep	9.56	10.40	Thr'u	2.48	5.23	Thr'u	Thr'u
St. Ann's Well	dep	9.59	10.43	Thr'u	2.51	5.26	Thr'u	Thr'u
Thorneywood	dep	10.03	10.47	Thr'u	2.54	5.31	Thr'u	Thr'u
Nottingham High Level	dep	10.07	10.51	1.05	2.58	5.35*	9.16	10.50
Nottingham Victoria	arr	10.10	10.55	1.09	3.20		9.20	10.53
			Wednesday and Saturday only	Wednesday and Saturday only	Bank Holidays excepted	Bank Holidays excepted * Arrives at London Road Low Level		* Saturdays Only

Basford and Bulwell to Nottingham Victoria on Suburban Line

Down Line		Pass.	Pass.	Pass.
		am		pm
Basford and Bulwell	dep	7.33		5.38
Nottingham Victoria	dep	7.44	9.55	5.50
Nottingham High Level	dep	7.47	9.59	5.54
Thorneywood	dep	7.52	Thr'u	5.58
St. Ann's Well	dep	7.55	Thr'u	6.01
Sherwood	dep	7.58	Thr'u	6.04
Daybrook	dep	8.02	10.09	6.09
Basford and Bulwell	arr	8.06	10.13	6.13
				From Pinxton

(right, top) **The 1st May 1909 GNR 'Guide to Holiday Resorts' for the Midland Counties District and containing entries for Sherwood station.** *GNR.* (right, bottom) **Short date and long date tickets to Norfolk Coast, including from Sherwood station, from the 1909 GNR guide.** *GNR.*

Up Line		Pass.	Pass.
		pm	
Basford and Bulwell	dep	2.08	7.05
Daybrook	dep	2.13	7.10
Sherwood	dep	2.16	7.13
St. Ann's Well	dep	2.19	7.16
Thorneywood	dep	2.22	7.20
Nottingham High Level	dep	2.27	7.26
Nottingham Victoria	arr	2.29	7.34
Basford and Bulwell	arr		7.40
			To Pinxton

SHORT DATE and LONG DATE TICKETS to NORFOLK COAST, &c.

	Hunstanton.		Cromer, West Runton, Sheringham, Overstrand, Trimingham, Mundesley-on-Sea, Weybourne,		FROM	Aldeburgh, Caister-on-Sea. Gorlest'n-'n-Sea Lowestoft (Central), Lowestoft (North), Southwold, Yarmouth,		Clacton, Dovercourt, Felixstowe, Frinton-on-Sea, Harwich, Walton-on-the-Naze.	
	Short date.	Long date.	Short date.	Long date.		Short date.	Long date.	Short date.	Long date.
	1 · 3	1 · 3	1 · 3	1 · 3		1 · 3	1 · 3	1 · 3	1 · 3
	s d · s d	s d · s d	s d · s d	s d · s d		s d · s d	s d · s d	s d · s d	s d · s d
	16 0 · 8 0	23 0 11 6	19 0 · 9 6	27 6 13 9	Basford	23 0 11 6	32 0 16 0	23 0 11 6	32 0 16 0
	16 0 · 8 0	23 0 11 6	20 0 · 9 6	27 6 13 9	Bingham	23 0 11 6	32 0 16 0	23 0 11 6	... · ...
	15 0 · 7 6	22 0 11 0	10 0 · 9 0	27 0 13 0	Bottesford	22 0 11 0	31 0 15 6	22 0 11 0	... · ...
	17 0 · 8 6	25 6 12 9	19 6 · 9 9	30 0 15 0	Breadsall	23 0 11 6	34 0 17 0	23 0 11 6	34 0 17 0
	17 0 · 8 6	25 6 12 9	19 6 · 9 9	30 0 15 0	Burton	23 0 11 6	34 0 17 0	23 0 11 6	34 0 17 3
	18 0 · 9 0	26 0 13 0	20 6 10 3	30 6 15 3	Codnor Park	24 0 12 0	34 6 17 3	24 0 12 0	34 6 17 3
	17 0 · 8 6	25 6 12 9	19 6 · 9 9	30 0 15 0	*Derby, F'gate	23 0 11 6	34 0 17 0	23 0 11 6	34 0 17 0
	18 0 · 9 0	25 0 12 9	20 6 10 3	30 0 15 0	Eastwood G.N.	24 0 12 0	34 0 17 0	24 0 12 0	34 0 17 0
	16 0 · 8 0	23 0 11 6	19 0 · 9 6	27 6 13 9	Gedling	23 0 11 6	32 0 16 0	23 0 11 6	32 0 16 0
	18 0 · 9 0	25 0 12 9	20 6 10 3	30 0 15 0	Heanor	24 0 12 0	34 0 17 0	24 0 12 0	34 0 17 0
	17 0 · 8 6	24 6 12 3	19 6 · 9 9	29 0 14 6	Hucknall	23 0 11 6	33 0 16 6	23 0 11 6	33 0 16 6.
	15 0 · 7 6	22 8 11 0	18 6 · 9 3	28 0 14 0	Humberstone	23 0 11 6	32 6 16 3	23 0 11 6	32 6 16 3
	17 0 · 8 0	24 6 12 3	19 6 · 9 9	29 0 14 6	Ilkeston	23 0 11 6	33 0 16 6	23 0 11 6	33 0 16 6
	15 0 · 7 6	22 8 11 0	18 6 · 9 3	28 0 14 0	Ingersby and John o' Gaunt	23 0 11 6	32 6 16 3	23 0 11 6	32 6 16 3
	17 0 · 8 6	24 6 12 3	19 6 · 9 9	29 0 14 6	Kimberley	23 0 11 6	33 0 16 6	23 0 11 6	33 0 16 6
	15 0 · 7 6	22 8 11 0	18 6 · 9 3	28 0 14 0	*Leicester (Belg've Rd.)	23 0 11 6	32 6 16 3	23 0 11 6	32 6 16 3
	15 0 · 7 6	23 0 11 6	18 6 · 9 3	28 0 14 0	Loseby	23 0 11 6	32 6 16 3	23 0 11 6	32 6 16 3
	16 0 · 8 0	23 0 11 6	19 0 · 9 6	27 6 13 9	Netherfield and Colwick	23 0 11 6	32 0 16 0	23 0 11 6	32 0 16 0
	16 0 · 8 0	23 0 11 6	19 0 · 9 6	27 6 13 9	*Nottingham	23 0 11 6	32 0 16 0	23 0 11 6	32 0 16 0
	17 9 · 9 3	26 0 13 0	21 0 10 6	31 0 15 6	Pinxton	24 0 12 0	34 6 17 3	24 0 12 0	34 6 17 3
	... · ...	... · ...	... · ...	... · ...	Pleasley	24 6 12 3	35 0 17 6	... · ...	... · ...
	16 0 · 8 0	23 0 11 6	19 0 · 9 6	27 6 13 9	Radcliffe-on-Trent	23 0 11 6	32 0 16 0	23 0 11 6	32 0 16 0
	17 0 · 8 0	23 0 11 6	19 0 · 9 6	27 6 13 9	Sherwood	23 0 11 6	32 0 16 0	23 0 11 6	32 0 16 0
	... · ...	... · ...	... · ...	... · ...	Shirebrook	24 6 13 0	... · ...	... · ...	... · ...
	... · ...	... · ...	... · ...	... · ...	Skegby	24 6 12 9	... · ...	... · ...	... · ...
	21 9 13 0	22 9 16 0	26 6 14 6	35 0 19 3	Stafford (Com. & Town)	27 9 15 3	37 3 20 3	34 3 17 0	42 6 22 0
	... · ...	... · ...	... · ...	... · ...	Sutton-in-Ashfield	24 6 12 9	... · ...	... · ...	... · ...
	15 0 · 7 6	23 0 11 6	18 0 · 9 3	28 0 14 0	Thurnby	23 0 11 6	32 6 16 3	23 0 11 6	32 6 16 3

For Notes and Routes, see pages 23 and 24.

FORTNIGHTLY RETURN TICKETS to LINCOLNSHIRE COAST.

Skegness, Sutton-on-Sea, Mablethorpe, Theddlethorpe, Saltfleetby.		FROM	Woodhall Spa.	
1	3		1	3
s d	s d		s d	s d
10 0	7 0	Barnstone	16 0	7 3
10 0	7 0	Basford	12 0	6 6
10 3	7 0	Bestwood	13 6	7 0
10 0	7 0	Bingham	14 6	7 3
10 0	7 0	Bottesford	14 6	7 3
11 0	8 0	Breadsall	14 3	7 3
10 0	7 0	Bulwell Forest	13 0	7 0
12 9	9 9	Burton	16 6	8 6
10 3	7 0	Butler's Hill	14 0	7 0
10 3	7 0	Codnor Park	16 0	8 0
10 0	7 0	Daybrook	12 0	6 6
11 0	8 0	*Derby (Friargate)	14 3	7 3
10 3	7 0	Eastwood and Langley Mill	16 0	8 0
10 0	7 0	Gedling and Carlton	12 0	6 6
10 0	7 0	Harby and Stathern	16 0	7 3
10 6	7 0	Heanor	16 0	8 0
12 9	9 9	Horninglow	...	7 0
10 3	7 0	Hucknall	14 6	7 0
11 0	7 0	Humberstone	15 9	7 0
10 6	7 0	Ilkeston	13 9	7 0
10 6	7 0	Ingersby	15 9	7 0
10 6	7 0	John o'Gaunt	15 9	7 0
10 6	7 0	Kimberley	13 9	6 9
11 0	7 0	*Leicester (Belgrave Rd.)	15 9	7 0
10 3	7 0	Linby	15 0	7 0
10 6	7 0	Loseby	15 9	7 0
10 0	7 0	Melton Mowbray	13 0	6 6
10 3	7 0	Netherfield and Colwick	15 0	7 0
10 3	7 0	Newstead	16 0	8 0
10 0	7 0	Newthorpe	12 0	6 6
10 0	7 0	*Nottingham	16 0	8 0
10 3	7 0	Pinxton and Pye Hill	16 0	8 0
10 3	7 0	Pleasley	16 0	8 0
10 0	7 0	Radcliffe-on-Trent	12 0	6 6
10 0	7 0	Redmile	16 0	7 3
10 0	7 0	Sherwood	12 0	6 6
10 3	7 0	Shirebrook	16 0	8 0
10 3	7 0	Skegby	16 0	8 0
15 9	12 0	Stafford Common and Town	20 3	12 0
10 0	7 0	Sutton-in-Ashfield	16 0	8 0
11 0	7 0	Thurnby	15 9	7 0
10 6	8 0	West Hallam	13 9	7 0

For General Conditions, see pages 4 and 5.
* Tickets are also issued at Town Offices shown on page 5.

Routes :—Same as for Tourist Tickets (see page 22).

Holders of fortnightly tickets to Sutton-on-Sea via Willoughby and Mumby Road may alight at and rejoin at Mumby Road those trains which are advertised to stop at that station.

Extension.—Passengers holding these tickets and wishing to stay for a longer period may do so by paying the difference between the Fortnightly and the Tourist fares.

SHORT and LONG DATE TICKETS to NORFOLK COAST (continued).

Week-End (Long and Short Date) Tickets by Mid. & G.N. Joint Route may be used as under Instead of to and from station printed on tickets :—

CROMER, WEST RUNTON, SHERINGHAM, OVERSTRAND, TRIMINGHAM AND WEYBOURNE tickets to and from Holt.
MUNDESLEY-ON-SEA tickets to and from Paston and Knapton, or North Walsham.
YARMOUTH tickets to and from North Walsham. Stalham, Catfield, Potter Heigham, Martham, Hemsby, Great Ormesby, or Caister-on-Sea.
LOWESTOFT tickets to and from Hopton or Corton.
GORLESTON-ON-SEA tickets to and from Gorleston North, Hopton or Corton.

Tickets issued to Weybourne, Sheringham, West Runton, Cromer, Mundesley-on-Sea, Overstrand, Trimingham, Caister-on-Sea, Yarmouth, Gorleston-on-Sea, and Lowestoft are available to return from either of these places, also from Holt. Passengers must pay the ordinary fare when travelling from one station to the other. Example:—A passenger holding ticket to Cromer may return, for instance, from Yarmouth, but an ordinary ticket must be taken to cover the journey from Cromer to Yarmouth.

SHORT and LONG DATE TICKETS to LINCOLNSHIRE COAST, &c.

Skegness, Sutton-on-Sea, Mumby Road, Mablethorpe, Theddlethorpe, Saltfleetby.				FROM	Woodhall Spa.				Grimsby, Cleethorpes.			
Short date.		Long date.			Short date.		Long date.		Short date.		Long date.	
1	3	1	3		1	3	1	3	1	3	1	3
s d	s d	s d	s d		s d	s d	s d	s d	s d	s d	s d	s d
8 0	5 0	...	...	Barnstone	10 0	5 0	...	...	10 6	6 0	13 0	8 3
8 0	5 0			Basford	11 0	5 0			10 6	6 0	13 0	8 3
9 0	5 6			Bestwood Colliery	11 0	5 6			13 6	8 3	13 6	8 3
8 0	5 0			Bingham	10 0	5 0			12 0	6 0	14 6	8 3
8 0	5 0			Bottesford	10 0	5 0			14 0	7 0	16 6	9 6
9 0	5 6			Breadsall	10 6	5 6			10 6	6 0	13 0	8 3
8 0	5 0			Bulwell Forest	10 6	5 6			10 6	6 0	13 0	8 3
10 0	6 0			Burton	12 0	6 0			15 0	7 6	26 0	11 3
9 0	5 6			Butler's Hill	11 0	5 6			10 6	6 0	13 0	8 3
9 0	5 6			Codnor Park	11 0	5 6			10 6	6 0	13 0	8 3
8 0	5 0			Daybrook	11 0	5 6			14 0	7 0	16 6	9 6
9 0	5 6			*Derby (G.N.)	11 5	5 6			10 6	6 0	13 0	8 3
8 0	5 0			Eastwood (G.N.)	10 0	5 0			10 6	6 0	13 0	8 3
8 0	5 0			Gedling	10 0	5 0			12 0	6 0		
8 0	5 0			Harby & Stathern	10 0	5 0			10 6	6 0	13 0	8 3
9 0	5 6			Heanor	11 0	5 6			10 6	6 0	13 0	8 3
10 0	6 0			Horninglow								
9 0	5 6			Hucknall	11 0	5 6			10 6	6 0	13 0	8 3
9 0	5 6			Humberstone	11 0	5 6			14 0	7 0	20 6	10 0
9 0	5 6			Ilkeston	11 0	5 6			10 6	6 0	13 0	8 3
9 0	5 6			Ingersby and John o'Gaunt	11 0	5 6			14 0	7 0	20 6	10 0
9 0	5 6			Kimberley	11 0	5 6			10 6	6 0	13 0	8 3
9 0	5 6			*Leicester (Bel. Rd.)	11 0	5 6			14 0	7 0	20 6	10 0
9 0	5 6			Linby	11 0	5 6			10 6	6 0	13 0	8 3
9 0	5 6			Loseby	11 0	5 6			14 0	7 0	20 6	10 0
11 0	5 6	17 3	11 9	Market Harboro'	11 0	5 6	23 0	11 9	14 0	7 0	25 9	12 3
8 0	5 0			Melton Mowbray	10 0	5 0			12 0	6 0	18 6	8 3
8 0	5 0			Netherfield and Colwick	10 0	5 0			10 6	6 0	13 0	8 3
9 0	5 6			Newstead	11 0	5 6			10 6	6 0	13 0	8 3
9 0	5 6			Newthorpe	11 0	5 6			10 6	6 0	13 0	8 3
11 0	5 6	17 3	11 9	Northampton (Cas.)	11 0	5 6	23 0	11 9	14 0	7 0	25 9	12 3
8 0	5 0			*Nottingham	10 0	5 0			10 6	6 0	13 0	8 3
9 0	5 6			Pinxton	11 0	5 6			10 6	6 0	13 0	8 3
9 0	5 6			Pleasley	11 0	5 6						
9 0	5 6			Pye Hill	11 0	5 6			10 6	6 0	13 0	8 3
8 0	5 0			Radcliffe-on-Trent	10 0	5 0			10 6	6 0	13 0	8 3
8 0	5 0			Redmile	10 0	5 0			12 0	6 0		
9 0	5 6			Sherwood	11 0	5 6			10 6	6 0	13 0	8 3
9 0	5 6			Shirebrook	11 0	5 6						
9 0	5 6			Skegby	11 0	5 6						
13 0	7 6			Stafford (Common & Town)	15 0	7 6			17 0	8 6	29 0	14 3
9 0	5 6			Sutton-in-Ashfield	11 0	5 6			10 6	6 0		
9 0	5 6			Thurnby	11 0	5 6			14 0	7 0	20 6	10 0
9 0	5 6			West Hallam	11 0	5 6			13 0	6 0	16 6	8 6

For General Conditions, see pages 4 and 5. For Routes and Notes, see page 22.
*Tickets are also issued at the Town Offices shewn on page 5.

Short date and long date tickets to Lincolnshire Coast, including from Sherwood station, from the 1909 GNR guide. *GNR.*

Additional notes for Norfolk and Lincolnshire destinations taken from the 1909 GNR Guide. *GNR.*

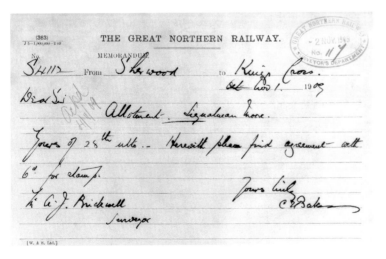

A GNR Memorandum from the Sherwood Station Master, Charles Edward Baker, and Surveyor A.J. Brickwell, dated 1st November 1909 regarding an Agreement about an allotment to be cultivated by Signalman Mr. Moore. *GNR.*

Going back in time to the penultimate year of the 19th Century. Howitts of Nottingham produced a pocket book timetable called the *ABC Railway Guide.* Below and opposite are the extracts for the NSR departures in the Down direction for July 1898. The GNR trains that were listed as running over the Suburban were:-

Nottingham (Victoria) and Newstead.

Nottingham (Victoria) and Ilkeston, Derby and Burton; Outbound departs Nottingham 3.15 p.m., Inbound arrives Nottingham 3.11 p.m. and 5.28 p.m.

Nottingham (Victoria) and Nottingham Suburban Railway.

Nottingham (Victoria) and Pinxton; Outbound departs Nottingham 3.15 p.m., Inbound arrives Nottingham 5.28 p.m. and 7.11 p.m.

A Nottingham to Basford local passenger train hauled by GNR locomotive No.1520. Note the reversible destination headboard, which was carried by most of the local passenger services. *R.H. Blencowe, T. Etches Collection.*

Down Line

Nottingham London Road	Thorneywood	St. Ann's Well	Sherwood	Daybrook	Newstead	Skegby
Fares from Nottingham	3d and 1½d	5d and 2½d	6d and 3d	-	-	-
7.45 am	7.49 am	7.52 am	7.55 am	7.58am	-	-
9.05 am	9.09 am	9.12 am	9.15 am	9.19am	9.42am	-
11.15 am	11.19 am	11.22 am	11.25 am	11.29am	11.58am	12.05pm
12.05 pm	12.09 pm	12.12 pm	12.15 pm	12.19pm	-	-
12.55 pm	12.59 pm	1.02 pm	1.05 pm	1.15pm	1.35pm	1.45pm
2.45 pm	2.49 pm	2.52 pm	2.55 pm	2.59pm	3.28pm	3.35pm
3.15 pm	3.19 pm	3.22 pm	3.25 pm	3.29pm	-	-
4.43 pm	4.47 pm	4.50 pm	4.53 pm	4.57pm	5.26pm	5.29pm Sutton in Ashfield
5.45 pm	5.51 pm	5.56 pm	6.02 pm	6.09pm	-	-
6.05 pm	6.09 pm	6.12 pm	6.15 pm	6.19pm	6.43pm	6.48pm
7.05 pm	7.09 pm	7.12 pm	7.15 pm	7.19pm	7.48pm	7.56pm
8.40 pm	8.44 pm	8.47 pm	8.50 pm	8.54pm	9.21pm	9.20pm

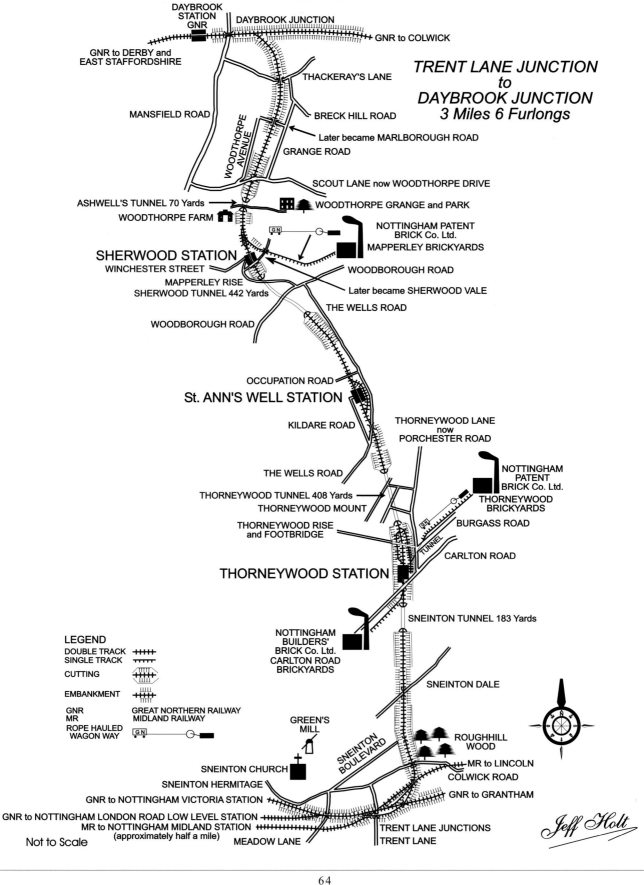

THE NOTTINGHAM SUBURBAN RAILWAY
- Circa 1916 -

DAYBROOK STATION GNR

DAYBROOK JUNCTION

GNR to COLWICK

GNR to DERBY and EAST STAFFORDSHIRE

TRENT LANE JUNCTION
to
DAYBROOK JUNCTION
3 Miles 6 Furlongs

THACKERAY'S LANE

MANSFIELD ROAD

BRECK HILL ROAD

Later became MARLBOROUGH ROAD

WOODTHORPE AVENUE

GRANGE ROAD

SCOUT LANE now WOODTHORPE DRIVE

ASHWELL'S TUNNEL 70 Yards

WOODTHORPE GRANGE and PARK

WOODTHORPE FARM

GN

NOTTINGHAM PATENT BRICK Co. Ltd.
MAPPERLEY BRICKYARDS

SHERWOOD STATION
WINCHESTER STREET

WOODBOROUGH ROAD

MAPPERLEY RISE
SHERWOOD TUNNEL 442 Yards

Later became SHERWOOD VALE

WOODBOROUGH ROAD

THE WELLS ROAD

OCCUPATION ROAD

St. ANN'S WELL STATION

THORNEYWOOD LANE
now PORCHESTER ROAD

KILDARE ROAD

THE WELLS ROAD

NOTTINGHAM PATENT BRICK Co. Ltd.
THORNEYWOOD BRICKYARDS

THORNEYWOOD TUNNEL 408 Yards

THORNEYWOOD MOUNT

GN

BURGASS ROAD

THORNEYWOOD RISE and FOOTBRIDGE

TUNNEL

CARLTON ROAD

THORNEYWOOD STATION

SNEINTON TUNNEL 183 Yards

NOTTINGHAM BUILDERS' BRICK Co. Ltd.
CARLTON ROAD BRICKYARDS

SNEINTON DALE

LEGEND

DOUBLE TRACK

SINGLE TRACK

CUTTING

EMBANKMENT

GNR   GREAT NORTHERN RAILWAY
MR   MIDLAND RAILWAY

ROPE HAULED WAGON WAY

GN

GREEN'S MILL

SNEINTON BOULEVARD

ROUGHHILL WOOD

MR to LINCOLN

COLWICK ROAD

SNEINTON CHURCH

SNEINTON HERMITAGE

GNR to NOTTINGHAM VICTORIA STATION

GNR to GRANTHAM

GNR to NOTTINGHAM LONDON ROAD LOW LEVEL STATION
MR to NOTTINGHAM MIDLAND STATION (approximately half a mile)

MEADOW LANE

TRENT LANE JUNCTIONS
TRENT LANE

Jeff Holt

Not to Scale

Chapter 11: THE END OF THE NOTTINGHAM SUBURBAN RAILWAY COMPANY 1910-1922

By 1910, the NSR passenger train services were gradually being whittled away with only five trains in the Down direction and three stopping trains on the Up line. Of the ten Down trains to Shirebrook, five were routed via Gedling, three travelled by the NSR and the remaining two went direct (*see* tables on page 67).

One of the engines used by the GNR over the Suburban in 1910 was the Stirling 0-4-4 Well Tank No.654, which was recorded as a Shirebrook departure from Nottingham Victoria.

On 22nd June 1911 the Coronation of King George V was celebrated and again the NPBC repeated their previous show of patriotism by organising another enormous bonfire on the site of their Mapperley Brickyard to act as a beacon for the people of Nottingham.

The post and five-rail fence along the boundary of Scout Lane adjacent to bridge No.13 with the newly built Grange Road houses at the rear.

Grange Avenue, the road off Scout Lane adjacent to bridge No.13 was built, forming a junction with the east end of Marlborough Road. The houses on the east side of Grange Avenue backed onto the west fence line of the NSR.

As many readers will be aware, there are not many photographs of trains operating on the Suburban, particularly when it was operated by the GNR. There was one taken by F.H. Gillford at Thorneywood station, which has been reproduced many times. It is of Stirling Class R 0-4-4T No.822 entering the station on the Up platform in 1911.

Two more recent photographs have been taken of the rail chairs that were used on the NSR permanent way. Mr G.H.F Atkins took a photograph in 1948 of a chair which was used for supporting a rail joint, the location of which was Sherwood station. The note that goes with the print states that it is a special fishplate and chair. It is not clear from photographic evidence whether or not these chairs were used along the whole length of the NSR. The other photograph is of a GNR chair dated 1918 which is in the collection of Mr B. Walker and was found near the NSR's Daybrook junction after the NSR's single line had been taken up and removed.

By 1912 the GNR had decided to paint some of its goods locomotives grey with white lining, instead of the light green with white and black lining. There is a photograph of GNR 0-4-2 No.598 in this livery on a Nottingham Suburban train at Basford in 1912 again taken by Gillford.

Despite the apparent decline in the use of the Nottingham Suburban Railway's lines for passenger traffic, the Great Northern gave Notice on 29th November 1912, for the 1913 Parliamentary Session, to acquire lands along the Suburban line. The Engineer for the works was Mr Charles J. Brown. The Bill included land and works throughout many areas of the GNR system but there were works named specific to the Suburban and these are listed on page 70 as follows:-

CORONATION BONFIRE MAPPERLEY. 1911.

The Coronation Bonfire at the NPBC's Mapperley brickworks as beacon for the 22nd June 1911 King George V Coronation.

(left) **The Nottingham Suburban Railway 1916.** *Jeff Holt*

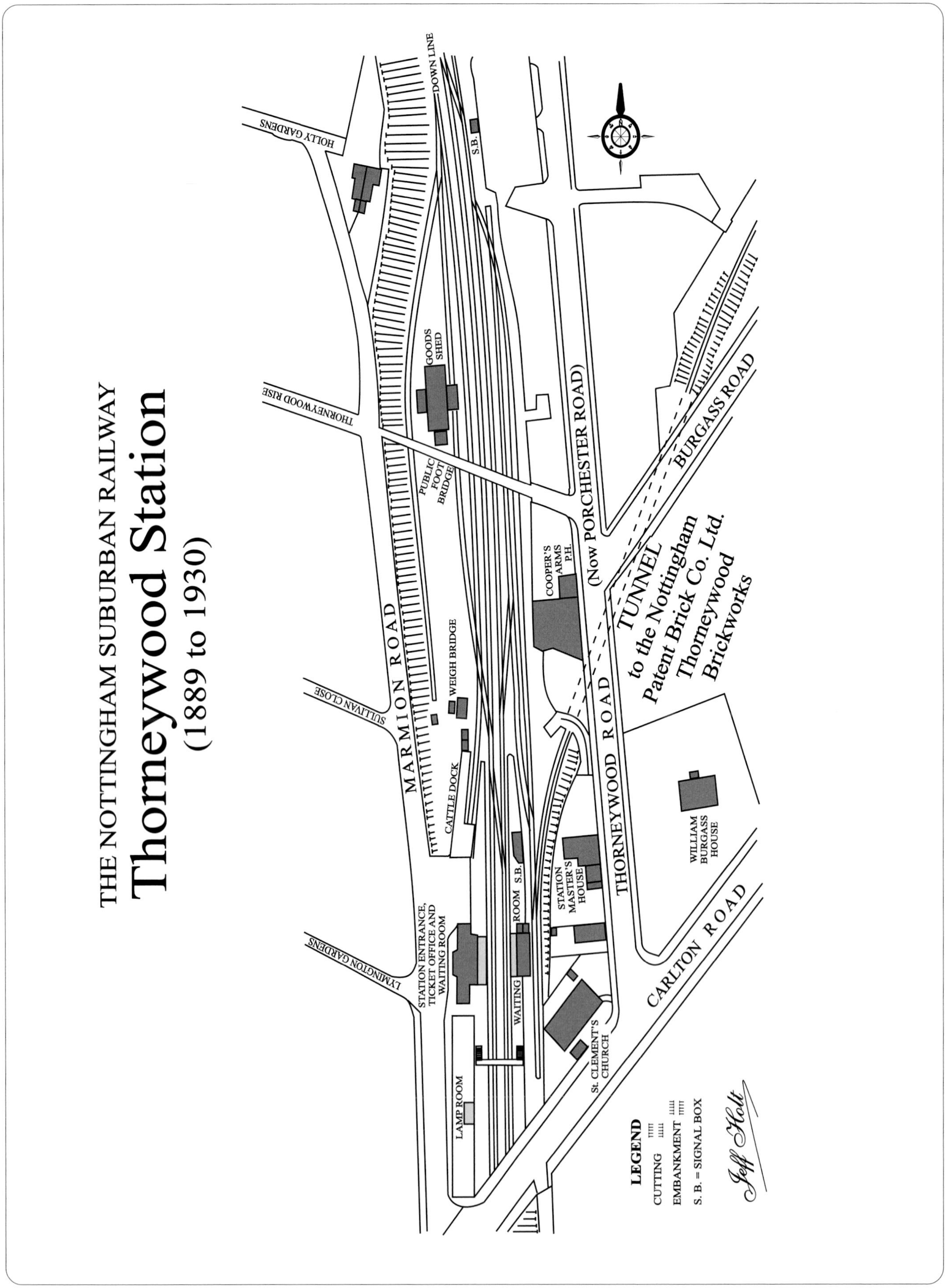

THE NOTTINGHAM SUBURBAN RAILWAY
Thorneywood Station
(1889 to 1930)

DOWN LINE

HOLLY GARDENS

S.B.

THORNEYWOOD RISE

MARMION ROAD

GOODS SHED

PUBLIC FOOT BRIDGE

WEIGH BRIDGE

SULLIVAN CLOSE

CATTLE DOCK

COOPER'S ARMS P.H.

(Now PORCHESTER ROAD)

TUNNEL
to the Nottingham
Patent Brick Co. Ltd.
Thorneywood
Brickworks

BURGASS ROAD

STATION ENTRANCE, TICKET OFFICE AND WAITING ROOM

LYMINGTON GARDENS

ROOM S.B.

WAITING

STATION MASTER'S HOUSE

THORNEYWOOD ROAD

WILLIAM BURGASS HOUSE

LAMP ROOM

St. CLEMENT'S CHURCH

CARLTON ROAD

LEGEND

CUTTING

EMBANKMENT

S. B. = SIGNAL BOX

Jeff Holt

Thorneywood Station 1889 to 1930. *Jeff Holt.*

Nottingham, Basford and Bulwell, Newstead and Shirebrook, via Suburban Extracted from Bradshaw's April 1910

Down Line		am			pm							
Basford and Bulwell	dep.	7.33					5.35					
Nottingham Victoria	arr.	7.42					5.42					
Nottingham Victoria	**dep.**	7.44	9.00	11.25	1.08	4.47	5.50	7.05	8.34	9.37	11.10	
Nottingham High Level	**arr.**	7.46	9.02		1.10	4.49	5.52	7.07				
Nottingham High Level	**dep.**	7.47	9.03	11.28	1.12	4.50	5.54	7.09	8.38	9.40	11.13	
Thorneywood	**dep.**	7.52	9.08	Thr'u	1.17	4.55	5.58	7.14	Thr'u	Thr'u	Thr'u	
St. Ann's Well	**dep.**	7.55	9.11	Thr'u	1.20	4.58	6.01	Thr'u	Thr'u	Thr'u	Thr'u	
Sherwood	**dep.**	7.58	9.14	Thr'u	1.23	5.01	6.04	Thr'u	Thr'u	Thr'u	Thr'u	
Daybrook	**dep.**	8.02	9.21	11.38	1.27	5.05	6.06	7.23	8.48	9.50	11.23	
Basford and Bulwell	dep.	8.06					6.13					
Bulwell Forest	dep.		9.28	Request	1.34	5.12		7.30	Set Down	Thr'u	Thr'u	
Bestwood Colliery	dep.		9.31	Thr'u	1.37	5.15		7.33	8.56	9.58	11.31	
Butler's Hill	dep.		9.34	Thr'u	1.40	5.18		7.37	8.59	10.01	11.34	
Hucknall	dep.		9.37	11.49	1.43	5.21		7.41	9.02	10.04	11.37	
Linby	dep.		9.41	11.53	1.47	5.25		7.45	9.06	10.08	11.41	
Newstead	dep.		9.45	11.57	1.51	5.29		7.49	9.10	10.12	11.45	
Sutton-in-Ashfield for Huthwaite	dep.		9.56	12.08	2.02	5.41		8.00	9.21	10.23	11.56	
Skegby	dep.		9.59	12.11	2.05	5.44		8.03	9.24	10.26	11.59	
Pleasley	dep.		10.04	12.16	2.10	5.49		8.08	9.29	10.31	12.04	
Shirebrook	arr.		10.09	12.21	2.15	5.54		8.13	9.34	10.36	12.09	
											Sat. Only	

Up Line		am		pm						
Shirebrook	dep.		9.47	12.08	1.55			8.25	9.55	
Pleasley	dep.		9.53	12.14	2.01			8.31	10.01	
Skegby	dep.		9.59	12.20	2.07			8.37	10.07	
Sutton-in-Ashfield for Huthwaite	dep.		10.03	12.24	2.11			8.41	10.11	
Newstead	dep.		10.13	12.34	2.21			8.51	10.21	
Linby	dep.		10.17	12.38	2.25			8.55	10.25	
Hucknall	dep.		10.21	12.42	2.29			8.59	10.29	
Butler's Hill	dep.		10.24	12.45	2.32			9.02	10.32	
Bestwood Colliery	dep.		10.27	12.48	2.35			9.05	10.35	
Bulwell Forest	dep.		10.30	Sat.	2.38			Thr'u	Thr'u	
Basford and Bulwell	dep.	8.13				2.08				
Daybrook	**dep.**	8.18	10.37	12.57	2.45	2.13	2.45	9.14	10.43	
Sherwood	**dep.**	8.21	Thr'u	Thr'u	2.48	2.16	2.48	Thr'u	Thr'u	
St. Ann's Well	**dep.**	8.24	Thr'u	Thr'u	2.51	2.19	2.51	Thr'u	Thr'u	
Thorneywood	**dep.**	8.27	Thr'u	Thr'u	2.54	2.22	2.54	Thr'u	Thr'u	
Nottingham High Level	**dep.**	8.33	10.46	1.05	2.58	2.27	3.00	9.22	10.51	
Nottingham Victoria	**arr.**	8.35	10.50	1.09	3.02	2.29	3.02	9.26	10.54	
				Weds. And Sats. Only						

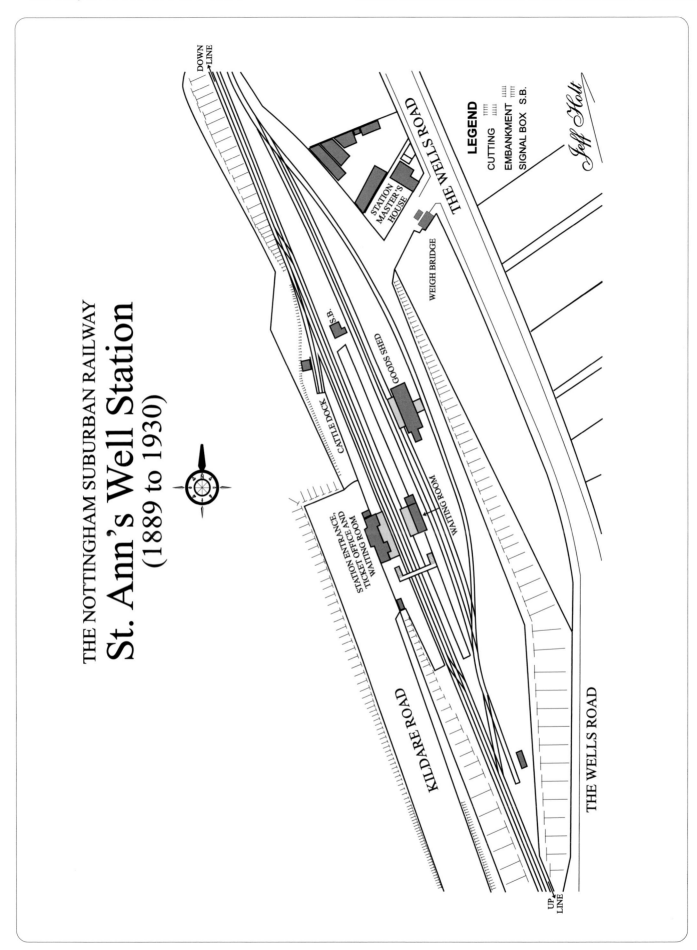

THE NOTTINGHAM SUBURBAN RAILWAY

St. Ann's Well Station
(1889 to 1930)

Jeff Holt

LEGEND

CUTTING

EMBANKMENT

SIGNAL BOX   S.B.

The 2.08 p.m. train from Basford approaching Thorneywood station on the Up line in 1910. Consisting of teak coaches, the consist is hauled by green liveried GNR 0-4-4T Stirling R class No.822. Station Master Leo Faunthorpe prepares to meet the train. *F.H.Gillford*

Close up of the special GNR fishplate and chair used along the NSR where rail joints occurred. Taken at Sherwood station in 1948. Photograph reproduced by kind permission of Phil Atkins. *G.H.F. Atkins.*

Sheep graze in a small patch of land adjacent to the NSR line and Woodthorpe Avenue. On the other side of the tracks, and the two lines of post and five-rail fencing, can be seen the Grange Road houses viewed in the previous photograph.

Additional Lands at Nottingham - A piece of land at Thorneywood station bounded on the east by Marmion Road and on the north by Holly Garden and extending a distance of about 42 yards and 30 yards measured along Marmion Road and Holly Garden respectively;

(Part of this piece of land has recently been involved in a study regarding its history. The area in question was two of the houses on the east of Marmion Road. Referring to the accompanying map, the two semi-detached properties have each been marked with a cross. The main road horizontally along the bottom of the map is Thorneywood Lane. The NSR was constructed in the gap between the properties on the east (top) side of Thorneywood Lane and to the underside of the two properties being discussed. The properties on Buxton Terrace, towards the bottom of this map, and the immediate buildings above and to the left, were all demolished to make way for the NSR. The research started when an enquiry was received from Mr J. Radford asking whether the NSR built any other properties along the line for its employees other than the three Station Masters' houses. The Author's reply was 'no, not as far as I was aware'. Mr Radford pointed out that his wife had lived in one of the two houses on Marmion Road between 1950 and 1965 and the property at that time was owned by British Railways. The property is No.2 Marmion Road and is also shown on page 65 of Volume One. (Located by looking at the upper photograph, the pair of semi-detached houses are directly above the central pier of the pedestrian bridge. The outcome of research has revealed that the two properties were within the boundaries for the construction of the NSR line and as such they were purchased by the NSR Company. The properties were subsequently found to be surplus to requirements and could remain standing, if rather close to the top of the west embankment. Who lived in the houses at that time has yet to be determined. These houses were included in the above notice and as a consequence, along with the other properties were transferred to the ownership of the GNR. At the grouping they were transferred to the LNER and upon Nationalisation transferred to British Railways and that is how these two NSR properties became British Railway owned).

Land at Sherwood station bounded on the east by the NSR and the south by Winchester Street;

Land near Sherwood station bounded on the north by Winchester Street and on the south by Mapperley Rise;

Land near Sherwood station bounded on the east by the Nottingham Suburban Railway and on the west by Mapperley Rise and on the north by Sherwood Vale;

Land at Sherwood station bounded on the west by the Nottingham Suburban Railway, on the north by Sherwood Vale and on the north-east by the site of a proposed road connecting with Sherwood Vale;

Land at Sherwood station bounded on the south-west by the site of the new road and on the north-west by Sherwood Vale;

Land bounded on the west by Sherwood station and on the south by Sherwood Vale;

Land bounded on the south by the Nottingham Patent Brick Company incline branch and on the east by Sherwood Vale;

Land partly in Nottingham and Arnold bounded on the east by the Nottingham Suburban Railway and being field and slope;

Land in Arnold forming the north-western slope of the road adjoining and lying to the north and west of the land bullet pointed above."

The conveyance of this NSR surplus land was raised at a meeting of the NSR on 22nd June 1914 when Mr S.H. Sands affixed the Seal of the Company to the Conveyance.

A register of the additional lands was provided, which included eight plots of land all owned by the Nottingham Suburban Railway Company at Thorneywood and Sherwood and three plots adjacent to Scout Lane in Nottingham and Arnold. The exercise may be a tidying up exercise by the GNR, as none of the land appears to be required for development purposes.

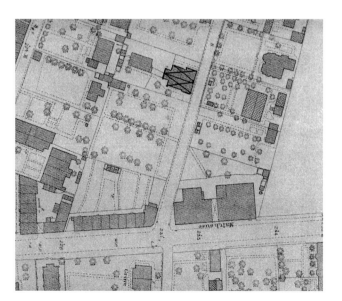

(left) **Ordnance Survey map dated 1882 of land to the west of Thorneywood Lane to be occupied by the Thorneywood station prior to it being developed.** *Ordnance Survey*

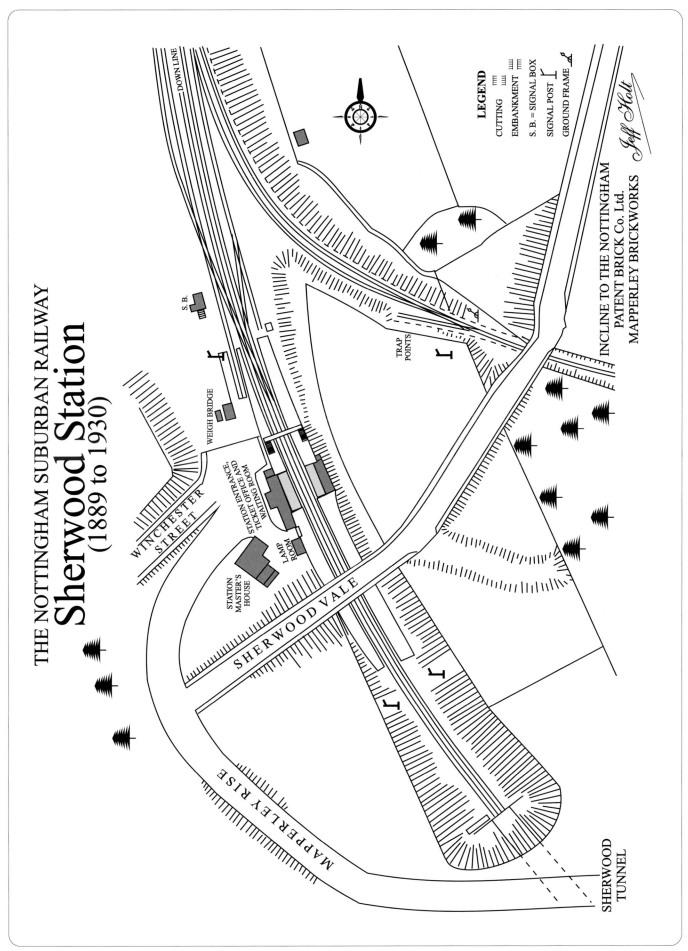

THE NOTTINGHAM SUBURBAN RAILWAY
Sherwood Station
(1889 to 1930)

LEGEND

CUTTING

EMBANKMENT

S. B. = SIGNAL BOX

SIGNAL POST

GROUND FRAME

Jeff Holt

DOWN LINE

S. B.

WEIGH BRIDGE

WINCHESTER STREET

STATION ENTRANCE, TICKET OFFICE AND WAITING ROOM

LAMP ROOM

STATION MASTER'S HOUSE

TRAP POINTS

SHERWOOD VALE

MAPPERLEY RISE

INCLINE TO THE NOTTINGHAM PATENT BRICK Co. Ltd. MAPPERLEY BRICKWORKS

SHERWOOD TUNNEL

A GNR chair rescued from the NSR near Daybrook junction dated 1918 and now treasured by Barry Walker. *D. Birch.*

It is interesting at this stage to look at two maps that were included in the *Kelly Directory* of 1913. We have already seen how the NSR, along with the GNR, had rejected the idea of building the two new stations in Sneinton and between Scout Lane and Marlborough Road. In order to get out of this they had used the argument that development in these areas had not reached the criteria as contained in the agreements for land purchase. This would have been easy to prove and an acceptable argument, for looking at the two maps, there had been little generation of new housing developments along the line since it had been built. Anyone taking a nice stroll adjacent to the line would be able to count the new properties that had been built in the previous fifteen or so years since the line opened; the line was still primarily a rural route.

Some developments were taking place in Sneinton to the west of the line but none of the Earl Manvers's proposals to the east of the formation had even been started. The only sign of development in the Thorneywood and St. Ann's areas was over the top of the Thorneywood tunnel. The Wells Road residential housing schemes had yet to have even been thought of. The only area where roads were starting to surround the NSR was in the Arnold area between Scout Lane and Thackeray's Lane but as we have seen, the construction of new properties had not reached the agreed level by this time. Although the reasons given to the property owners were that the requisite number of houses had not yet been built, it is more likely that the NSR and GNR would have been thinking of the expense that would have been incurred in building two new stations at that time. It would clearly have been a total waste of money, as they would have been fully aware that the tram services had already taken most of the custom away from the suburban railway systems in Nottingham. The passenger train timetable for the NSR had already been pruned to an almost minimal service.

By 1914, the only trains to service the NSR stations were those destined to terminate at Shirebrook. Again the timetable for trains stopping on the Suburban was reduced so that of the eight daily trains to Shirebrook on a Saturday, only three stopped at the three Suburban stations, and in the return direction only four stopped from the six timetabled. All the remainder of the GNR trains ran non-stop over the Suburban rails between the Nottingham (London Road High Level) station and Daybrook station, achieving a journey time between the Nottingham (Victoria) station and Daybrook station of thirteen minutes, which whilst being quicker than the trams, was more expensive and was a far less frequent service. Most of the GNR trains, which ran between Nottingham (Victoria) and Shirebrook, either travelled by way of Bulwell Common and the GCR main line, and returned via the Suburban, or vice versa, in order to avoid reversal at Nottingham (Victoria).

In 1915 it was reported that Mr G.B. Kid, who had been a NSR's Auditor since 1901, had retired and Mr J.N. Derbyshire was subsequently formally adopted as a replacement as one of the two Auditors for the NSR Company, a role that he retained until March 1923.

Within the year of 1915, a frequently repeated story occurred that was told by Mr J.A.B. Hamilton in the March 1932 edition of *The Railway Magazine*. When he went to the Victoria station to buy a ticket in order to go to Sherwood station, the booking clerk advised him to go by tram!

The late Sid Checkley recalled those days of trains going to Shirebrook from Victoria station via the Suburban. *"A Shirebrook train in the bay at Victoria station, headed by a 0-4-4T [No. 768]. The train consists of a six-wheeler, a bogie coach and three more six-wheelers' with the possibility of a horse box at the rear." "The GNR coaches were a mixed bag. Some were in articulated sets of three or five but there were plenty of six-wheelers' around. I remember several things about these coaches. Each compartment door had the coach number painted on the window rail. Some of the articulated sets had the initials G.N.R. applied in white paint, instead of the usual transfer, on the waist panels. The upholstery for the seats was in several shades of red. The articulated sets had picture frames built into the compartment partitions above the seats and the luggage racks were fastened to the partitions. There were three picture frames each side and four luggage rack brackets. The six wheelers had separate picture frames screwed to the partitions. The coaches were all gas-lit using Pope's Patent system. When the coaches were new out of the works, the roofs were white but that rapidly turned grey and then dirty black as the sulphur from the coal reacted with the lead in the roof paint."*

The passenger usage of the Thorneywood, St. Ann's Well and Sherwood stations on the Suburban declined to such an extent that in 1915 the GNR reduced the stopping trains by one each way. By March 1916, the Suburban only had three weekday stopping trains visiting the three stations each way plus others which ran along the whole line without stopping.

On 13th July 1916, the GNR sadly withdrew all the passenger facilities from the Suburban, presumably with prior agreement with the NSR Company. Also, due to the start of the First World War, the GNR were looking to implement financial and operating economies and in addition to the above closures, the Suburban rails were from this time only to carry the two daily non-stop through passenger trains from Nottingham to Shirebrook, with none in the reverse direction. The trains now took thirteen minutes to travel from the Nottingham (London Road High Level) station to Daybrook over the NSR rails. On the same date as closing the three NSR stations to passenger traffic, the GNR also closed Linby station.

Mrs I. Hill, the niece of Mr L. Faunthorpe, Thorneywood's Station Master from approximately 1911 to 1922, wrote to the *Evening Post* of her memories regarding her visits to him. She said that people from around the station flocked to the tunnels to shelter when the Zeppelins came over in the Great War of 1914-1918. She added that at the rear of the Station Master's house there was a winding path of wooden steps from the house to the station, hewn out of the bank [which was still there in 1983 when the house was visited]. When he left the Suburban, her uncle went to Mickleover and then Bestwood.

It is alleged that during the First World War Thorneywood station was chosen as a station to receive special trains that carried wounded soldiers, who would then be transported to hospitals in Nottingham for care. Despite the closure of its stations to passenger

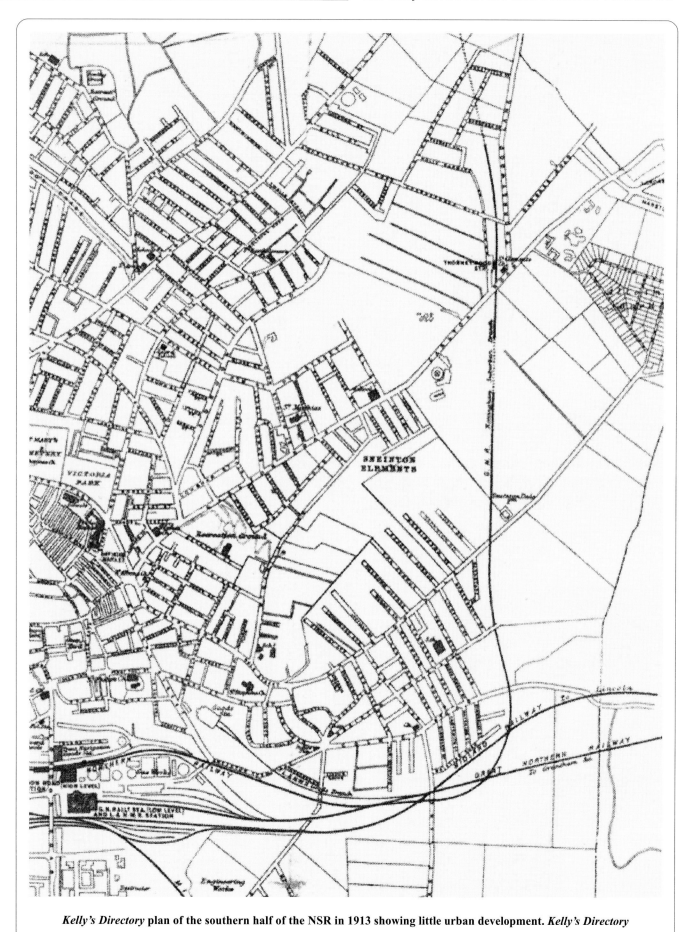

Kelly's Directory **plan of the southern half of the NSR in 1913 showing little urban development.** *Kelly's Directory*

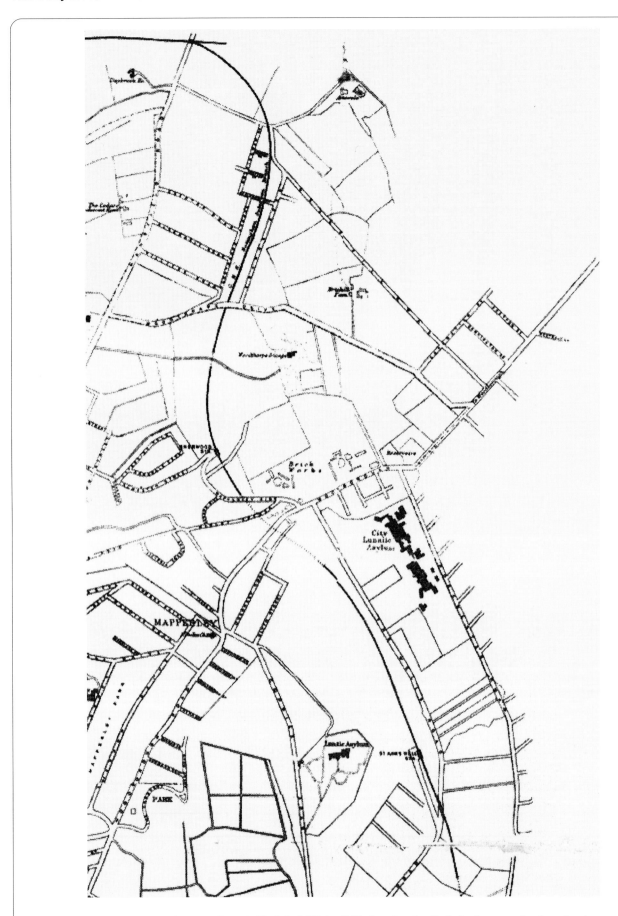

Kelly's Directory **plan of the northern half of the NSR in 1913 also showing little in the way of urban development.**

traffic, the NSR Company kept the line open, principally to maintain the transportation links with the two NPBC's two brickyards, in which most of its Directors had a financial and a commercial interest, and also retain the services for the merchants and the NBBC at the various station goods yards.

In 1919 one of the long serving Directors of the NSR Company died. Jesse Hind, known as the entrepreneurial lawyer, had been a Director since 1894, when he took the place of the late Edward Gripper. Jesse Hind's replacement on the Board was Oliver Watts Hind JP, Jesse's son, who was voted on to the Board on 23rd December 1919. He would remain a Director until the end of the NSR Company. Oliver Hind was born in Sneinton during the last quarter of 1873 and lived his early life with his parents at Papplewick Grange before moving to Edwalton Hall. He had two sisters and two brothers, he being the second eldest of the children. After becoming qualified as a solicitor, he became a partner in his father's old established firm of Wells & Hind at 16 Fletcher Gate, Nottingham. He was, for thirty years, the Captain of the 2nd Nottingham Company of Boys Brigade and also formed the Lads Club in Dakeyne Street, Sneinton, where over 350 boys were members. The Dakeyne Street property that the Lads Club used was once the Sneinton Asylum. In the same year as becoming a Board member, Oliver Hind purchased the George Green's windmill in Sneinton and four years later replaced the rotting wooden cap with one covered in copper to keep out the weather.

(right) **Jesse Hind (1843 to 1919). Pike & Co.**
(below) **Jesse Hind's residence at Papplewick Grange in 1890.**

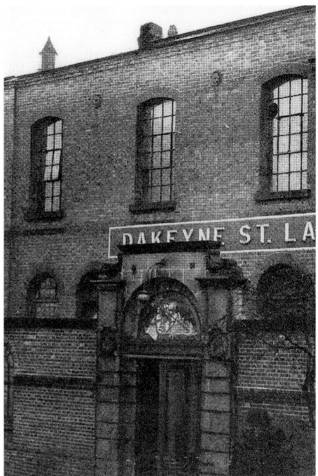

Oliver Watts Hind (1857 to 1932). *(right)* **Dakeyne Street Lads Club**, **of which Oliver Hind was its founder.**

On 7th May 1920 it was reported at a NSR Board meeting that the GNR had written to the NSR Company expressing their concern about the poor state of repair of the verandas overhanging the platforms at all three stations. They stated that they were all in decay and required repair. However, as the stations were no longer used for passengers they suggested that they should be removed. The NSR Directors considered this was a matter for the GNR Company but expressed that they had no objection to their removal.

At this same meeting, the Directors also considered a suggested Government Scheme for leased lines to be absorbed by larger companies at terms to be agreed upon. They decided to write to the Ministry of Transport for more definite proposals and a copy of the recommendations, as they may wish to make suggestions before coming to a decision.

At the beginning of August 1920 the NSR Company Board members and other post holders were;
Chairman and Director, Samuel H. Sands.
Director, Robert Mellors.
Director, Harry L. Birkin (for the GNR).
Director, Oliver Watts Hind.
Secretary, Thomas G. Mellors.
Engineer, Edward Parry.

However, many changes to the above were about to happen quite quickly. On the 25th August 1920 the NSR's long serving Director, and current Chairman, Mr. Samuel Herrick Sands passed away. He had been a Director of the Company for 34 years and it's Chairman for the past 25 years. He was 88 years old when he died. Mr. Robert Mellors, who was the only surviving member of the

original Board, was appointed Chairman in his place. Mr. Charles Sneath Wright was appointed as a new Director, again replacing Mr Sands. He was a Nottingham man born in 1851 and by trade he was a corn merchant.

This August meeting was quite eventful as far as personnel were concerned for Mr. T.G. Mellors resigned as Secretary for the Company, a post he had held for 30 years. Mr. Frank Pragnell, also of Mellors, Basden & Mellors, was appointed in his place. He was to stay with the firm until after 1936 but his job as Secretary was to end when the NSR Company ceased to exist in 1923. Perhaps the saddest news reported at the meeting was that Edward Parry M.I.C.E., the Engineer for the NSR had passed away on 11th August 1920 in Leamington Spa, aged 75.

In August 1921, Major Harry Birkin, the GNR's Board representative, resigned his seat on the NSR Board as he no longer worked for the GNR. Lt Col. The Hon. F.S. Jackson M.P. was nominated to take his place as the GNR representative. Jackson was a national celebrity as he had been a first-class cricket player. He was born on 21st November 1870 at Allerton Hall, Chapel Allerton in Leeds, Yorkshire. He played cricket for Cambridge University, Yorkshire and England, as a right-hand batsman and as a right-arm fast to medium paced bowler. His nickname was Jacker and his first-class career spanned from 1890 to 1907. His international debut for England came on 17th to 19th July 1893 where he played at St. John's Wood, Lords, against Australia. He captained England in 1905 and his last test was against the Australians at the Kennington Oval from the 14th to 16th August 1905.
After retiring from cricket he took up the following posts:
from 1915 to 1926 Member of Parliament for Howdenshire.
from 1922 to 1923 he was Financial Secretary to the War Office.

(above) **Edward Parry (1844 to 1920).** *NPBC.*
(above right) **Thomas Galland Mellors (1865 to 1944).** *Pike & Co.*
(right lower) **Frank Stanley Jackson MP (1870 to 1947).**

(below) **The residence of Samuel Herrick Sands (1833 to 1920) in September 2009. This property is now in the grounds of the Nottingham University.** *D Birch*

Jackson's batting, fielding and bowling records were as follows:

Batting and Fielding Record	1st Class	Test
Matches	309	20
Innings	505	33
Not out	35	4
Runs	15901	1415
Highest score	160	144
Average score	33.83	48.79
100's	31	5
50's	76	6
Wickets Caught	195	10

Bowling Record	1st Class	Test
Balls	37516	1587
Runs	15767	799
Wickets	774	24
Best Bowling Innings	8/54	5/52
Average	20.37	33.29
4 wickets		1
5 wickets	42	1
10 wickets	6	0

from 1923 to 1926 he was Chairman of the Conservative Party. and from 1927 to 1932 he was the Governor of Bengal.
He died on 9th March 1947 at Hyde Park, London aged 76 years. A detailed history of Colonel Sir Francis Stanley Jackson, P.C., G.C.I.E., is provided in *Wisden Crickers' Almanac*.

Extract from the Nottingham (Victoria) station Timetable November 1921:

Trains departed on a Wednesday and Saturday only at:-
11.55 a.m. from platform 10.
1.20 p.m. from platform 12.
5.05 p.m. from platform 11.
6.40 p.m. from platform 10 (did not stop at Bulwell Forest).
All the above trains went to Shirebrook over the NSR rails, visiting Daybrook (via Thorneywood), Bulwell Forest, Bestwood, Butler's Hill, Hucknall, Newstead, Sutton, Skegby, Pleasley, and Shirebrook. There was also an arrival on a Wednesday and Saturday Only at:-
10.22 a.m. on platform 4 which also ran over the NSR tracks but did not stop at Bulwell Forest.

The business discussed at the NSR's Board meeting held on 16th December 1921 was principally about the 1921 Railway Act. They had received a letter from the Association of Smaller Railway Companies, to the effect that the NSR Company was not considered as being entitled to participate in the distribution of the sum of £24,500,000 referred to in Section 12 (1) (a) of the Railways Act 1921. They had requested the NSR Company to sign an authorisation that the Company will not claim to participate in the said amount. The Secretary, Mr Pragnell, reported that Council's opinion had been obtained prior to the meeting on this matter and as a result of their advice; he had signed the authorisation and returned the document to the Association.

The Secretary added that under the amount set aside under the 1921 Railways Act as compensation for the Railway Companies having been taken over by Government, it was considered that the NSR Co. could only participate in the £500,000 provided by Section 12 (1) (b), but it was doubtful whether they were entitled to anything even under this sub-section. The matter was left over for a future Board meeting.

At the Board meeting held on 1st September 1922, it was reported that the Auditor Mr. W.J. Grinling had deceased and his replacement was approved to be Mr. C. Lewis Edwardsbe at the next meeting which was held on the 22nd September.

The Board was again reduced in numbers on 30th November 1922 when they received the resignation of The Hon. F.S. Jackson M.P., who had resigned his position on the Board of the GNR following his appointment as Financial Secretary to the War Office.

Bradshaw's Railway Guide for July 1922, which is my last source of timetable prior to the Grouping, shows that there were now only three trains a day passing over the NSR rails.

In November the NSR Company received a letter from the General Manager of the GNR relating to their future absorption by the Amalgamated Company which was to be formed by the amalgamation of the North Eastern, Eastern and East Scottish Group, under the Railways Act 1921. The GNR were requesting to know the terms that the NSR Company was prepared to agree to the absorption provided for in the Act. A decision was made that Mr Oliver Hind and the Secretary should meet with the GNR and discuss the matter with them.

Just before the end of the NSR Company and its Agreement with the GNR, the through passenger trains were generally hauled by GNR 4-4-2T engines, which would have been resplendent in their beautiful green livery. Trains were probably made up of a three or five coach articulated set with one or two six-wheelers attached.

On 1st January 1923 the railway Grouping took place and the Nottingham Suburban Railway Company, along with all its assets were absorbed by the newly formed London & North Eastern Railway (LNER), finally loosing its status as a private and independent company. As part of the LNER absorption of the GNR's 'subsidiaries', the Nottingham Suburban Railway only received 1st. guarantee, below par. The tribunal had previously approved an 'absorption scheme' in June 1921, which included the NSR. On the same day, the Great Northern Railway was amalgamated along with the Great Central Railway and others to form the LNER.

Despite the passing of the 'absorption date' of midnight on 31st December 1922, the NSR Company continued to meet and sort out unresolved business. Their first Board meeting in 1923 was held on 11th January when they appointed a replacement Director in the name of Mr. F. Liddell Steel to replace the retired Lt. Col. The Hon. F. S. Jackson M.P. At the same meeting, Mr Oliver Hind, Solicitor to the Company, reported that he had held an interview with the General Manager of the GNR Company and their Solicitor. He reported to them that the outcome of the meeting was that, subject to the approval of the Tribunal, there be issued to the Shareholders in respect of each £100 stock held in the NSR Company by them, £87 10s 0d of 4% First Guaranteed Stock of the London & North Eastern Railway Company. (This is a straight forward transaction as £100 of NSR stock at 3⅛% first guaranteed stock, equates to £87 10s of LNER stock at 4% first guaranteed stock.) Further, that there should be paid to the NSR Company as compensation, the sum of five times the annual payment of £300 for expenses of management. In addition the Company would be paid their costs for winding up the Company.

The next meeting of the Board was held on 2nd March 1923. After certifying the Annual Accounts and Report, the Secretary was requested to draft a letter to all shareholders concerning the Company's absorption under the Railway Act 1921, after consulting with the Chief Legal Adviser of the LNER Company. Messrs. Wells and Hind were also requested to prepare a schedule of the Deeds and Documents in their possession for submission to the LNER Company.

The last Board meeting of the Nottingham Suburban Railway Company that was minuted, and is recorded in the archives, was held on 27th March 1923. Following the presentation of the Directors' Report and the Statement of Accounts for the year ending 31st December 1922, the Board received and adopted them and the dividends for both 30th June and 31st December 1922, were confirmed and declared respectively. Not surprisingly, Mr. F.L. Steel and Mr. C.S. Wright were re-elected as Directors of the Company, and also Mr. J.N. Derbyshire was re-elected as an Auditor to the Company, as the winding-up procedures still had to be concluded. The following is the concluding minutes of the NSR Company:-

"Absorption by the London and North Eastern Railway:-
On the motion of Mr. R. Mellors, seconded by Mr. J.W. Hind, it was resolved that, this Company and its undertaking having by the Railways Act 1921 been absorbed by the London & North Eastern Railway Company, as from the 31st December last, and it having been provisionally agreed by and between the Directors of this Company of the one part, and the London and North Eastern Railway Company of the other part-

1.   *That the 3⅛% stock of this Company be exchanged for 4% 1st Guaranteed Stock of the London & North Eastern Railway Company at the rate of £87.10.0 for each £100 stock of this Company.*

2.   *That the sum of £1500 be paid to this Company in respect of the annual sum payable under the Agreement with the Great Northern Railway Company for expenses of Management &c.*

The terms of absorption be hereby approved and adopted.

On the motion of Mr. R. Mellors, seconded by Mr. O.W. Hind, it was resolved that the £1500 to be received from the London & North Eastern Railway Company, together with the sum of £249.00.05 carried forward on the Balance Sheet as at 31st December 1922, be paid to the Directors, to be appropriated by them for the following purposes:-

1.   *For compensation to the Directors for the abolition of their Offices, and not as salary.*
2.   *For compensation to the Auditors of the Company.*
3.   *And that the balance be paid to the Secretary for the following purposes –*
        1.   *As compensation for the loss of his Office, and not as salary.*
        2.   *For the payment of any outstanding Accounts owing by the Company.*
        3.   *For the expenses of winding up the Company.*

Deeds and Documents:-
On the motion of Mr. R. Mellors, seconded by Mr. O.W. Hind, it was resolved that the Directors be and are hereby authorised to take all steps and do all acts necessary for the transfer of this Company's undertaking and assets to the London & North Eastern Railway Company.

Register of Stockholders;-
The Seal of the Company was affixed to the Register of Stockholders.

Vote of Thanks:-
On the motion of Mr J.W. Hind, a unanimous vote of thanks was passed to Mr. Robert Mellors for his services for many years past on behalf of the Company, and for presiding at the present meeting."

The Nottingham Suburban Railway Company had a devoted and enthusiastic membership during its thirty-seven years plus existence. Only one man was to run the full course of the Company and that was Robert Mellors, who held the post of Chairman during the last three to four years. The full membership of the Committee, sourced from *Allen's Nottingham Red Book* and the NSR Company minutes was as follows:-

Registered Office: - Nos.1 and 2 King John's Chambers, 15, Bridlesmith Gate, Nottingham

Nottingham Suburban Railway Committee

Chairmen

Thomas Hill	1885 - 1888
Alderman Edward Gripper JP	1888 - 1894
Samuel Herrick Sands JP	1894 - 25 August 1920
Robert Mellors	1920 - 1923

Directors	Committee		Inc. Committee
Ald. Edward Gripper JP.	1885	&	1886 - 1894
Samuel Herrick Sands JP	1885	&	1887 - 1920
Robert Mellors	1885	&	1886 - 3/1923
Thomas Hill	1885	&	1886 - 1888
Henry Milward Baines			1886 - 1887
John Wesley Lewis			1886 - 1887
Jesse Hind JP			1894 - 1919
Major Harry Birkin			1902 - 8/1921
Oliver Watts Hind			12/1919 - 3/1923
Charles Sneath Wright			1920 - 3/1923
Lt Col. The Hon. F S Jackson M.P			8/1921 - 11/1922
Mr. F. Liddell Steel			1/1923 - 3/1923

Solicitors

Messrs. Wells & Hind,	
20 Fletcher Gate, Nottingham	1886 - 1893
then 14 & 16 Fletcher Gate, Nottingham	1894 - 3/1923

Engineer

Edward Parry   1885 - 1920

Secretary

Duncan F. Basden   1886 - 1890
Thomas G. Mellors   1891 - 1920
F. Pragnell   1921 - March 1923

Auditors

G.B. Kid   1901 - March 1915
Mr J N Derbyshire   1915 - March 1923
W.J. Grinling   1902 - 1922
Mr. C. Lewis Edwardsbe   1922 - March 1923

Bankers

Nottingham Joint Stock Bank Ltd.   1886 – 1903

Robert Mellors (1835 to 1931). *Pike & Co.*

Chairman	Director 1	Director 2 (of GNR)	Director 3	Director 4	Secretary	Auditor 1	Auditor 2	Solicitor
Edward Gripper 1886 to 1894	Edward Gripper 1886 to 1894	L.C. Probyn 1887 to 1902	S.H. Sands 1887 to 1920	Robert Mellors 1886 to March 1923	D F Basden 1886 to 1890	G B Kid 1901 to March 1915	W J Grinling 1902 to 1922	Messrs. Wells & Hind 1886 to March 1923
S.H. Sands 1894 to 25th August 1920	Jesse Hind 1894 to 1919	H L Birkin 1902 to August 1921	C Sneath Wright 1920 to March 1923		T G Mellors 1891 to 1920	J N Derbyshire 1915 to March 1923	C Lewis Edwardsbe 1922 to March 1923	
Robert Mellors 1920 to March 1923	Oliver W. Hind December 1919 to March 1923	F S Jackson August 1921 to November 1922			F Pragnell 1921 to March 1923			
		F Liddel Steel 1923 to March 1923						

A table of the persons who held the Board positions on the Incorporated NSR Company's Committee

Chapter 12: THE EARLY YEARS UNDER THE OWNERSHIP OF THE LONDON & NORTH EASTERN RAILWAY 1923-1932

On 1st January 1923 the Nottingham Suburban Railway (NSR) was just one of 123 British railway companies who were either absorbed or amalgamated into the four new major companies; the London and North Eastern Railway (LNER) Company being the one absorbing the NSR.

The LNER didn't waste any time in trying to sort out the issue of the terms for the absorption of the NSR. On 2nd January 1923 the LNER Finance Committee had a meeting, chaired by The Rt. Hon. Lord Faringdon, C.H., during which a report was discussed regarding the NSR and the negotiations for its absorption into the LNER. It was reported that an agreement with the representatives of the NSR Company had already been completed, subject to the approval of the Board.

The agreed terms as reported were:-

'That there be issued to the Shareholders of the Nottingham Suburban Railway Company in respect of each £100 stock held by them £87.10.0 of 4 per cent first Guaranteed Stock of the London and North Eastern Railway Company.

That £1,500, i.e. five years' purchase of the £300 paid annually by the Great Northern Company for expenses of management, including Directorial and Secretarial fees and salaries, be paid to the Nottingham Suburban Railway Company.

That the amalgamated Company pay any necessary expenses incurred in carrying the scheme into effect.'

The Finance Committee met twice more to discuss the NSR's absorption on the 11th and 18th January 1923 and it was at the latter meeting that they finally approved the scheme as stated above.

On 19th January 1923, the LNER Board, chaired by William Whitelaw, approved the terms which their Finance Committee had finally agreed the previous day. The terms, which had been somewhat abbreviated, were:-

'£87. 10. 0., of the LNER Company's 4% 1st Guaranteed Stock will be allotted in respect of each £100 Stock of the Nottingham Suburban Company, plus a cash payment of £1,500 in full quittance of all Directors' and other claims.'

The LNER carried out some minor changes to the local passenger train timetables but its effect on the NSR was slight in terms of use. The three stations remained closed to passengers but the main double track line remained open throughout its whole length providing a permanent way to both through passenger trains and goods handling facilities at the three stations.

The initial through passenger services to be seen on the line were three daily trains and one Saturday train from Nottingham (Victoria) to Shirebrook and one train from Basford to Nottingham (Victoria). On a Wednesday and Saturday there was a train from Shirebrook to Nottingham in the reverse direction plus another on a Monday, Tuesday, Thursday and Friday only.

Overleaf is an abstract from *Bradshaw's* 1923 showing only those trains that passed over the Suburban's rails.

Between 1925 and 1929 the 1.03 p.m. weekday and 11.55 a.m. Saturday departures from Nottingham (Victoria) to Shirebrook

(below) **Sherwood station in 1923. Although this is a poor print, the photograph was taken from the west looking east at the station. It shows wagon movement activity on the NPBC sidings, the signal box, weighbridge, footbridge and Station Master's house.** *Nottingham Newspaper.*

NOTTINGHAM, NEWSTEAD AND SHIREBROOK (All via the Suburban Line)

Down Line	am	pm		
Nottm. Victoria	11.55	1.20	5.05	6.40
Nottm. High Level	11.58	1.24	5.08	6.44
Daybrook	12.08	1.34	5.18	6.54
Bulwell Forest	12.15	1.41	5.25	Thr'u
Bestwood Colliery	12.18	1.44	5.28	7.02
Butler's Hill	12.21	1.47	5.31	7.05
Hucknall	12.24	1.50	5.34	7.08
Newstead	12.30	1.58	5.40	7.14
Sutton-in-Ashfield	12.41	2.09	5.51	7.25
Skegby	12.44	2.12	5.54	7.28
Pleasley	12.49	2.17	5.59	7.33
Shirebrook	12.54	2.22	6.04	7.38
	Wed. & Sat. Only			except Sat.

Up Line	pm	
Shirebrook	2.00	5.10
Pleasley	2.06	5.16
Skegby	2.12	5.22
Sutton-in-Ashfield	2.17	5.26
Newstead	Thr'u	5.36
Hucknall	2.35	5.42
Butler's Hill	2.38	Thr'u
Bestwood Colliery	2.41	Thr'u
Bulwell Forest	Thr'u	Thr'u
Daybrook	Thr'u	5.52
Nottm. High Level	Thr'u	6.00
Nottm. Victoria	2.51	6.03
	Mon, Tues, Thurs, Fri. Only	Wed. and Sat. Only

(North) service were extended to the Lancashire, Derbyshire & East Coast Railway's (LD&ECR) Chesterfield (Market Place) station and was routed over the NSR rails. This service to Chesterfield was to become the extent of the GNR services in the area.

An incident happened at about 8.30 a.m. on Friday 23rd January 1925, which was to give a crumb of life back to the NSR lines and be a saviour to the LNER. It was at this time that some bricks from the roof were found on the track of the 1132 yard long Mapperley tunnel, which is located between the Gedling and Daybrook stations on the Derbyshire Extension Railway.

Fortunately the discovery was made in time to prevent an accident. A breakdown gang were tasked to repair the damage and the line was reopened at 11.45 a.m. At 8.45 p.m., on the same day, approximately twelve yards of the same tunnel's roof collapsed. The tracks within the tunnel were blocked with about 150 tons of bricks and clay. The reason that was suggested at that time as to why the section of the tunnel's roof should collapse was that it was caused by a combination of wet clay above the arch ring and subsidence resulting from its close proximity to the Gedling coal mine. Again, fortunately, there were no oncoming trains at the time. The outcome was that the 'Back Line' had to be closed in both directions whilst the repair works were carried out and many passenger and goods trains, particularly those conveying coal, to and from the Leen Valley were diverted from Saturday 24th January either along the Suburban line or by the former GCR route through Nottingham (Victoria) station. The return empties and the iron-ore Stanton Ironworks trains, which were diverted along the Suburban, had to reverse in the London Road goods yard to be forwarded onto Colwick, as the NSR's only access to and egress from the Nottingham to Grantham line at its southern end was to and from the west.

The engines and passenger stock frequenting the 'Back Line' at this time, as recorded by A.G. Cramp in his *'Basford via Gedling'* article, were old GNR articulated coaches and a few six-wheelers, hauled by C12 and C14 4-4-2Ts, D2 and D3 4-4-0s and J2, J3, J5, J6 and J11 0-6-0s from Colwick shed. He adds that two services were operated by one of five Sentinel steam railcars, which were also stationed at Colwick. Three were named, COMMERCE, EXPEDITION, and RISING SUN and there were two un-named examples. How many trains were actually diverted along the NSR during the Mapperley tunnel closure has not been determined. It would be interesting to find out which engines and rolling stock from the above list made an unusual appearance and passed over the NSR rails for this brief period of time. There were no reported incidents on the Suburban whilst diversions were in progress but it must have been a train enthusiasts' delight to see a coal train of

(left) **A photograph taken in May 1922 looking north from the top of the north portal of Ashwell's tunnel with the Scout Lane bridge No.13 constructed of wrought iron troughs and face girders in the centre of the photograph. *Reg Baker.***

Sentinel Camel steam railcar No.45 COMMERCE in its green and cream livery about to depart in a southerly direction from Nottingham (Victoria) station in 1931 probably to travel over NSR rails on its way to Daybrook station and Shirebrook.

thirty or more loose coupled wagons tackling the 1 in 70 inclines and the steeper Down gradients and associated curves.

In 1926 the General Strike, which had a major impact on the running of the railways, showed that privately owned lorries could handle the extra volume of work which wasn't being carried out by rail. New factories and warehouses were already being built some distances away from the existing railway network and the private lorry companies were creating and enlarging their own transportation fleets to cope with these deliveries. Whilst these private sector road transport companies were using motorised lorries and vans, the railways were still using horse drawn carts right up to the Second World War, which were slower and less cost effective or efficient. Hence, rail goods traffic declined, which again had an adverse affect on the overall use of the NSR's three stations and goods yards, which now were only used for goods transfer.

From September 1927, the 11.55 a.m. Victoria departure via the Suburban ran Saturdays only to Chesterfield and there were only three other passenger trains passing over the NSR routed to Shirebrook, and two on Saturdays. In the southbound direction the Suburban traffic was limited to the daily pick-up goods from Leen Valley Junction to Nottingham and a single light engine working.

The Suburban was to receive another single day's reprieve on Tuesday 10th July 1928 on the occasion of the visit to Nottingham by King George V and Queen Mary. Subsequent to opening the Royal Show at Wollaton Park, but before moving on to open the new University College at Highfields, the Royal couple were entertained by about 17,000 children aged between 10 and 14, in Woodthorpe Park which had been owned by the Nottingham Corporation since 22nd June 1921. About 6,550 of the children, accompanied by 284 teachers were transported to and from the park

by the NSR to and from the Sherwood station. The LNER supplied thirteen special trains to accommodate this mass transportation requirement, which terminated at Sherwood from the stations at Basford & Bulwell, Nottingham (London Road Low Level) and Thorneywood. As both the Thorneywood and Sherwood stations had only been used as goods stations since 1916 and closed to all passenger traffic, the LNER had to carry out a repair and maintenance operation on both these stations in order to make then safe and presentable for the passengers for this special occasion. Both stations were staffed for the day.

The trains started to arrive at Sherwood station at about 11.00 a.m. and continued depositing their passengers until after 1.30 p.m. Sherwood station sidings were not large enough to accommodate the rolling stock of thirteen passenger trains and so it is anticipated that some of the trains will have continued onto St. Ann's Well, Thorneywood or Daybrook stations, depending on their direction of travel. As the NSR now had very little other use it would have been quite easy for the locomotives to perform a run round operation and prepare themselves for the return journey from Sherwood. At 1.50 p.m. the Lord Mayor of Nottingham Alderman E. Huntsman and the other important invited guests left the Guildhall to go to Woodthorpe Grange Park. The King and Queen arrived at 2.30 p.m. There were presentations to Their Majesties at the City Boundary by His Grace the Duke of Portland. A bouquet of flowers was presented to the Queen by Miss Barbara Wright. Some 7,000 children then sang the National Anthem, which was played by the 7th (Robin Hood) Battalion, The Sherwood Foresters, just before Their Majesties departed to go to the New University College at 2.45 p.m. by way of Mansfield Road to the Market Place and out on Castle Boulevard and Beeston Road. Mr. Jesse Boot, Bart., presented each child with a commemorative medal of the visit.

The front cover of the official souvenir programme for the Royal visit by His Majesty King George V and Her Majesty Queen Mary for the opening of the Nottingham New University on the 10th and 11th July 1928. *Nottingham City Council.*

Down line, its cross over points to the Up line, and the most westerly of the sidings were lifted but the cattle dock remained.

Moving along north to the Daybrook junction, the Down line was lifted leaving just the Up line for two-way traffic. At Daybrook junction the new track layout must have been quite difficult to implement whilst keeping rail traffic moving. The NSR's Up line junction with the 'Back Line' was removed completely. At some distance from Daybrook junction the NSR's Up line was slewed over in a westerly direction on a new transition to join to the NSR's Down line, the Down line south of this point being removed. As a consequence of this new single track layout, all future trains wishing to enter onto or egress from the NSR had to do so from the 'Back Line's' Down or most southerly line via the Suburban's original Down line junction and after negotiating the new transition between the NSR's Down line and Up line, continue their journey along the Up line.

The two signal boxes at Thorneywood and St. Ann's Well had already been closed by this time. However, as part of this rationalisation to single line working, it was decided to close the remaining signal box at Sherwood station, along with its associated signals. To replace it, a ground frame was installed at the north end of the Up platform. As a consequence the NSR was now operated with a train staff which unlocked all the ground frames, which had now replaced all the signal boxes. The LNER also decided that, as the line would never be used for passenger traffic again, all the footbridges at the Thorneywood, St. Ann's Well and Sherwood stations (Nos. 7A, 9A and 11A respectively) should be removed. This instruction was not carried out immediately and it took something like ten years before the last remaining one at St. Ann's Well station was dismantled.

It was on Sunday 23rd February 1930 that the last of the NSR stations, St. Ann's Well, received direct competition from public road transport. A trolley-bus terminus was created just west and adjacent to The Wells Road Bridge No.9. The 'Railless' Service No.10, as it was called, attracted a good crowd and many onlookers on its first day of service, even though it was about fourteen years too late to poach any passengers from the NSR.

On the 14th March 1931, the last remaining gentleman who had worked to promote the NSR sadly passed away. Robert Mellors was not just a part of Nottingham's history; he also recorded it as an author of numerous books and booklets based on the history of Nottingham and its suburbs. To record all the achievements of this great man would require a complete book but it is only right that the main ones are recorded here, for probably without his input, the NSR would not have been what it was, if at all.

(opposite, top) **The first trolley bus service at The Wells Road terminus, registration TV 743, on 23rd February 1930. Photograph reproduced by kind permission of Phil Atkins. *G.H.F. Atkins. (opposite)* Demonstrator trolley bus Thorneycroft BD, fleet No.28, registration TV 3460, at The Wells Road terminus with the NSR railway embankment, south of bridge No.9 on the left. Photograph reproduced by kind permission of Phil Atkins. *G.H.F. Atkins.***

Although the Suburban Railway enjoyed a very limited renewed use from the above two occasions, the LNER decided in 1929 to reduce the NSR to a single line. Work began on 9th February 1930 to produce the single line from the existing two track main line. Commencing from the southern end of the line, the Down line junction with the GNR Nottingham to Grantham line was disabled and the Down line track was lifted from a point just clear of the Trent Lane Junction to a point just north of the Sneinton tunnel, but before the trailing junction with the NBBC's siding. A rail-built buffer stop was positioned here. At this point in time the Up line remained untouched along its full length, except for the junction with the 'Back Line' as described later. The track from north of Sneinton tunnel through to the Thorneywood tunnel remained completely untouched with all the original trackwork left in situ to allow the freight services for the merchants and the NPBC and NBBC brickworks to carry on functioning as normal. At the entrance to the Thorneywood tunnel, the Down line was terminated and another rail-built buffer stop was provided. The Down line from this point right through to Daybrook Junction was removed leaving only the adjacent Up line for future two way traffic.

At St. Ann's Well station, in addition to the Down line being removed, the line to the cattle dock on the Down platform was removed along with the two cross-over points between the Down and Up lines. All the track work for the goods sidings on the east side of the Up line were left in situ for the coal merchants and the Somnus bedding to utilise. As stated, the Down line between the St. Ann's Well and Sherwood stations was completely removed. At Sherwood station the Up line and the entire trackwork to its east side, which were primarily used by the NPBC's Mapperley brickyard, weren't affected by the singling operation. However the

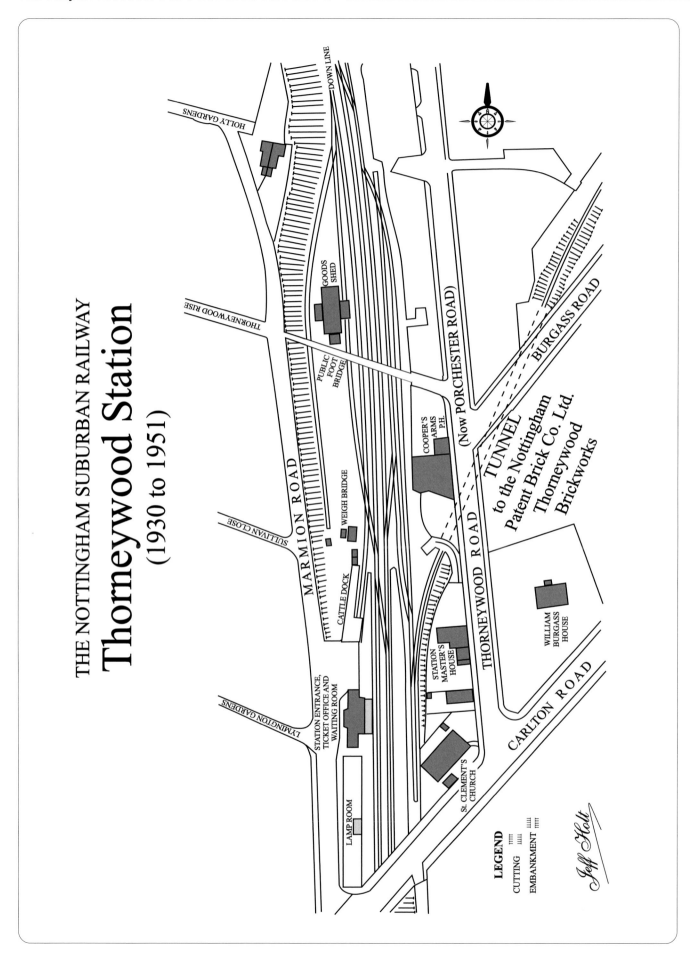

THE NOTTINGHAM SUBURBAN RAILWAY
Thorneywood Station
(1930 to 1951)

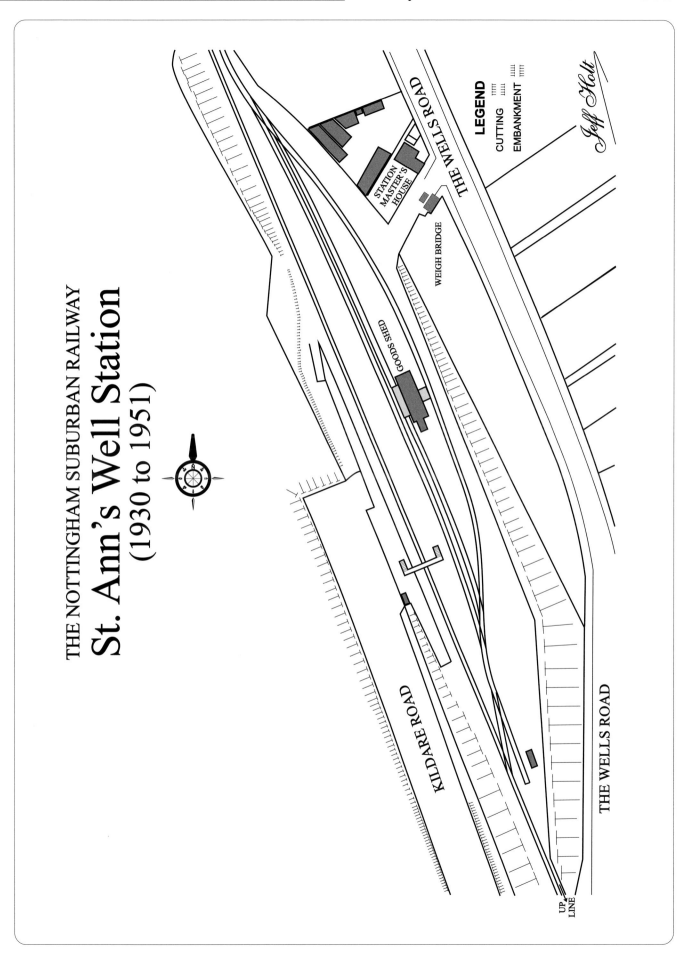

THE NOTTINGHAM SUBURBAN RAILWAY
St. Ann's Well Station
(1930 to 1951)

Jeff Holt

LEGEND

CUTTING

EMBANKMENT

STATION MASTER'S HOUSE

WEIGH BRIDGE

GOODS SHED

THE WELLS ROAD

KILDARE ROAD

THE WELLS ROAD

UP LINE

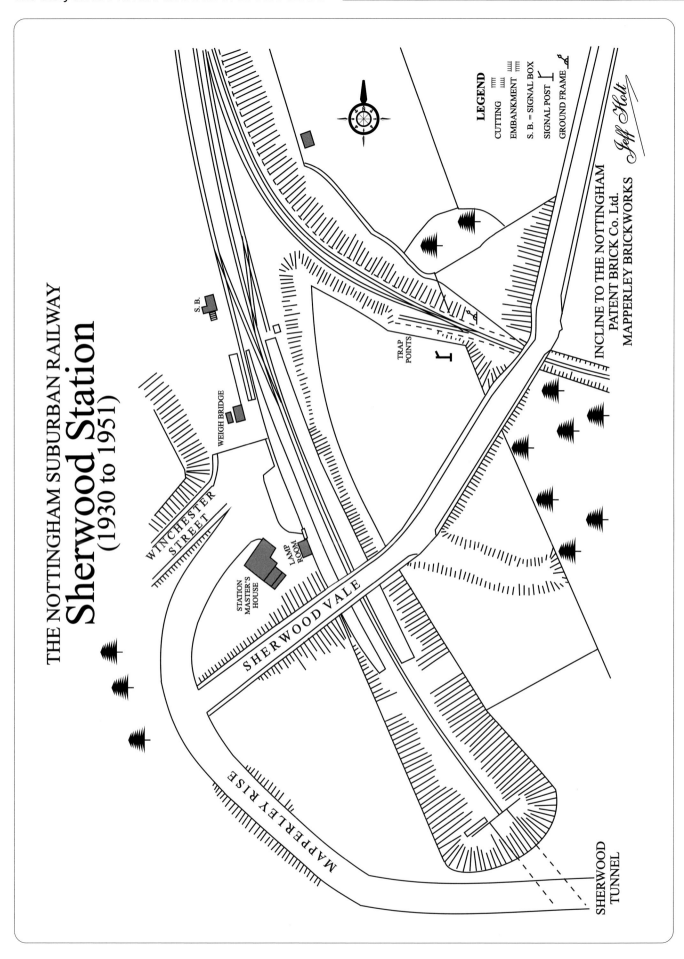

THE NOTTINGHAM SUBURBAN RAILWAY
Sherwood Station
(1930 to 1951)

LEGEND
CUTTING
EMBANKMENT
S. B. = SIGNAL BOX
SIGNAL POST
GROUND FRAME

Jeff Holt

INCLINE TO THE NOTTINGHAM
PATENT BRICK Co. Ltd.
MAPPERLEY BRICKWORKS

S. B.

WEIGH BRIDGE

TRAP POINTS

WINCHESTER STREET

STATION MASTER'S HOUSE

LAMP ROOM

SHERWOOD VALE

MAPPERLEY RISE

SHERWOOD TUNNEL

AEC 663T demonstrator, fleet number 26, at The Wells Road terminus on 26th October 1930 with Kildare Road and the NSR bridge No.9, either side in the distance. Photograph reproduced by kind permission of Phil Atkins. *G.H.F. Atkins.*

continued from page 85./ Robert Mellors was born on 26th April 1835, the son of Paul and Elizabeth Mellors, a farmer on the Duke of Portland's estate. In 1857 Robert married Mary Galland the daughter of the Reverend T.J. Galland, Vicar of Laneham, Nottinghamshire. Robert and Mary had eleven children together; seven sons and four daughters.

Robert, who wanted to become an accountant, was articled to Messrs. Taylor & Mosley in 1850. Four years later after qualifying, he went into partnership with Mr Taylor to form the new firm of Taylor & Mellors. It was in 1860 that Robert made the decision to start his own business called simply 'Robert Mellors'. In 1861 he was the founder of the Nottinghamshire and Midland Merchants' & Traders' Association, which was incorporated in 1880 for the protection of members and the improvement of commercial law. By 1888 it had about 1000 members from Nottinghamshire, Derbyshire, Leicestershire and Lincolnshire. He was its Secretary from the day it was started until 1904.

From 1866 to 1887 his offices were at 17 Pelham Street, Nottingham, where he advertised his business as Accountant, Estate Agent, Insurance Agent and Bill Discounter. In 1883 he qualified as a Fellow of the Institute of Chartered Accountants of England and Wales.

During the period 1867 to 1887 he was the Chairman of the Nottingham Patent Brick Company and from 1867 to 1912 he was also a Managing Director of the same company. From 1886 to 1923 he was Director of and Financial Agent to the Nottingham Suburban Railway and its Chairman from 17th September 1920 to March 1923. In 1895 he was appointed the Local Agent for the purchase of property and adjustment of compensations during the construction

of the Great Central Railway through Nottinghamshire and for the Nottingham Joint Station Committee.

In 1878 he joined with Duncan Frederick Basden to form the partnership of Mellors & Basden. In 1887 the company moved to 1 & 2 King John's Chambers which was between 13 and 15 Bridlesmith Gate, Nottingham. Also in 1887 one of his sons, Thomas Galland Mellors, qualified as an accountant and was approved as another partner in his father's business now being called Mellors, Basden, Mellors (MBM). From 1893 MBM opened branches in Mansfield, London, Manchester and an additional office in London.

He was the Chairman of the Arnold School Board between 1877 and 1886 plus from 1898 to 1901. From 1889 to 1925 he was a County Councillor for Arnold and Bestwood and from 1892 to 1922 a County Alderman. From 1912 he was a County Magistrate.

As a local historian and antiquarian, he was the author of many books and booklets some of which are listed below:-
'In and About Nottinghamshire' (1909)
'Old Nottingham Suburbs: Then and Now' (1914)
'Men of Nottingham and Nottinghamshire' (1924)
'The Gardens, Parks and Walks of Nottingham and District' (1926)
'Scrooby: Transactions of the Thoroton Society' (1905)
'Stapleford: An Address to the young folks of Stapleford' (1906)
The *'Then and Now'* series of booklets*:*
Sneinton (1913), Basford (1914), Bulwell (1914),
Kingston-on-Soar (1914), Lenton (1914),
Mapperley and Carrington (1914),
Radford and Hyson Green (1914), West Bridgford (1914),
Wilford (1914), Beeston (1916),
Attenborough, Chilwell and Toton (1920) and *Scrooby (1920).*

(left) **Robert Mellors (1835 to 1931).** *NPBC.* *(above)* **Robert Mellors reading congratulations on his 95th birthday.**

(below) **The north portal of Sneinton tunnel on 16th June 1951, showing the buffer stop on the Down line just short of the tunnel and the build-up of rubbish on the Up line. The track to the right used to go to the Nottingham Builders' Brick Company's sidings and the petrol distribution yard, which was now no longer used.** *A.G. Forsyth.*

By July 1931 there were only two daily trains to use the NSR line. These were the daily goods train from Daybrook which worked through to the London Road (Low Level) goods depot in the afternoon and the staff was returned to Daybrook on the 5.05 p.m. Nottingham to Shirebrook. The Leen Valley services were all diverted over the GCR line. However, due to competition from bus services, the LNER decided to withdraw its Shirebrook passenger service in 1931 and as a consequence the 5.05 p.m. along the Suburban made its final run on Monday 14th September 1931, hauled by an Ivatt Class C12 4-4-2 tank engine. This was the last time the NSR was to host a timetabled passenger service.

The single track Nottingham Suburban Railway line had now been reduced to a goods line facilitating a thrice-weekly pick-up goods operating from the Leen Valley junction through to Thorneywood station and return, with stops at Sherwood and St. Ann's Well. These were mostly hauled by one of Colwick's retiring Ivatt 0-8-2 tanks, the final one, No.3150, being withdrawn in December 1933. After this date the pick-up goods could be seen with one of the GNR's 0-6-0's or even a saddle tank in charge of the working.

The LNER again took the opportunity to carry out further track alterations allowing for the NSR's decline in use. In 1932 the Down line connection at Trent Lane junction was removed and the Up line was reorganised to run into the Nottingham (London Road Low Level) yard. The cross-over from the Up line, together with the resulting through running to the High Level station and Nottingham Victoria, was now not possible and the late Edward Parry's dream was at an end.

A superb photograph of Sherwood taken from bridge No.11, showing the reconfigured track layout following the NSR being reduced to a single track. Apart from the Down line, much of the west sidings have been removed with only the cattle dock and an extended siding remaining. The sidings used by the NPBC remain as originally designed. *E.C. Haywood, Michael Vanns collection.*

Thorneywood station as viewed from just inside Thorneywood tunnel, looking south. The Down line has been removed from the buffer stop on the right, through to just short of Daybrook junction. *John Wilson.*

Trent Lane junction, track relaying in progress in 1930. Work appears to be proceeding on the removal of the NSR's Down line junction with the GNR Nottingham to Grantham line, although this may not be so. New sections of track and sleepers await to be laid on the right with NSR's Up line bridges Nos.1 and 2 in view to the left of the lamp post. *R.B. Parr, Graham Jelly collection.*

Looking south at the north portal of Thorneywood tunnel with the 1 in 70 and 1 in 50 gradient post and the sleeper-built permanent way workers hut on the left. *R.B. Parr, Michael Vanns collection.*

The south face of St. Ann's Well station footbridge, No.9a. The decorative lamps at each end of the bridge have been removed. The station buildings and the timber-built Up platform are still in situ. *R.B. Parr, Michael Vanns collection.*

(below) Trent Lane Junction rail alterations taken at the same time in 1930 as the illustration opposite. *R.B. Parr, Michael Vanns collection.*

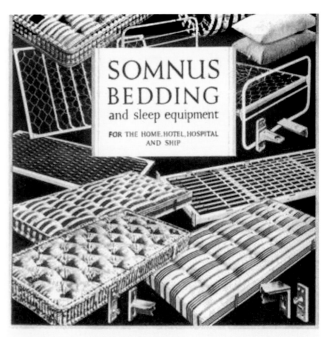

SOMNUS AND RHODOSTEEL SLEEP SPECIALITIES
are built in clean and airy surroundings by qualified craftsmen, with experience and intelligence, plus a desire to produce only those things in which, they themselves can take real pride. By selecting only the finest materials, the most efficient methods of production and good design, we have made sure that SOMNUS specialities are of value unequalled elsewhere. Sleep equipment bearing our various branded names will provide enduring bed comfort and real luxury for a very reasonable outlay. Such expenditure will prove an investment and not an expense.

SOMNUS products are known and praised all over the world. They are giving satisfaction in the best homes, hotels and ships everywhere, and have acquired a reputation which fully justifies our slogan,

FOR THE *REST* OF YOUR LIFE.

(*upper left*) **Somnus bedding lorry as used at the St. Ann's Well station goods shed to collect bedding parts and deliver completed mattresses for transportation back to Leeds.** *William Rhodes Ltd.* (*above*) **Somnus bedding advertisement.** *William Rhodes Ltd.* (*left, centre*) **The St. Ann's Well station Station Master's house still standing at the junction of The Wells Road and Dooland Drive. Apart from The plastic double glazing, the house is more or less the same on the exterior as originally built. The red bricks and tiles were supplied by the NPBC, the blues are Hathern bricks.** *D. Birch*

(*above*) **A photograph of the Rugby (Central) station staff in 1960, on the occasion of the station being awarded a prize for the cleanest and tidiest station. From the left are a Foreman, the Station Master Mr. Potts, a Porter and another Foreman. Mr Potts was the Station Master at St. Ann's Well station and most of the rest of the NSR from 1928.** *V.W. Long, Will Adams collection.*

No.1				
Guard's Working 177				
Speed B				
Class of Engine 3		Goods	K – Train Staff Stop	
	UP		**DOWN**	
Thorneywood	Arrive	12.00pm	Depart	1.49pm
St. Ann's Well	Depart	11.55am	Arrive	1.51pm
	Arrive	11.27am	Depart	2.04pm
Sherwood	Depart	11.19pm	Arrive	2.15pm
	Arrive	10.49am	Depart	2.27pm
Daybrook	Depart	10.42am	Arrive	2 36pm K
	Arrive	10.36am K	Depart	2.37pm
Leen Valley Junction	Depart	10.32am	Arrive	2.40pm

Chapter 13: THE LATER YEARS UNDER THE OWNERSHIP OF THE LONDON & NORTH EASTERN RAILWAY 1933-1947

In 1933 the NPBC purchased a steam locomotive No.6, works No.373. The locomotive had previously worked from April 1917 for the Ministry of Defence at Purfleet, on the north bank of the River Thames. It was then sold to the Mapperley Colliery Company in Derbyshire and the Stanley Colliery, West Hallam until 1933. It remained at the NPBC brickyard until 1947 when it was returned to Stanley Colliery and then to Mapperley Colliery in 1954. The locomotive was eventually withdrawn from service and scrapped by Bush of Alfreton in 1957, on the site of Mapperley Colliery.

Although the work on singling NSR began in February 1930, it wasn't until August 1934 that work commenced to convert the Daybrook junction to the NSR Down side single line working, which was completed in September 1934. As part of the works, the Daybrook Junction signal box, which was on timber supports, was demolished and the bracket signal was removed. Subsequently the single connection to the Down line was operated from a ground frame. The LNER managed to find a small GNR somersault signal from somewhere and this they installed to control entry onto the NSR line. The NSR was now connected with the 'Back Line' from Colwick by a trailing junction, controlled by the previously mentioned ground frame, adjacent to the Down track, just east of Daybrook station. To gain access to the NSR rails from the north, the trains now had to reverse from the 'Back Line' Up track to the Down line over the trailing crossover. The pick-up train wishing to enter the Suburban now had to manoeuvre and set back over the Daybrook station cross-over.

The annual returns and receipts for 1935 revealed that the three NSR goods stations were still providing a significant service when compared to some of the other local LNER stations which were still open to passenger traffic. This is shown in the following table.

Station	A	B
Sherwood	1197	195
St. Ann's Well	1096	8
Thorneywood	1330	930
Daybrook	2856	572
Hucknall Town	1214	374
Newstead LNER	1030	80

A = *Number of Received Loaded wagons.*
B = *Number of Forwarded loaded wagons.*

If the Up and Down line connections at the Daybrook and Trent Lane Junctions had not been radically altered by this time, the NSR may have seen another day's significant use. This was because of a derailment which happened at the Nottingham (Victoria) station which necessitated trains to be diverted over the Leen Valley route via Colwick.

As can be gleaned in the next chapter, during the LNER ownership years, the St. Ann's Well station became key to the management and operation of the NSR. Both Sherwood and Thorneywood ceased to have their own resident Station Master; Thorneywood from 1933 and Sherwood from 1922. Mr. J. E. Potts had been the Station Master at St. Ann's Well since 1922 and when Harry Sparsholt left Thorneywood in 1932 and Frederick Martin, the Relief Station Master, left Sherwood in 1922, the LNER appear to have carried out a bit of rationalisation and decided not to replace them. Instead Mr Potts was asked, or told, to manage the extra lengths of the line as each Station Master left.

From all accounts Potts did a fine job and a flavour of the NSR under the rule of Mr Potts can be read in the next chapter. Although St. Ann's Well station never enjoyed the brickyard goods traffic that the other two stations had, it appears that it did have much more private merchant goods traffic, with many more coal merchants plus Somnus Bedding generating a lot more pick-up wagons than the other two stations put together. Mr Potts left the NSR in 1948 and after failing to get a post at Ruddington on the GCR main line; he applied for the job of Station Master at Rugby (Central) station, which he was successful at being appointed. Potts is referred to many times in David Holmes's book *The Life and Times of the Station Master*, published by Silver Link.

Will Adams made significant contributions to this book with a photograph of Potts and many examples of his paper work, some of which he has kindly agreed to have reproduced in this book. From examples of correspondence in Mr Holmes's book J.E. Potts was employed at Rugby (Central) before 1949 and after January 1960. He obviously kept up his reputation for cleanliness and tidiness as the photograph opposite shows the station under his management winning an award.

On 6th and 8th April 1937 the *Nottingham Guardian* ran a couple of pictures of the Thorneywood station with its buildings looking very sorry for themselves. Both the Up and Down tracks were still running through the station and the station footbridge No.7A still stood. The caption beneath the photograph states that all the three stations on the NSR were now being demolished. It confirms that the line was exclusively used for goods traffic and the depots at the stations were retained for this purpose. The photograph published on the 6th was used again in the *Evening Post* on 8th December 1969.

The LNER (GN Section) Working Time Table for the Nottingham District from 27th September 1937, page 53, gave the following information for the Daybrook & Thorneywood Branch as the NSR was then called. The Suburban was defined as a single line between Daybrook junction and Trent Lane junction, with only one engine in steam permitted. Week days only. A typical goods work along the 'branch' appears opposite as 'Guards Working 177'.

On 8th April 1938, work commenced on the demolition of the Thorneywood, Sherwood and St Ann's Well stations. Using photographic evidence, it would appear that the following buildings at each station were demolished:
Sherwood station - Waiting room on the Up platform; Waiting room and ticket office unit on the Down line. [The lamp room on the Down platform, the weighbridge, the signal box, Station Master's

Thorneywood station with both the Up and Down lines still in place *after* the singling of the NSR had been completed! *Douglas Thompson.*

(above) Another view of the track layout at Thorneywood station. The signal box at the north end of the Up platform has been demolished as has some of the ticket office on the Down platform. *Douglas Thompson, Michael Vanns collection.*

(left) The LNER cast iron footpath sign at the west end of the pedestrian footbridge No.8. *Barry Walker.*

A reproduction of a newspaper cutting dated 8th April 1937 showing that the footbridge is still in situ. The line, bottom left, came from the rope-hauled wagon-way of the NPBC's Thorneywood brickyard. The two chimneys in the distance are of the NBBC's kilns. *Nottingham Guardian.*

house, the sleeper-built linesman's cabin and both platforms were left insitu.]

St. Ann's Well station - All buildings including the lamp house, waiting room and ticket office [excluding their rear walls) and small hut by the cattle siding on the Down platform; Timber-built Up platform; The signal box on the Up platform. [The Down side platform, the Up side waiting room, goods shed and weighbridge were left insitu].

Thorneywood station - The Up side waiting room; The signal box on the Upside platform; Part of the Down side ticket office and waiting room. [The lamp room and part of the Down side waiting room, the weighbridge and the goods shed were left insitu].

The line continued to be used exclusively for freight traffic, worked occasionally by a Colwick based J50, the goods depots at the stations being retained after this date.

The exact dates for the removal of the three station pedestrian footbridges have not yet been ascertained, but from photographs the following has been determined:

Thorneywood footbridge No.7a: still there in April 1938, gone by 16th June 1951.

St. Ann's Well footbridge No.9a: still there in 1939, gone by 1943.

Sherwood footbridge No.11a: still there in April 1938, gone by 16th May 1951

The same scenario applies to the three signal boxes:

Thorneywood signal box: still there April 1938, gone by 16th June 1951

St. Ann's Well signal box: still there in 1939, gone by 1945.

Sherwood signal box: still there in May 1952, gone by June 1954.

The story of the NSR, as most railway enthusiasts and local historians will know, is not exempt as far as the Second World War was concerned.

Mr Barry Elliott relates an interesting event that he witnessed around 1941. He remembers seeing, from his home front windows, a biplane, probably a Gloucester Gladiator, diving down from a south-westerly direction towards the Thackeray's Lane bridge. He thinks that this plane was using the bridge as a practice bombing raid target by the way it flew. There was, at the time of this fly over, about thirty or so ARP or Home Guard military personnel 'on the ground'.

Tragedy was to befall the Suburban during the Second World War. Of the 479 high explosive devices (bombs and land mines) that were dropped on Nottingham throughout the conflict, some 428 fell within a mile radius of Newark Street, Sneinton. The area between Carlton Road and Colwick Road was the worst hit area

The western portal of the NPBC's brickyard wagon way. *Tony Hill.*

The intricate wrought iron lattice work of the pedestrian footbridge No.8 with the blue brindle brick arched retaining wall to the rear. *Barry Walker.*

(above) Thorneywood station viewed from the pedestrian bridge No.8 looking south. The NPBC's wagon-way can be seen entering the shunt siding and buffer stop on the left, its short length giving an indication of the limited number of wagons that could be hauled up and down the wagon-way at a time. The cattle dock and the weighbridge is on the right, along with the goods yard gates. *Douglas Thompson, Michael Vanns collection.*

(left) One of the refuges inside Thorneywood tunnel designed to allow a safe location for railway personnel in the tunnel from passing trains. *John Wilson.*

A view of St. Ann's Well station Up platform, the only platform on the line to be of timber construction. The station sign and platform rear fence still remain as does the goods shed to the behind.

St. Ann's Well station looking north with Bentley's Bridge No.10 in the distance. The Down platform buildings have all been demolished and the Up timber platform has been removed. The Up platform waiting room and goods shed remain. This view was captured in May 1952, just after closure but all the track still remains. *Douglas Thompson.*

View looking south at Bentley's Bridge No.10 with the Up side single track and the permanent way cabin on the right. St Ann's Well station can be seen under the arch in the distance. *John Wilson.*

(opposite, top) The north face of bridge No.11 under Sherwood Vale. The fogman's hut at the end of the Up platform remains, as does the bridge identifying number plate. *J.P. Wilson.*

The north portal of Sherwood tunnel on 11th June 1951. The 'Sherwood 442 yards' board remains but the telegraph wires from the tunnel are now supported by telegraph poles instead of being housed in underground ducting when the Down platform was in situ. *F.E. Quenby.*

Looking north through the arch of bridge No.11 also on 11th June 1951. The Up track remains along with some redesigned sidings to the west. The signal box and weighbridge office remain, as does the permanent way cabin at the end of the Up platform. *F.E. Quenby.*

(opposite, bottom) The Sherwood station Up platform and footbridge No.11a. The station signboard is still standing despite the fact that the station ceased timetabled passenger use in 1916! *E.C. Haywood, Michael Vanns collection.*

Sherwood station looking south. The place looks quite complete except for the footbridge lights, which are missing, whilst the platform lamp looks a bit worse for wear. The Down line was removed through the station as part of the singling operation. *E.C. Haywood, Michael Vanns collection.*

continued from page 97./ and it was clear that the railways and its bridges were the main target areas of the Luftwaffe. The German's carried out their major air-raid over Nottingham on the night of the 8th and 9th May 1941 when they dropped 424 bombs. During the raid on that night, 159 people were killed of which 93 were men, 36 women and 30 children. In addition 274 people were injured, 122 seriously. Because of war reporting restrictions the *Nottingham Evening Post* could only report that a *'N. Midland Town was Bombed by Nazis and that there was considerable damage done but casualties were not unduly heavy.'*

In fact the "The Nottingham Blitz", as it became to be known, was the worst air-raid that the city was to experience, the Luftwaffe killing 181 people in total throughout their air raids. Ninety-five aircraft attacked Nottingham and carried out destruction from Mapperley Park, across Woodborough Road, St. Ann's Wells Road, The Lace Market, Meadow Lane, Midland station, Sneinton Dale, Leenside, Carlton Road, Carlton Hill and Colwick Road. Apparently London Road Sneinton, Colwick Road and Carlton Road suffered the most. [It is possible that the Luftwaffe pilots and navigators were in fact following the Suburban line from north to south thinking that it was the GCR, which would have led them straight into the heart of Nottingham.]

Sadly for the NSR it was hit by three bombs during the raid. The first two bombs landed adjacent to St. Ann's Well station, the first in the goods yard, which caused little damage and the second in the cutting between the north portal of Thorneywood tunnel and The Wells Road bridge. This bomb blew out a section of the single line track clean across The Wells Road and came to rest in a school.

The story of these two bomb explosions have been explained in more detail by Alan Westby and Aubrey Gibson in Chapter 14. The third bomb to hit the NSR that night was to have a much more damaging effect – which would last until the closure of the line. One of the German bombs landed and exploded on the Suburban's embankment just north of bridge No.3's north abutment, adjacent to the MR's Nottingham to Lincoln line. The explosion removed part of the NSR's embankment, damaged the north abutment of the bridge and breached the line.

It is amazing that the line was not hit more than once, particularly around Sneinton Dale bridge No.6 where there was a very heavy concentration of bombs landing very close to the structure. Another report recorded in the "Bygones" paper was sent in by Mrs. P. Bray of Carlton who recalls the night of the blitz. She had spent the night in an Anderson shelter in Bradbury Street, Sneinton, a hundred yards from the Suburban bridge No.3 over the Nottingham to Lincoln line. She reports, *'During the night, I can remember the terrifying whistle of a bomb which landed with a dull thud on the railway. Luckily for us, it was a time bomb which was later detonated by the Army and caused superficial damage to our house.'* As this section of the NSR had little or no use, the LNER decided not to sanction repairs but instead carry out extensive remedial works to the bridge's north abutment and superstructure by using timber supports. The NSR's embankment and damaged bridge abutment were never repaired.

The NSR line was now breached and no live loading was permitted on the damaged bridge from this date. As a consequence, the NSR on the morning of 9th May 1941 became either two branch lines, or a branch line and a siding may perhaps be a more accurate description. As there was now little use for the line south of Sneinton Tunnel to be used other than for storage of railway stock, the LNER decided to lift the section of track that included the length over bridge No.3. In addition to the bridge, several lengths of track were lifted either side of the bridge to fully ensure that no loads from the track could be transferred to the weakened structure. At

Bridge No.3 with the track removed and the north abutment strengthened with timbers following the bombing of the north embankment in 1941. Note the buffer stop at the end of the original UP line, which was now used as a siding to store wagons, which some say were either ordnance or condemned wagons. The Down line track has already been removed. *John Wilson.*

The buffer stop on the original Up line just north of bridge No.3 over the MR Nottingham to Lincoln line following the bombing of the NSR's embankment which was never repaired. *John Oxley.*

The north end of Sherwood station in May 1952, with a close-up of the boarded-up signal box. *Douglas Thompson.*

The north face of bridge No.11 under Sherwood Vale on 23rd July 1951, just seven days before closure. The Down platform is looking poorly kept but the Station Master's house, on the right, is still occupied but not alas by railway staff working on the Suburban. A stack of sleepers in good condition are piled between the tracks, and the permanent way cabin looks well kept and possibly still used. Note the small trolley wagon adjacent to the buffers. *F.E. Quenby.*

The Sherwood goods yard weighbridge building. *Tony Hill.*

An LNER 'Trespass' cast-iron notice located at the north-west corner of the Thackeray's Lane bridge No.15. *Barry Walker.*

A close-up of the Sherwood station Station Master's house gable end. Note the tiles at the top of the gable and the octagonal chimney stacks.

the two 'new' ends of the track the LNER placed rail-built buffer stops.

The loss of the use of the NSR south of Thorneywood did not significantly affect the working of the line, as the Leen Valley thrice-weekly pick-up goods, from Daybrook to Thorneywood, was the only timetabled train. From this date the short branch or stub on the Up line between the bridge No.3's south buffer stop and the London Road Goods Yard junction was used for storing wagons, most, allegedly condemned, a situation which continued until at least 1950.

At various times during the war, the tunnels along the Suburban, as with many more throughout the country, were employed as air-raid shelters by the local population, a situation similar to that found in the underground tube stations in London.

The LNER *Appendix to the Rules and Regulations and Working Time Tables* from 4th May 1942 sheds light on how the NSR was operated at this time. On page 139, the maximum speed at the Trent Lane junction, the Up NSR over the bridge No.2, and on the curve opposite the signal box, was 15 m.p.h. On page 195 the standard code of engine whistles at the Trent Lane junction box was:

The south portal of Ashwell's tunnel after the Down line has been removed. Both the two sidings to the east and west of the remaining Up line have differently constructed buffer stops. The sleeper and earth construction one on the right is provided for the NPBC siding where as a traditional rail construction type is provided for the merchants' siding. *John Oxley.*

Suburban to Low Level station	2 long whistles
Suburban to Victoria	2 long, 2 short whistles
Suburban	2 long whistles
Down Main and Suburban	4 short whistles

In addition to the above, there were *Special Instructions* for working on the Suburban, on page 375 as follows:

'Drivers of trains working through from Daybrook to Nottingham must take the train staff forward to Nottingham Goods Yard Box and from there it must be taken by the London Road Passenger Station staff and sent to Daybrook by Passenger train. The staff must be handed to the Station Master at Daybrook and he must see that it is placed in the Daybrook Signal Box in readiness for the Freight train the following morning.

Freight trains from the direction of Daybrook requiring to work at Sherwood will stop on a sharp rising gradient and the special attention of Guards is drawn to the necessity for securing their trains in accordance with the instructions in Rule 115(c) before uncoupling the engine.

The Signalman at Trent Lane must be advised by telephone when the train is ready for leaving Thorneywood'.

Clearly, although the above instruction is written for trains travelling from Daybrook right through to the London Road station, which of course was not possible after May 1941, this instruction provides insight on how the trains were operated before this date.

It was around this time that the Nottingham Builders' Brick Company closed down but their site continued to be used as an oil storage depot, which allegedly opened in 1910, still being accessed by the trailing junction off the NSR's Down line into Thorneywood station. By the 1940's Jeff Holt recalled – in *Bygones 119* – seeing the trackwork for the tramways of the Nottingham Builders' Brick

Company on Carlton Road still in place but he was not sure that they were still in use. The book *Oil on the Rails* by Alan Coppin refers to Redline Glico having a siding at Thorneywood which confirms eye-witness accounts that following the demise of the NBBC, an oil company continued to use the two sidings south of Thorneywood station to receive oil wagons from which their loads were transferred into road transport tankers for delivery to their customers.

It was reported that on the 14th October 1942 the Nottingham City Council took over the ownership and hence the maintenance of the Carlton Road bridge No.7 from the LNER.

It is surprising, but factual, that during the War years, Mr A.G. Cramp wrote in *The Guardian* on 1st December 1942, about a plan for improving the Nottingham suburban railway services after the war, by providing a more equal distribution of traffic between road and rail, thus relieving road congestion. The plan called the Nottingham District Railway (NDR), which was being considered by the Post-War Railway Reconstruction Commission. It was suggested that the new railway would be jointly operated by the LNER and the LMS and would serve Alfreton, Heanor, Hucknall, Kirkby-in-Ashfield, Long Eaton, Loughborough, Newark, Mansfield, Ripley, Sutton-in-Ashfield, West Bridgford and suburban areas of Nottingham. The report mentions the use of the NSR as being part of the scheme and being upgraded to become double track once more. In addition to this the three stations would be re-opened to passengers. The report also recommended *'the building of a new station at Sneinton, where the railway crosses Sneinton Dale and another at Woodthorpe near Marlborough Road. Both these new stations would serve areas with large populations. Further comment included that the two stations at St. Ann's Well and Sherwood would provide transport for two districts which are a considerable distance from a bus route. The new stations should be of modern design with a large booking hall provided with ticket machines and quick access to the platforms. The three existing stations would be refurbished and/or rebuilt and be provided with electric lighting. The trains on*

The Up line curves to the left to meet the original Down line at Daybrook junction. Note the check rail adjacent to the inner rail on the curve. It was in this area that a transition was put in to join the Up line with the Down line as the Up line junction with the 'Back Line' was to be removed.

derequisition these premises so that the owners can resume their pre-war production of 250,000 bricks per week.'

'Sir S. Cripps responded that the brickyard and kilns of the Nottingham Patent Brick Company at Nottingham have been occupied by the Royal Air Force for storage purposes. The stores have now been removed and the owners are free to enter into possession of the premises at any time.'

the service would be hauled by "*powerful tank locomotives in a streamlined casing and modern saloon-type coaches with large self opening sliding doors, which would permit quick entrance and exit, thus eliminating long stops at stations.*' '*For services where traffic was not so heavy and also for use on the steam operated routes during slack periods, diesel or diesel electric railcars could be used.*'

I have not been able to follow this scheme through to an outcome, but suffice it to say, the part involving the re-doubling of the NSR track and the opening of existing and new NSR stations to passengers never came about. There are two main interesting issues relating to this report. Firstly, it is interesting that this Commission was now considering building new stations on the NSR which had been originally proposed by land owners along the line back in 1886. Although the levels of population had not been achieved in the early years of the NSR, and thus the two suggested stations had never been built, housing development and associated population growth had manifested themselves and, by the 1940's, were considered a necessity. Secondly, it is surprising to learn that plans for an integrated road and rail system around and within Nottingham was being considered in the 1940's. It is a pity that the opportunity does not appear to have been taken at that time, for when it appears to have been considered again in the late 1950's, too much of the NSR's infrastructure had either been demolished or built upon to achieve a through route along the line.

During the Second World War it is said that the areas around St. Ann's Well station and goods yard were used to store aircraft wing fuel tanks. My thanks to Ron Hawthorne for this information. It has also been said that St. Ann's Well station was used for oil storage by the Ministry.

Mapperley brickyard also contributed towards the war effort. Either all or parts of the works were used by the Royal Air Force for storage purposes. It wasn't until 18th February 1946 that the Government allowed the NPBC at Mapperley to resume its normal working practices. It was reported in Hansard Commons sitting, Trade and Commerce (HC Deb 18th February 1946 vol .419 cc779-80:

'*Mr S Shephard asked the President of the Board of Trade if he is aware (780) that the brickyard and kilns of the Nottingham Patent Brick Company at Nottingham are still occupied by the military authorities as a storage depot; and what steps is he taking to*

Regarding bridge No.6 over Sneinton Dale, Mr Brian Goulding reported in *Bygones 86* that '*During the war, a line of old trucks, other vans, were parked along the line across the bridge, said to be a 'decoy' to draw the attention of enemy bombers away from the main lines in the area.*' Perhaps this could be one reason why the Germans aimed their bombs along the NSR during the night of the Nottingham Blitz.

In 1945 the Mapperley Brickyard bought a 2' 0" gauge, four-wheel mechanical transmission diesel locomotive from Ruston & Hornsby Ltd. of Lincoln, maker's number 235715. However, this locomotive was reported by the Industrial Railway Society as 'out of use and that all rail traffic within the yard had ceased by 1968'. Throughout the war the brickyards are thought to have continued production but on a limited scale due to the loss of some of their workforce who was serving their country and that certain areas of the brickyard were occupied storing items for the War Ministry. It would have also been the case that the demand for bricks significantly reduced as many of the men employed to lay them would have been deployed in His Majesty's Forces.

There are a couple of entries in the LNER 1947 *General Appendixes* relating specifically to the NSR. These are;

Trent Lane Junction – speed limit on NSR, over bridge No.2 and on curve opposite signal box 15 m.p.h.
Trent Lane Junction – Down Suburban, 90 yards after passing junction facing points, 1 in 49 rising gradient with catch point.
Custodian of train staff for the Nottingham Suburban is Daybrook.
List of tunnels:
Sneinton tunnel between Trent Lane junction and Thorneywood 183 yards, Thorneywood tunnel between Thorneywood and St Ann's Well 408 yards, Sherwood tunnel between St. Ann's Well and Sherwood 442 yards.

At midnight on the 31st December 1947 the LNER Company ceased to exist as it was part of the Government's Nationalisation scheme for all the railways in Britain. From 1st January 1948, the NSR rails formally became part of the new public body known as British Railways.

(above) **A view from a train which has just left Daybrook station and is heading east on the 'Back Line' in 1951. Apparent is the small summersault signal, and the ground frame which operated the points to access the NSR's original Down line, which quickly transitioned into the Up line.** *F.E. Quenby.*

(below) **A NPBC advertisement stating the location of their three brickworks, their offices and the two LNER sidings.** *NPBC.*

(right) **An advert poster for the NPBC detailing the types of bricks manufactured at the three brickyards.** *NPBC.*

(top) **NPBC's Mapperley brickworks viewed from the north with the new road known as Mapperley Rise on the right.** *(above)* **Thorneywood brickworks viewed from the west. The row of houses to the right are on Burgass Road and the road at the bottom is Thorneywood Lane, later Porchester Road.** *both Mike Chapman collection.*

Chapter 14: MEMORIES OF THE NOTTINGHAM SUBURBAN RAILWAY

It is not very easy to still find people who can reminisce about the NSR during the days when it still operated prior to August 1951. However, we are fortunate to be able to read the memories of five such people who are willing to share their thoughts with us.

Most of the memories that are included in this chapter have been generated from members of the Friends of The Nottingham Suburban Railway group, which was created at the same time that Volume 1 of this series was published in 2010. You will note that the contents of this chapter, as well as providing you with some wonderful anecdotes, also gives readers access to some previously unpublished photographs of live steam in action on the NSR.

The memories have been faithfully reproduced from each person's dialogue and as such this book's author does not accept responsibility for any inaccuracies in their content or the correctness of data. Sincere thanks needs to go to the following gentlemen who have given their time, valued memories and photograph collections for us all to enjoy: Alan Westby, Aubrey Gibson, Sid Checkley, Peter Mackness and George Allen.

The Alan Westby Interview – The following is a transcription of an interview that was carried out by the author on 19th April 2010 with Alan Westby.

I was born in 1931 and it was around 1932 or 1933 when we moved to 451 The Wells Road. The house, which is still there, is four houses down the hill on The Wells Road from the St. Ann's Well station house. Our house, at the rear, looked over the St. Ann's Well station goods yard.

My father had worked on the railway. He had been in the signal box at the Leen Valley Junction in GNR times. He spoke the same language as the St. Ann's Well Station Master, who was John Potts, and they had quite a bit in common. At St Ann's Well station it was John Potts, and his wife Connie, who ran the railway. John Potts came from Accrington and I do believe that he started with the Manchester, Sheffield and Lincolnshire Railway, which went on to become the Great Central and then the LNER. Quite how he came to Nottingham I don't know but he was at St Ann's Well. From the time that I recall, he was in charge of the whole of the Nottingham Suburban Railway from Daybrook, I suppose, through to Trent Lane before the War. After the line was bombed at Sneinton and was truncated, he was probably only responsible up to there.

A friend of mine Aubrey Gibson and myself used to spend a lot of time round about St Ann's Well station. Sometimes we would walk up to the Sherwood tunnel and we would stand at the south end and wait to hear the engine start away from Sherwood. It would come rattling through the tunnel and, as I say my pal was more hair-brain, he would stand silhouetted in the mouth of the tunnel waving. The driver of the engine would see him and anchor up and by the time he came by, realising that the gradient to St Ann's was 1 in 50 downhill, we just about managed to hare along and hop onto the brake van. We would go to St. Ann's, shunt that place, then continue to Thorneywood, to shunt there before returning to St Ann's where we would drop off.

The trains would shunt Sherwood, drop off and pick up wagons, then do the same at St Ann's and Thorneywood and shunt the brake van to the rear of the train at Thorneywood. We often came back on the footplate, which was a good experience. But the driver never stopped to drop us off. He would shut down to about

4 m.p.h. and as soon as we had jumped off onto the ballast, as there was no platform against the Up line anymore, the regulator was pushed wide open again.

When the train proceeded to Thorneywood from Daybrook, the locomotive hauled the wagons and as usual the brake van was at the back. The brake van was always parked in the same place at Thorneywood and then everything was drawn away from the brake van. Because the track gradient was 1 in 50, the brake van was allowed to roll down the slope, with the guard winding the handbrake down. Occasionally my pal and I were allowed to do this manoeuvre; Health and Safety eat your heart out. My pal was more of a devil or a free spirit than I. He said *'we'll let the brake van run a bit'* and so it ran under the Carlton Road bridge and down towards Sneinton tunnel. Nothing had been down there since the crippled wagons had been pushed further down the track to Sneinton, so the rails were well and truly rusty, rough old things. We got a good telling off for doing this but we had to get out of this hole, so the loco backed down with the wagons and now everything was on the rusty track. When they came to start away, the climb back up through Thorneywood and Thorneywood tunnel and back to St Ann's Well, it was more than hard work. We were banished from the brake van for a considerable length of time after that.

My cousin had a shop on Carlton Road opposite the end of Marmion Road. At the rear of the shop his father had a garage where he kept his car before the War. Behind the garage was the siding to the Nottingham Builders' Brick Company yard. I remember the siding was used by Redline Glico Oil wagons that were part of the Anglo American Oil Company, which is now Esso. The Redline Glico lorries were petrol blue (a purple blue), with a red stripe. The tank wagons were shunted into the siding and the fuel was discharged into lorries. I remember, only once, seeing a bogie petrol tank wagon in the Thorneywood yard.

The entrance to the St. Ann's Well goods yard was where the Station Master's house was. On the opposite side of the entrance was a weighbridge office, which really was the hub of the railway. There was no electricity in the place. All the lighting was by paraffin lamps and a big coal fire in one corner, which blazed away, for coal was readily available. Before the War, the Babbington Coal Company had a wooden office there, but I'm not so sure when that disappeared. It was shiplap, a typical shed. One of the coal merchants that took delivery of coal at St Ann's was Sanders, whose house was on Hill View Road, parallel with Porchester Road. There was also Jones of Querneby Road, parallel to Woodborough Road, Heyhoe who was from Porchester Road way, and he was quite friendly with Potts. There was also William Gell and also another company Burtons who were on Mansfield Road. These were all coal merchants. Burtons had a fleet of Sentinel steam lorries.

We always had our coal from Sanders. If Mr Jones was coming down The Wells Road, when we were coming back from school, he would give us a lift on the back of his Ford lorry, sitting on the back in the coal dust. There was another coal merchant called Henson who had a yard in Westminster Street and he had a horse and cart.

There was a fire lighter place next door to the goods' entrance called Dawson's Fire Lighters and Dry Salters. The best advert they had was that the whole lot caught fire in about 1941 time. Two new Council houses were built in its place. The business was primitive in the extreme. They employed women who sat at a bench

Unless otherwise indicated, the photographs illustrating this chapter have been taken and supplied by Aubrey Gibson and Alan Westby.

In the winter of 1947 an unidentified J52 approaches the south portal of Sherwood tunnel with a NSR pick-up goods. The train is climbing the last length of 1 in 50 gradient before the section of level track (the sumit of the NSR), and then the 1 in 70 gradient down through Sherwood tunnel. Enjoy the wonderful visiual display of billowing smoke and steam!

Sherwood station signal box looking north-west in the winter of 1947. The box has several of its windows boarded up and had long since been out of use. It was however the last of the NSR's signal boxes to be in service.

and they had a little device in front of them. They put two sticks in the bottom of the devisc, then a handful of chippings off a planning machine, followed by another two sticks on the top. Two clips were then brought over, the woman pressed the foot treadle, which crushed it all together and then she used a piece of black iron binding wire to tie round it. That was the start of the fire lighter. They spent all morning doing that. There were about four women employed on this with 'Music While You Work' playing on the radio. In another shed they'd got the old fashioned coppers that you used to have in the corner of the scullery, with the fires underneath them. They'd got about four of these in which they boiled naphthalene, which if you know the smell of moth balls; it was like that but a thousand times worse. These bundles of sticks were dipped about 1½" each end in this naphthalene, which were then allowed to dry, and they were then bundled up and a piece of very cheap paper was wrapped round them. They were then sold in the shops. They also made another type of fire lighter, which was sawdust mixed with naphthalene, which was compressed to form a large block, like that of Cadbury's chocolate, so that you could break bits off and put a match to it and it lit your fire! You could also get from there big blocks of salt for salting down vegetables. During the War you were encouraged to grow your own, so everybody grew kidney beans and they were cut up and then placed into a jam jar. A layer of beans were put into the bottom of a jar and on the top was placed a layer of salt. Then another layer of beans was put in followed by more salt until the jar was full of alternate layers of beans and salt.

The real business at St. Ann's Well goods yard was Somnus bedding, which had two factories on The Wells Road near Kildare Road, and they also had another factory on Lotus Street. Every day there would be three or four railway goods vans arriving at St. Ann's Well from William Rhodes, the proprietors of Somnus Beds. Three or four vans would come from Leeds, the main factory, to St Ann's Well station, with components for Somnus bedding. A road van was employed continuously from the factories. A road vehicle van, the size of a transit, came up to St Ann's Well and it 'shunted' backwards and forwards between the station and the factories emptying the railway vans and bringing stuff from the factories to go into the vans to go back to Leeds. This provided everyday work, five days a week. There was a train everyday at this time particularly during the War and occasionally there were more. The main goods shed was used by Somnus bedding. As you will know from the track plan, on The Wells Road side of the Goods Shed, there was road access to the shed and on the other side there were twin tracks and one track provided rail access to the shed. Somnus put staff into that goods shed and possibly had a couple of blokes emptying and filling railway vans. The road van would then come up and either picked stuff up or dropped things off as required.

The old St. Ann's Well station building, which was on the wooden Up platform, was still there but the platform had gone. I can't remember the wooden Up platform being there. I remember that about every six foot there was a creosoted 6" x 6" cut stump that stood 2" to 3" above the ground. The station building's floor was 1½" flooring on about 7" x 3" joists and the floor was reinforced by 11" x 4" timbers, which were underneath, and had been used as a depot by Earl's Cement.

At Sherwood station there had been a footbridge. At Thorneywood station there had been a footbridge. There was also a footbridge at St. Ann's Well station. The footbridges at Sherwood and Thorneywood went years ago but the one at St Ann's Well didn't. It stayed but one day my Dad told me to look out of the window. There was a Colwick breakdown crane and they were taking the footbridge down because somewhere had been bombed and where was a spare footbridge? - St. Ann's Well. Why the one at St Ann's had been left I do not know, but that footbridge was dismantled and taken away at the beginning of the War, about 1941

time. It was carefully dismantled and re-erected somewhere else. I don't know where it went to.

The area around Bentley's Bridge, was always known to the kids as 'Brownies Field'. There were allotments on the other side of this bridge, right up to Ransom Road, or Coppice Road as it was called when I was a kid. Right at the top there was Blyth Street and adjacent was Mason's Farm, which during the War was a gun site. A lot of timber was stored at Sherwood during the War.

With regard to the bombing at St. Ann's Well station, this was the same night as the Sneinton bomb. The bomb was dropped in the cutting at the north end of the Thorneywood tunnel, just before it went into fill. Morley school was just on the north side of The Wells Road, west of The Wells Road railway bridge. When this bomb dropped, two 30 feet lengths of rail were blown right out of the cutting, right over The Wells Road and one landed in the Morley School playground. The other came vertically down through the school roof in the men's staffroom and there was a big table in the middle of the room and the rail went straight through that! The line was only single track at that time.

There was also a third bomb. This landed in the St Ann's Well station yard just off the back line on a roadway adjacent to the houses. That roadway was built up quite a bit from the track. My father was 'fire watching' on there that night because Mr Potts organised fire watching. He dropped down at the side of the line, sort of tucked down under the wagon when he heard this thing coming down. It dropped but it was only a small bomb otherwise he wouldn't have lasted afterwards. All the muck it lifted out of the hole vertically dropped back in. At the bottom of the embankment the people who lived at 429 The Wells Road had a greenhouse and I think two panes of glass got broke. The railway was untouched. I remember my Mother asking my Dad 'Are you alright Ernest?' as he came back in. He sort of shook a few bits of muck out his clothing and that was it.

Up to the Mapperley brickyard, sometime after the War, a wagon of coal broke away on the incline and ran back down through the catch points and was wrecked at the bottom. I don't know whether the rope broke or a coupling broke or what happened but somewhere I have a photograph of the wagon. I am sort of standing next to it inspecting it. The coal was like nutty slack stuff, which was burnt at the brickyard. But there was quite a lot of traffic up to the brickyard at Mapperley. These were part of the pick-up goods trains. The railway at Mapperley used to go up the incline but there was another part to it. If you go down Mapperley Rise from Woodborough Road, just before Maurice Drive, on the right there used to be an entrance to the brickyard and the standard gauge railway ran to there. There was a kiln near there. If the bricks being transported by wagon were facing bricks they would come down the incline packed in straw. Commons were canched in properly but facing bricks were treated with a bit more respect.

John Potts was not there till the end of the line. He possibly left around 1947 time. He realised that the NSR wasn't a very remunerative thing and he decided to look for pastures new. He wanted to go to Ruddington but ended up at Rugby Central and I believe he retired from there. He has been dead many years. He was a 'big man' in the St John's Ambulance. During the War, in order to boost moral, there was a church service every Sunday morning and parade in Nottingham and people marched to St Mary's Church or St Peter's Church. Most of these Sunday mornings you would see John Potts striding down The Wells Road to Kildare Road in his St. John's Ambulance Brigade uniform with peaked hat and straight cane with a silver top on it. It was a power in the land as far as the St John's Ambulance was concerned because the railway had set a great store on First Aid and he had been in the Medical Corps in the First World War.

Alan Westby inspects a wagon which became derailed whilst being lowered down the rope hauled incline from the NPBC's Mapperley brickworks in the winter of 1947. The wagon belongs to the Amalgamated Anthracite Collieries, Swansea.

J6 No.4202 has just passed beneath Bentley's bridge, No.10, as it journeys northwards in the summer of 1948 towards Daybrook, the driver gives a glance at the photographer, who he probably knew quite well - *see* the Memories.

In another view from the summer of 1948, we see St. Ann's Well goods yard as seen from the guards van of the pick-up goods train. This area of the yard was given over to the coal merchants who had to unload the coal wagons by hand either onto the coal heaps in the yard or onto their horse carts or into sacks. The covered wagon at the rear of the goods shed probably contained *Somnus* bedding parts.

That first summer of Nationalisation saw a number of NSR views captured on film. This 'pick-up' goods heads north towards Daybrook after completing a day of shunting. Bentley's bridge can be seen in the murky distance and the coal merchants' coal piles are adjacent to the wagons on the right.

(below) A group of railway workers and coal merchants stand around a trolley adjacent to the coal yard at St. Ann's Well station in the summer of 1948.

On the day of the RCTS Special I just photographed it at St Ann's Well station as it went to Thorneywood. I then left because I had a meeting with the Nottingham Society of Model Engineers and we were taking a portable track somewhere as it was a Saturday because I was helping to run the model railway.

Connel's of Coatbridge dismantled a lot of the Suburban Railway. They took the bridge down over The Wells Road as well taking down everything else including track etc. It was very interesting to see when they took the bridge down over The Wells Road. Strangely the ballast on the bridge was all round pebbles and flint; it wasn't stone or granite like everywhere else. The Wells Road was lined with horse chestnut trees and at a certain time of the year all the kids from the St Ann's area would go 'conkering'. They would get up on the railway bridge and would pick up the 'duck' stones, as we would call them, and pelt them at the conkers off the bridge. Well, one or two cars got clobbered, there weren't many cars about then and 'PC Plod' was around but he wasn't very effective, he wasn't speedy enough for the local urchins.

Connel's was responsible for the demolition of The Wells Road bridge. They had about a 5-ton Bedford lorry with a crane on the back; nothing very spectacular and six men took that bridge down. They got some pieces of wood which came from Glasgow, some pieces of ship's mast, guy ropes and pulley blocks etc. Fortunately, the big horse chestnut trees on The Wells Road provided a good anchorage for guy ropes. They stripped all the decking off the bridge, they took the hand-railing off [parapet] and then the lorry manoeuvred with a piece of the ship's mast up The Wells Road and into Dooland Drive and through the station to the north side of the bridge. The crane lowered the mast between two of the longitudinal beams/girders that went across the road. The lorry then had to go all the way to Thorneywood with another mast and came back travelling through the Thorneywood tunnel to do likewise at the south side of the bridge. These two poles were then set upright and tied back to the trees. They put a ring of sleepers round the trees to protect them and used the trees to support the guy ropes which were about three-quarter inch steel rope, probably old ship's cabling. Around the base of the north abutment they had about 100 oxygen bottles and they were all piped together. They then cut through the girders along the line of the face of each abutment wall with an oxygen lance. They had put sleepers down across the road underneath the bridge. The pulley blocks took the weight and they lowered each girder down onto the carpet of sleepers and then cut it up into chunks.

In 1954, when I came out of the Air Force, I went to work for a firm named George Harrison, who was at the top of Mapperley Rise/Woodborough Road. I obtained a load of railway sleepers for a firewood business and I also had all the timbers out of that Up platform's waiting room and the lead that was still there. The roof was slate but the kids had knocked a lot of the slates off. I had the lead off the roof, all the roof timbers, the flooring, all the joists, and the extra timbers that were underneath to support the floor. I borrowed a pole ladder from work so that I could get up to get the roof timbers down. My Dad met me at work and we walked down Woodborough Road like the 'Hall's Distemper' men, one each end of the ladder with the ladder on our shoulders. Fortunately I got the lorry to pick it up, so we didn't have to walk back up the hill with it. I left St Ann's Well Road in 1959.

Aubrey Gibson's Memories of the NSR:

The area around St Ann's Well station was my playground for many years as I lived on The Wells Road along side the station.

Later I was helping out with shunting, unloading coal and coke wagons which saved demurrage charges. All this was "unofficial" and helped me earn my pocket money.

During the air-raid over Nottingham on May 8th 1941 a bomb burst alongside the rail track, fifty yards or so to the north from the north end of Thorneywood tunnel. This resulted in a length of track being thrown out of the cutting, across allotments, houses and The Wells Road, finally coming to rest in the playground of The Morley School where I was a pupil. The impact remained visible for many years in the playground's asphalt surface. There was only minor damage caused to the railway's embankment. Likewise, another bomb exploded on the railway in the St. Ann's Well goods yard on the edge of the hardcore/embankment top facing No.439 The Wells Road. The blast caused no damage to any property and there was not even a window broken. It left only a small crater.

In the late 1940's, on Saturdays, I used to help Sam, who was the regular guard on the Suburban, with his shunting duties. I would ride either on the locomotive's footplate or in the guards van between the St Ann's Well and Thorneywood stations. On more than one occasion I was left in complete charge of the locomotive and wagons at Thorneywood station whilst the driver, fireman and Sam the guard went off for a "quick one" at the local hostelry. Their instructions to me were that if they were needed to blow the whistle. This of course was all "unofficial".

The passenger footbridge (No.9A) which was originally between the St Ann's Well station platforms was removed during the early days of the war for use elsewhere. I cannot recall there being any platform adjacent to the 'Up' line, it must have been removed prior to 1932.

Alan and I were "roamers"; we roamed together all over the area between the Sherwood and Thorneywood stations. The Station Master, Mr. Potts, soon decided to look the other way rather than to be constantly chasing us off railway property.

Sherwood Station - During the period up to the outbreak of the Second World War, the sidings at Sherwood were utilised to receive full wagon loads of imported sawn timber with the surrounding area used for storage of the timber. The Station House was occupied by the Signalman who worked at Daybrook, cycling along the track to his box. The Sherwood signal box was used as a track storeroom and subsequently vandalised. It was finally demolished in the 1950's. Coal was brought in for the brickyard's boilers, usually in "SC" wagons. The upper sidings were also used by a Mapperley coal merchant who bagged his coal for delivery by horse and cart. Coal by the wagon load was hauled up the incline for Mapperley Hospital. All the necessary "lower" shunting was undertaken by the goods train guard in the absence of any Station staff. There was a fixed telephone on Ashwell's tunnel wall, direct to Daybrook signal box, to alert the signal man that the train was now en route back to Daybrook.

St. Ann's Well Station - In the 30's and 40's right through to closure it was a busy station. Incoming seasonal freight consigned to Mapperley Hospital, consisted of seed potatoes, bales of peat, bag lime and fertiliser. Blocks of salt, bagged naphthalene, scrapped rail sleepers for cutting up into fire sticks consigned to Dawson's 'Salt and Firelighter' works located alongside the Station House with its own entrance to the sidings. The four main coal merchants were Heyhoe, Jones, Saunderson (who had his own two lettered coal wagons) and Gell's. Heyhoe purchased his coal from Gedling, Jones bought Bestwood and Hucknall, Gell's bought from anywhere buying coal and coke, being the only coal merchant dealing in coke holding considerable stocks around the Station yard. Keetchers Transport also received full loads of coke for their own use.

Messrs. William Rhodes, Somnus Bedding (for the rest of your life) had on average two van loads of bedding materials from their Leeds factory each trip. This was off-loaded into the large goods shed. The Up waiting room was hired out to Earles Cement Merchant who had van loads of bagged cement delivered for road distribution.

St. Ann's Well station goods shed in summer 1948 with the Up platform waiting room standing alone after the timber platform had been removed.

In another view from the summer of 1948, an unidentified ex-GCR 0-6-2T N5 shunts wagons in St. Ann's Well station goods yard. Note the correct lamp head-code for a branch line freight.

Colwick's solitary J11 gets a chance to visit the NSR in the summer of 1948 whilst in charge of the 'pick-up'. Here, at St. Ann's Well station, the former Great Central 0-6-0 slows ready to commence shunting duties. The Fireman alights to change the points on the ground frame to access the goods yard after the train has passed the access point.

In this summer scene from 1948, a Fireman, and a Shunter with his pole, pose for the camera at St. Ann's Well station. The Station Master's house can be seen behind the two wagons on the track to the rear of the goods shed.

The Driver and Fireman of J6 No.3591 want to get 'in the picture' as they shunt covered and open wagons in the St. Ann's Well goods yard during summer 1948. The covered wagons were probably full of *Somnus* bedding mattresses or parts, depending on whether the wagons were being delivered or collected!

It was busy on the NSR during the summer of 1948 for reasons other than routine. The Colwick breakdown train makes it's way home and is travelling northwards to Daybrook having just recovered a derailed locomotive further down the branch near Thorneywood. The rear ex-GNR 4-wheel coach is being used as a mess van.

There were occasional outward bound seasonal freight movements consisting of two or so wagon loads of sugar beet from Mapperley Hospital.

The Station Master, Mr E. Potts lived in the Station House; he was responsible for all three stations. He subsequently transferred to Rugby in the early 50's as Station Master there prior to his retirement. There was an early photograph of him with Alan Westby standing along side a 'South Normanton Colliery' coal wagon, watching a steam railcar pass through the station. Up to the early days of the war he was assisted by a traffic clerk/shunter, as the war progressed this man was transferred to LNER lorry driving. His clerical duties, weighbridge etc. being undertaken by Mrs Potts. The team of gangers kept the whole branch spotless, weeding, raking, scything, the result being the line resembled a municipal park.

Thorneywood Station - Again, an equally busy station with a number of coal merchants utilising the rail yard. One merchant in particular had her own marked coal wagons 'Mrs. Rose Smith'. There were occasional van loads of keg vinegar and onions for the pickle factory located on Porchester Road. I was told, on good authority, that prior to the war petrol tankers would be shunted down into the sidings off Carlton Road, previously used by the Nottingham Builders' Brick Company. From this site a petrol distributor would fill his tanker in the sidings for delivery locally. At the outbreak of war this activity ceased.

As the war progressed, considerable quantities of brick were consigned outwards with incoming empty railway owned wagons brought forward from Colwick for these loads. After the line was severed at Colwick Road by a bomb, a buffer stop was installed and the track was occupied by a long line of "cripples". These wagons stretched almost to Sneinton tunnel. Subsequently, when required for repair or scrapping they were hauled away twenty at a time. As traffic was now decreasing, there was only inward coal; the Traffic Clerk Mr Harry Flint was not replaced on his retirement. His duties were combined with the Station Master and the Goods Guard.

I previously mentioned that some of my happiest memories are of the times when I was sitting on the edge of the platform awaiting the arrival of the goods train from Sherwood in order to assist Sam, the permanent guard with shunting at both St Ann's Well and Thorneywood, allowing Mr Potts to go shopping with his wife. For this unofficial chore I was paid "pocket money". I rode to Thorneywood either on the footplate or with Sam in the brake van, returning back to Sherwood where I alighted on the platform - a very rare passenger indeed - either to walk back home through the tunnel or on my cycle which travelled in the brake van.

At one time there was a severe shortage of coal wagons. I was engaged by Gell's to empty their coal and coke wagons in the evenings to save them paying demurrage charges, with up to four truck loads a week it was a nice little earner. It was very hard work to throw coke out of a high sided coke wagon, it had to come out through its door and I have to admit I was pleased to be helped by my Father but then of course I had to share my earnings!

The Sid Checkley Interview: *In February 1989, Jeff Holt and I were fortunate to participate in an interview with the late Sid Checkley about his recollections of the NSR. The key points he raised have here been transcribed for your enjoyment.*

After the bombing, they used to go to the brickyards from the Daybrook end to Thorneywood and take the coal up and bring the bricks and empties back, with a J52 tank, usually in the afternoon. It also picked up bricks from Mapperley. It picked up bricks at Thorneywood right up to the 1950's. This was the cable hauled line up Burgass Road.

Aubrey Gibson poses in front of the boarded-up Down platform lamp room at the St. Ann's Well in the summer of 1948.

Under the Carlton Road bridge there was a turn-off, just around to where the school is now. In my school days it used to be Pratt's' Petrol, which later became Esso. They used to have one or two tanks at the time. There was no big demand for petrol in the 1920's and 30's. I do not know when the brick yard finished and the site became Pratt's.

The line up to the brickyard, up Burgass Road, was very ancient indeed. It was originally known as a puncheon yard, making these large bowls. This was going on before the First World War.

From the Sherwood brickyard a lot of bricks went out to the London sewers. They were very suitable for the London sewers. These came from the Mapperley yards, not the Thorneywood yards. They must have been a different type of clay.

All of the [pick-up] trains going down the Suburban started from Colwick. These were J52's. They were part of a roster working - a pilot gang. The driver would pick-up a train from Colwick and take it to Leen Valley/Daybrook. They took the train from what they called the 'western full' sidings and took it to Daybrook, where the engine would run round the train, and then go to Thorneywood. And of course the same thing would happen coming back. After the run round at Daybrook, the brake would be next to the engine. Apart from the driver and fireman, there used to be a checker who went with the guard to look after the wagons and their destinations. He would also do the labelling. They used to take quite a bit of coal up at one period. This was mostly for the brickyards.

The train crew made quite a little centre for themselves in Daybrook sidings at Daybrook station. This was while the engine ran round the train, they made tea, etc. This went on until the 1950's.

The RCTS trip's train had to borrow the engine from Annesley. The trip was on a Saturday. The engine was one of the "Dido" engines. A C12 tank cleaned up for the job. The trip went up as far as Thorneywood.

The last passenger trains that ran over the line were the 5.05 p.m. in the evening from Nottingham (Victoria) to Shirebrook. Sometimes that train was a railcar COMMERCE – a Sentinel railcar. It was the last one they had at Colwick where it was shedded. Several, at one time or another, came and went at Colwick [EXPEDITION and RISING SUN]. The Sentinel was a six cylinder unit. The first stop was Daybrook.

Quite a bit of through goods traffic ran over the line after 1931. It mostly ran as specials for one reason or another. During the period when the Mapperley tunnel collapsed there were quite a large number of trains run over the line and into the Nottingham Yard by Low Level station. They did not reverse there but were re-engined.

I was still at school when the Sherwood station was opened for school children on Tuesday July 10th 1928.

My first glimpse of the line was from a Nottingham tram when travelling over the Carlton Road bridge on my way to and from home in Netherfield. I couldn't remember seeing any traffic movement but there were a lot of wagons in the Thorneywood yard. There were the oil tanks on the left where the school is now. They were all GN 8 and 10 tonners in those days, and 5 planks. They were all railway owned wagons, no privately owned ones other than the coal and colliery wagons. The bricks were nearly always carried away in GN wagons. They were not sheeted over.

The bricks from Mapperley went to London for years and years. When the bricks came off the Suburban line they were taken to Colwick and shunted into general freight trains. These general, not coal, freight trains would be up to fifty wagons. These wagons ran to Ferme Park in London. [This is south of Hornsey on the East Coast Main Line]. This was most probably the receiving and distributing sidings for all Suburban goods traffic going to London. All the Suburban freight traffic left by the Daybrook end, even before the bombing of the bridge. Quite often when the train did leave the line from the south end, the trains would run over the bowstring bridge and halt at the Up junction. The brake van would stand foul of the bridge. These trains were usually trains of empty wagons.

The section of line between Thorneywood and Trent Lane Junction saw only through traffic. I never rode over the line.

One of the six-wheeled pilots used to go up there every day but which of the seven that was shedded at Colwick I do not know. They were the old J52 saddle tanks.

The 1 in 49 gradient on the Down line from Trent Lane junction used to make the old railcar grunt, although I never heard of it stalling. They usually ran it as a single railcar but sometimes they would run a six-wheeled coach as a trailer to it. It was nearly always driven by one man – Donkey Brown. If the railcar was not available they would run a C12 tank with three coaches, one of the triplets. In the course of the day it went to Shirebrook and Nottingham, and it also went to Chesterfield (Market Place), via Shirebrook.

Trains carried destination boards on the smoke box door. These were carried right up to the 1940's. Destination boards for Nottingham were always labelled 'Victoria', not Nottingham. They were two-sided and were changed over at the end of the journey, usually by the fireman. Most of the GN bogies had destination boards. The 7.19 p.m. from Grantham was always an Atlantic, this did not have any.

The checker at Colwick yard would be told by the brickyard that they wish to transport so many thousand bricks and he would have converted this to a number of wagons. These wagons would be ordered from the railway, and leased from them. Bricks could not be

put in the empty returning coal wagons as they were privately owned by the collieries. Separate wagons were used for hauling coal into the brickyards and hauling bricks out of the brickyards. Most of the coal wagons were either Gedling or Barber Walker wagons. Barber Walker came from the Erewash Valley, from collieries such as Harworth and Bentley collieries, they were the big ones. Coal also came from some of the smaller ones around Ilkeston.

Wagons for the bricks were Railway Company owned, usually GN and later NE. The coal was thought to be unloaded by hand.

The pick-up goods train was operated usually by the same crew every time. They were one of the shunt gangs who were known as the 'sick, lame and lazy'. They came off other jobs that they felt were too much trouble and none of them favoured night work. Night shunting at Colwick was done by men on standby, known as 'having a week on loose'.

I think that the wagons parked at the side of Colwick Woods during the war and after the bombing of the bridge had been shunted there out of the way. They belonged to the Royal Ordnance. They paid the rent for them. They were not thought to be condemned.

I think that the points at the bottom of the Mapperley Brickyard's incline were something that the company had devised for themselves.

The track was lifted from the Suburban over quite a long period of time. When the engineers had nothing to do during the week they went over the Suburban and lifted some more of the track. Although I can't remember where the Suburban track went to, most of the track at this time went to the engineers at Trumpington, Cambridge, after it was lifted."

Sincere thanks are given to Sid for his wonderful recollections of the NSR and his permission to record them.

Peter Mackness's Recollections recorded on 19th April 2010:

I was born shortly after the UK declared war on Hitler's Germany and grew up in a home overlooking what must have once been 'a railway station in the countryside'. I refer of course to 'Sherwood': a station whose platforms were simultaneously in a cutting and on an embankment.

In my childhood there was a signal box and a weighbridge. Tunnel nameboards remained and there were one or two ash covered remains of signal stumps. The Down platform sported a boarded-up lamp room, but no ticket office or waiting rooms. My father told me they were demolished and the woodwork, joists and rafters, sold on-site to local residents at knock-down prices in circa 1936. A neighbour built a greenhouse with timber from the station.

Mr and Mrs Holmes lived at the Station Master's House. He was a signalman at Leen Valley Junction and presided with authority over what remained of 'Sherwood'. One of his sons was my age and he allowed me to roam around the station yard when the pick-up wasn't due.

It was a time when children could have fun and be excited without having to spend money. We had the freedom to explore and imagine. My excitement was watching an engine arrive, shunt wagons laden with coal and bricks, and sometimes unload huge standards of timber for Sims Sons & Cook which was stored along the edge of the 'Downside' loop.

No matter what the weather, 'the pick-up goods' would provide me with endless fascination. Helping in the garden, or on the allotment (on LNER land rented at 5/- a year!), the arrival of the train and chatter of railwaymen and brickyard staff was the stuff of dreams for me.

I could scramble up or down the side of the cutting and run along Sherwood Vale to climb up and sit on the red brick parapet

Aubrey Gibson at the southern end of the St. Ann's Well station where, by summer 1948, the footbridge and timber Up platform have already been removed. Covered vans at the rear of the goods shed are probably providing transportation for *Somnus Beds*.

A view from the guard's van as it awaits the 'pick-up' at the end of the Thorneywood station Up platform. The locomotive carrying out the shunting during this summer day in 1948, is between the weighbridge and the goods shed on the left. On completion, the train will be reversed back onto the guard's van and commence the return journey.

A winter scene of The Wells Road bridge No.9 very early in its life as the adjacent trees are not very mature.

The view from the waiting Guard's van at the south end of the Up platform at Thorneywood. To the left of the van's ducket, the exhaust smoke from the shunting locomotive can be seen rising into the warm summer air.

Summer 1948 – The guard's van has been left in the charge of Aubrey Gibson, which, on one occasion, was not such a good idea, as Alan Westby recalled. The tracks on this side of the bridge, including the rails to the Nottingham Builders' Brick Company, look as if they haven't been used for some time.

wall of 'the brickyard bridge'. There, I would watch the detailed procedure for shunting and shackling loaded trucks for the brickyard.

I was doubly lucky in that my father grew up close to Thorneywood station. He recounted to me many stories of the comings and goings there between 1918 and 1933 at which point he moved to Sherwood.

What I haven't seen recorded are the occasional 'parspec' (party special) trains that ran over the line between 1932 and final closure. The famous pre-closure RCTS special is well known and photographed. There were others and I distinctly remember two.

The pattern of train movements at Sherwood was predictable – they were mainly in the afternoon, although Saturday mornings also featured. Watching the goods trains seemed to coincide with my mother's habit of an afternoon walk "for some fresh air", with me after school, through Woodthorpe Park, along Sherwood Vale and home for tea.

Apart from the final *RCTS* farewell special, I remember seeing two passenger trains travelling, non-stop, through Sherwood towards Daybrook. This must have been about 1947-48. One of these sightings remains very clear to me even now. It was a weekday, late one warm, sunny, summer afternoon. We broke our walk home to collect some vegetables from the allotment. As we walked through the gate onto the pavement, I heard an engine whistle and the familiar rumbling made when an engine was still in Sherwood tunnel. I ran the few yards to the bridge but too late. The train had burst out and into the cutting and under Sherwood Vale bridge. I dashed across the road and saw a tender engine, two or three coaches and a sea of arms waving and flailing from the windows drifting towards Woodthorpe Park and Ashwell's. Afterwards I couldn't stop talking about it. Why was a passenger train there? Who were the people waving? The other sighting, it may have been before or after the account just related. The details of the engine and coaches are not as strongly imprinted on my memory. Again, it was a warm, sunny weekday afternoon and it was me and my mother. We had just crossed Mapperley Rise to walk via Cresta Gardens and across the field to Dornoch Avenue. We heard a train and turned around to see, again, an engine two or three coaches going towards Daybrook. These 'unusual for the Suburban' events stayed with me. However, there was a sequel.

A few years later, around 1956, I was on a return train from Basford (North) via the 'Back Line'. The three-coach train formation was unusual in that it included an old GN clerestory corridor coach. A driver and fireman going off-duty to Colwick cheerfully hailed me and asked if I had collected many numbers. This started a conversation. As we drew out of Daybrook I drew their attention to the now closed single line of the NSR and that I had twice seen passenger trains at Sherwood during the 1940's. This prompted one of the footplate men – probably the driver – to confirm that 'some schools occasionally booked a 'parspec' (party special) over the line as far as Thorneywood.' For what purpose the parspecs were booked I never discovered but, it might have explained the arms I saw waving and flailing from the carriages.

Driver George Allen's Memories

In the 1980's Mr. David Page recorded several interviews he carried out with Mr. George Allen, who had previously been a steam locomotive driver, spending his entire footplate career at Colwick. The following are extracts taken from these recordings that specifically referred to George's memories of his work on the Nottingham Suburban Railway, both just before its closure to through passenger traffic to Shirebrook and subsequently on freight trains to Nottingham (Low Level) station and pick-up goods workings to the Suburban's three stations.

We didn't stop at the stations. There was one at dinner time what went over the Sub and there was one at 5.05 p.m. that went to Shirebrook. You would come in at Daybrook junction. Then, after they had withdrawn passenger services, we used to work [goods trains] over there to Low Level and pick-up goods once a day about 9.30 a.m. from Daybrook in the morning. Sometimes we used to get to Thorneywood and come back to Daybrook. We used to get some brick traffic and at Thorneywood, facing as if you were going to Low Level, there was a road that led off to the right and it went to the Nottingham Patent Brick Company (sic, [Nottingham Builders' Brick Company]) and on the other side they used to lower some wagons down with ropes from a brick works.

Then of course it got bombed and you couldn't get [any further] but that was much later of course. That stopped the through traffic. I can't remember ever such a lot about the Suburban. I fired over it; the ruling gradient was 1 in 49. I think there were three stations and four tunnels. The locomotive would be on a bunkey, a 1500, 4-4-2 side tank, a C12.

At night, the 6.40 p.m. from Nottingham Victoria to Shirebrook, we used to have a 6-wheel engine on that because then when we got to Newstead we used to hook off the train, nip to back of station on the turntable and turn. [We would then] finish the passenger train to Shirebrook tender first then load back from Shirebrook with a coal train and the same thing happened with the 9.07 from Nottingham to Shirebrook.

The pick-ups on the Suburban were worked by Baltics occasionally. You see it was only a 'dog and monkey' job, and they would put any old crock on it, when they were short [of locos], and occasionally they done it with a saddle tank, a J52. But if they had got plenty of engines you would perhaps get a six wheeler.

Although I worked over it I can't remember ever such a lot about it.

Interviews with railway personnel who have in the past actually had experience of working on the Suburban are rare and precious. My deepest thanks goes to George Allen for his memories and David Page for both supplying his recordings and granting his approval for its reproduction in this book.

N5 No.9286 has removed some empty wagons from the NPBC sidings in summer 1948 as it shunts at Thorneywood station; the points being operated by Aubrey Gibson at the ground frame.

J2 No.5018, proceeds southwards on a down gradient with loaded coal wagons just before passing under Bentley's bridge from which the photograph was taken on 31st July 1950, exactly a year before the last timetabled train was to run on the line. *E.N.C. Haywood*

The east face of bridge No.4 taken at 10 a.m. on 18th October 1957. British Railways must have been earning quite a lot from the advertising company judging by the number of banners located on the wingwalls, abutments and embankments. *Nottingham City Engineers Department*

The east face of the Sneinton Dale bridge No.6 with a good quota of advertisements. Adjacent to the right hand span can be seen a gas lamp, which provides illumination to the gentlemen's urinal below, the entrance of which is adjacent to the street lamp post. The view dates from 18th October 1957, at just 12.15 p.m.! *Nottingham City Engineers Department*

The day the RCTS travelled the 'branch' – Saturday afternoon, 16th June 1951. Immaculate C12 No.67363 exits Ashwell's tunnel on its journey over the northern section of the NSR with the special train of enthusiasts. This was the last passenger train to travel over the line, albeit un-timetabled and some decades since the GNR had run the passenger service. Appropriately, a former Great Northern locomotive was chosen as the motive power. A fitting tribute to a railway which didn't stand a chance as road transport started out on its burgeoning course. Nowadays, a tramway following the course of the NSR would be most welcome in a city which has once again embraced public transport with a renewed passion. *T.G. Hepburn*

Leaving Ashwell's tunnel behind, the special train of 16th June 1951 approaches the remains of Sherwood station to be greeted by a few spectators. History was indeed in the making. Volume 3 will include a whole chapter covering the RCTS event and its aftermath. Nearest to the camera are Mrs. Atkins and her son Philip, actually hidden behind her. Photograph reproduced by kind permission of Phil Atkins. *G.H.F. Atkins*

Contents of Volume 3:

Chapter 15 – The British Railways Years.

Chapter 16 – The Last Passenger Train.

Chapter 17 – Desolation, Deterioration. Dilapidation, Decay and Destruction.

Chapter 18 – Death and other Dastardly Deeds.

Chapter 19 – De-railed.

Chapter 20 – Demolition.

Chapter 21 – Developments.

Chapter 22 - Dawdling along the line.

Corrigendum

A detailed index for all the three volumes.

A bibliography for all three volumes.

Edward Parry's detailed financial accounts for the construction of the line.

The NSR Company's detailed accounts showing how they never made a deficit thanks to their agreement with the GNR.

Appendix on Tunnels and Bridges. .